Zabrze (Hindenburg) Yizkor Book

By William Leibner

Edited by Phyllis Oster and Tammy Forstater

Published by JewishGen

**An Affiliate of the Museum of Jewish Heritage - A Living Memorial to the Holocaust
New York**

Zabrze (Hindenburg) Yizkor Book

Compiled by William Leibner
Editors: Phyllis Oster and Tammy Forstater
Layout: Joel Alpert
Cover Design: Nina Schwartz

Published by JewishGen, Inc.
An Affiliate of the Museum of Jewish Heritage
A Living Memorial to the Holocaust
36 Battery Place, New York, NY 10280

"JewishGen, Inc. is not responsible for inaccuracies or omissions in the original work and makes no representations regarding the accuracy of this translation. Digital images of the original book's contents can be seen online at the New York Public Library Web site."

The mission of the JewishGen organization is to produce a translation of the original work and we cannot verify the accuracy of statements or alter facts cited.

Printed in the United States of America by Lightning Source, Inc.

Library of Congress Control Number (LCCN): 2017941797
ISBN: 978-1-939561-52-7 (hard cover: 270 pages, alk. paper)

JewishGen and the Yizkor-Books-in-Print Project

This book has been published by the **Yizkor-Books-in-Print Project,** as part of the **Yizkor Book Project** of **JewishGen, Inc**.

JewishGen, Inc. is a non-profit organization founded in 1987 as a resource for Jewish genealogy. Its website [www.jewishgen.org] serves as an international clearinghouse and resource center to assist individuals who are researching the history of their Jewish families and the places where they lived. JewishGen provides databases, facilitates discussion groups, and coordinates projects relating to Jewish genealogy and the history of the Jewish people. In 2003, JewishGen became an affiliate of the **Museum of Jewish Heritage - A Living Memorial to the Holocaust** in New York.

The **JewishGen Yizkor Book Project** was organized to make more widely known the existence of Yizkor (Memorial) Books written by survivors and former residents of various Jewish communities throughout the world. Later, volunteers connected to the different destroyed communities began cooperating to have these books translated from the original language—usually Hebrew or Yiddish—into English, thus enabling a wider audience to have access to the valuable information contained within them. As each chapter of these books was translated, it was posted on the JewishGen website and made available to the general public.

The **Yizkor-Books-in-Print Project** began in 2011 as an initiative to print and publish Yizkor Books that had been fully translated, so that hard copies would be available for purchase by the descendants of these communities and also by scholars, universities, synagogues, libraries, and museums.

These Yizkor books have been produced almost entirely through the volunteer effort of researchers from around the world, assisted by donations from private individuals. The books are printed and sold at near cost, so as to make them as affordable as possible. Our goal is to make this important genre of Jewish literature and history available in English in book form, so that people can have the personal histories of their ancestral towns on their bookshelves for themselves and for their children and grandchildren.

A list of all published translated Yizkor Books in the project with prices and ordering information can be found at:
http://www.jewishgen.org/Yizkor/ybip.html

Lance Ackerfeld, Yizkor Book Project Manager

Joel Alpert, Yizkor-Book-in-Print Project Coordinator

JewishGen
Yizkor Book Project

This book is presented by the
Yizkor Books in Print Project
Project Coordinator: Joel Alpert

Part of the
Yizkor Books Project of JewishGen, Inc.
Project Manager: Lance Ackerfeld

These books have been produced solely through volunteer effort
of individuals from around the world. The books are printed and
sold at near cost, so as to make them as affordable as possible.

Our goal is to make this history and important genre of Jewish
literature available in English in book form so that people can have
the near-personal histories of their ancestral towns on their bookshelves for themselves and for their children and grandchildren.

Any donations to the Yizkor Books Project are appreciated.

Please send donations to:
Yizkor Book Project
JewishGen
36 Battery Place
New York, NY 10280

JewishGen, Inc. is an affiliate of the
Museum of Jewish Heritage
A Living Memorial to the Holocaust

Dedicated to
Yeshayahu Drucker
and
The Staff at the Zabrze Orphanage

Acknowledgements

Avner Shalev, Chairman of the Yad Vashem Directorate, Rachel Barkai, Director of Commemoration and Public Relations, Yad Vashem; Dr. Robert Rozette, Director of Yad Vashem library; Rachel Cohen, Secretary of Yad Vashem library; Mimi Ash at the Yad Vashem Media Center in Jerusalem; David Sinai, Head of Human Resources Department, and all of Yad Vashem staff at the various research stations in Jerusalem and Dr. Daniel Uziel of the archive division at Yad Vashem, the library staff at Yad Vashem.

Many thanks are in order to my wife, Claudette Leibner, who helped with the artistic layout of the cover page..

Special thanks are in order for Emil Leibner who constantly provided technical media assistance. We also want to express our thanks to all the translators of the various documents that enabled us to write the book.

Special mention is in order for Dr. Zvi Fine who provided background material and guidance in the area of Joint operations in Europe.

Special thanks to Michlean Amir at the Museum for her assistance.

Also special thanks to the editors, Phyllis Oyster and Tammy Forstadt

Ingrid Rockberger deserves a special citation for the hard work of shaping the *Unlikely Hero of Sobrance* into a presentable and readable story.

We would also like to thank all the people that were interviewed and extended cooperation and goodwill to the project.

William Leibner and Larry Price (Jerusalem)

A Short History of the Jewish Community of Zabrze

The Jewish community of Zabrze began in 1825 with the arrival of the first Jews to the locality. The arrivals were from the area and saw economic opportunities as the coal mining industry expanded and the population grew in numbers. Slowly the Jews community grew and expanded. A cemetery, a synagogue, and a kehilla were established. Later a Jewish school and an old age were added to the Jewish compound. The Zabrze Jews created many Jewish clubs and associations that provided the Jewish community with a host of social and fraternal organizations.

The Jews helped the industrial development of the city namely by opening new industries. The Jews played an important role in the city but were never integrated into the population. There was no social mingling between the Jewish and non Jewish populations. The Jewish population reached 1200 souls prior to World War I. During the war the name of the city was changed to Hindenburg, the famous military leader and later President of Germany. The Jews of Zabzre contributed heavily to the war as attested by the large number of military graves.

Following the war, the area became contested between Poles and Germans. Zabrze-Hindenburg remained German. The Nazi party became very strong in Zabrze and Jewish persecutions began. Jews began to leave the city. The synagogue was torched during the pogrom of the "Broken Glass." The last Jews were rounded up in 1942 and deported to camps.

The city was liberated by the Russian army in 1945. There were a few mixed couples (Jews and Germans) left. Polish Jews began to settle the city. They created a vibrant Jewish community that included a a Jewish orphanage. By 1949 the home was closed as were most Jewish institutions, most of the Jews left Zabrze, Poland. At present, he city has no Jews .

Other Works by William Leibner

Wrote <u>Nowy Zmigrod Yizkor Book</u>

Wrote <u>Krosno by the Wislok River - Yizkor Book</u>

Wrote the <u>Brichah Military Organisation</u>

Translated <u>Blood Stained Feathers</u> from Hebrew to English

Wrote with Larry Price <u>The Unlikely Hero of Sobrance, Slovakia</u>

Translated the <u>Korczyna Yizkor Book</u> from Yiddish to English

Translated the <u>Yizkor Book of Jaslo</u> from Hebrew to English

Geopolitical Information:

Zabrze, Poland is located at <u>50°19' North Longitude, 18°47' East</u> Latitude

Alternate names for the town are: Zabrze [Pol], Hindenburg [Ger, 1915-1945], Zobrze [Silesian], Zabzhe [Yid], Zaborze, Hindenburg in Oberschlesien, Hindenburg O.S.

Region: Prussia

	Town	District	Province	Country
Before WWI (c. 1900):	Zabrze	Schlesien	Preussen	Germany
Between the wars (c. 1930):	Hindenburg	Oberschlesien	Preussen	Germany
After WWII (c. 1950):	Zabrze			Poland
Today (c. 2000):	Zabrze			Poland

Jewish Population: 789 (in 1895), 1,027 (in 1925)

Notes: Yiddish: זאַבזשע

In Upper Silesia, 53 miles WNW of Kraków, 11 miles WNW of Katowice, 8 miles WSW of Bytom (Buethen).

Nearby Jewish Communities:

Bobrek 4 miles ENE
Gliwice 6 miles WSW
Swietochlowice 6 miles ESE
Chorzow 8 miles E
Bytom 8 miles ENE
Tarnowskie Gory 10 miles NNE
Katowice 11 miles ESE
Siemianowice Slaskie 11 miles E
Mikolow 12 miles SSE
Czeladz 14 miles E
Grodziec 14 miles E
Toszek 15 miles NW
Bedzin 16 miles E
Modrzejow 17 miles ESE
Sosnowiec 17 miles E
Myslowice 17 miles ESE
Niwka 18 miles ESE
Zagorze 18 miles E
Rybnik 18 miles SW

Dandowka 18 miles E
Dabrowa Gornicza 18 miles E
Zory 19 miles SSW
Golonog 20 miles E
Niemce 21 miles E
Strzemieszyce Wielkie 22 miles E
Siewierz 22 miles ENE
Zabkowice 23 miles ENE
Szczakowa 23 miles ESE
Jaworzno 23 miles ESE
Lubliniec 25 miles N
Pszczyna 25 miles SSE
Strzelce Opolskie 25 miles WNW
Dębowa Gora 26 miles E
Wodzislaw Slaski 26 miles SSW
Slawkow 27 miles E
Oswiecim 28 miles SE
Lazy 29 miles ENE
Czechowice-Dziedzice 29 miles SSE

BALTIC SEA   LITHUANIA

RUSSIA   Vilnius ●

POLAND   BELARUS

GERMANY

● Poznan   Warsaw ●

● Lodz

● Prague   ● **Zabrze**

CZECH REPUBLIC   ● Krakow   UKRAINE

SLOVAKIA

|———————————————| 250 miles
0

|———————————————| 500 Km
0   250 Km   500 Km

POLAND - Current Borders

Map of Poland with Zabrze indicated

Notes to the Reader:

In order to obtain a list of all Shoah victims from Zabrze Poland, the reader should access the Yad Vashem web site listed below; one can also search for specific family names using family name option. These lists are continually updated by Yad Vashem, so it is worthwhile to periodically search these lists.

There is much valuable information available on this web site, including the Pages of Testimony, etc.

http://yvng.yadvashem.org

A list of this book and all books available in the Yizkor-Book-In-Print Project along with prices is available at:

http://www.jewishgen.org/Yizkor/ybip.html

Table of Contents

Notes

[Page 7]

Chapter I

Jewish History of Zabrze
Edited by Tammy Forstater

Synagogue of Zabrze

The City of Zabrze, Poland

Zabrze is an industrial mining town near the city of Katowice. It is an old historic city, already mentioned in 1243 as Biscupci and as Alt-Zabrze in 1295. In the late Middle Ages, the local Silesian Piast dukes invited German settlers into the territory resulting in increasing German settlement. Zabrze became part of the Habsburg Monarchy of Austria in 1526, and was later annexed by the Kingdom of Prussia during the Silesian Wars. With the discovery of coal in Zabrze by the Jewish mining engineer Salomon Izaka of Brabant, Belgium, the city became a coal mining town. The first mine named "Królowa Luzia", located in Zabrze, began to extract coal in 1791, becoming one of the largest mines in Europe. In 1791 it produced 120 tons of coal and in 1891 the production reached to 3,000,000 tons.

**Railroad cars transport the coal from the digging site to the exit site.
The trains also provided transportation for the workers.**

Coal attracted many industries and provided economic opportunities. The city grew.

With the booming economy, Jews began to move to Zabrze. In 1825, the first Jew reached and settled in Zabrze. He was Mozes Glaser, a builder. However, before Glaser, there were other Jews that dealt with or visited Zabrze, like Jakob Lebol or Jakoba Schlesingera. But Glaser was the first permanent settler. In 1840, 24 Jews lived in the village of Zabrze and several dozen Jews in the vicinity. The Jews who first settled in Zabrze at the beginning of the 19th century began to plan the organization of a Jewish community. Meanwhile they depended on the Jewish community of Bytom for all their spiritual needs, like burial services. The Jewish population slowly grew in numbers and wealth. Simon Hamburger started the first steam mill that Samuela Hoffman later acquired and expanded. Wilhelm Silber opened a brick factory. Lobel Haendler opened a brewery and Karol Sachs opened a factory that produced lubricating products. In addition other industrial enterprises were opened by Jews that helped the growth of the city of Zabrze.

As mentioned earlier, the Zabrze Jews depended on the religious services of the Jewish community of Bytom. By 1860, there were about 300 Jews in Zabrze and vicinity. There was a need for a Jewish communal organization in Zabrze.The Jews in the town organized the Jewish community to provide various services including burial services. The following Jewish inhabitants of Zabrze partook in the creation of a Jewish community organization:

Bohm, Max	Handler
Eisner, Wilhelm	Kaiser
Glaser, Noa	Kochmann
Handler, Heinrich	Markus
Schuler, Salomon	Pollack
Dantziger	Sachs
Grunwald	Schindler
Guthamer, Dr.	Wienskowitz
Eugen	

The organised Jewish community of Zabrze petitioned the authorities to grant the Jewish community of Zabrze full independence and the request was confirmed in 1872. Wit the arrival of the permit, elections were held to elect an official body of representatives of the Jewish population of Zabrze and immediate vicinity. The following people were elected to the Jewish community council of Greater Zabrze:

The official stamp of the Jewish community of Zabrze. Notice the coal hammers used by the miners as symbols of the Jewish community of Zabrze

The main objective of the community organization was to provide religious services and religious instruction for the Jewish population of the area.

In 1865, the Jews of Zabrze purchased a sizable plot of land that was located at the intersection of the present Brysza and Karłowicza Streets. The plot was much larger than was needed for a synagogue. The remainder of the plot was destined for an elementary Hebrew school and an old age home. Mateusz Kries, master mason, was commissioned to build the synagogue.

The Jewish cemetery at Zabrze

The Jewish cemetery was set up in 1871 by the Jewish community. The plot was a gift to the Jewish community of Zabrze from the town's last private owner, Guido Heckel von Donnersmarck. At the time, the plot was in the suburbs of the town. Several months after the establishment of the cemetery, a funeral house was built next to it It was the seat of the Chevra Kadisha or Burial Society. Prior to this period, the Jewish deaths of Zabrze had to be transported to the Jewish cemetery of Bytom. A grave had to be bought and paid for as assessed by the Bytom Jewish community. The entire process was handled by the Zabrze Chevra Kadisha. This voluntary association already existed for some time in Zabrze. In 1872, the Chevra Kadisha or Jewish burial society had about 70 members. In 1892 Max Böhm financed the extension of the funeral house, where apartments for the cemetery's caretaker and gardener were built. Because the the Jewish community grew in size, the surface of the cemetery was extended between 1894 and 1895.

Entrance to the Jewish cemetery in Zabrze

The inside of the Jewish cemetery behind the gate at Zabrze

The Jewish cemetery at Zabrze

The inscriptions on the tombstones underwent changes with time, namely less and less Hebrew letters. The cemetery was used until most of the Jews of Hindenburg were rounded up in 1943 and sent to the death camps. A few " *mishling* " or mixed families remained but disapeared with time. At the end of the war, there were no known Jews in Hindenburg. With the end of the war, the name of the town was changed to Zabrze. Repatriated Jews from the Soviet Union began to settle in Zabrze and began to use the Jewish cemetery that would be used until 1953. A unique aspect of the cemetery is that, in addition to Hebrew inscriptions, many tombs feature texts in both German and Polish. Typical tombstone decorations and inscriptions in German and Hebrew continued to be placed on the tombstones. The most impressive tombstones date back to the 19th and 20th centuries when the well to do Jewish families built family plots. Special attention should be paid to the tombs of the following families: the Deckos, the Borinskis, the Herzbergs, the Goldmanns and the Leschnitzers. The most splendid tomb, made of black Swedish granite, belongs to Max Böhm (died in 1904). With time, some of the tombstones collapsed or were damaged extensively. The caretaker collected the parts and placed them in a special location called the "wailing wall".

Family tombs at the Zabrze cemetery

A special place was of course reserved for the fallen German Jewish soldiers of World War One. Russian prisoners of war of World War One and Soviet soldiers killed in the area during World War II were buried next to the walls at the front and back of the cemetery. Within the cemetery there was an area where the Germans dumped the bodies of inmates from the nearby labor camp that was a subsidiary of of the Auschwitz-Birkenau concentration camp complex. This camp was located in the city of Hindenburg. The Nazi local authorities encouraged the people of Hindenburg to dump their garbage on this plot, so that nobody would know what was buried there. The mass grave was discovered by Mr. Dariusz Walerjañski, a local historian. He and the municipality cleared the plot and the bodies were reburied in a mass grave

At the cemetery one can admire a beautiful stand of trees, consisting of more than 200 trees; most of them are robinias, with the rest being tall European ash, maples, sycamores and others. Family tombs are fitted into the framework of columns, semi-columns and pilasters. With the disappearance of the Jewish community of Zabrze in the fifties following the closure of the Joint organisation, the Jewish organisations and the vicous anti-Jewish attacks, the Jews of Zabrze left the place as did most of the Jews of Poland. The cemetery became neglected and overgrown. Lately, a historical group started to clean the cemetery area and restore it to its former state.

The main entrance to the Zabrze synagogue

The synagogue building was completed in 1873. The synagogue was a free-standing English is two-story red brick building, with the elements typical of Romanesque and Moorish architecture. All decorative elements, such as corners, window frames and friezes, were made in plaster. The synagogue was rebuilt once more in 1909. It resembled the one of Kaiserslauter, and had three entrances. Over the main entrance there was a Hebrew inscription which was a citation from the First Book of Moses (the Book of Genesis) 28:17 - " This is none other than the house of God, and his is the gate of heaven." The main prayer room was surrounded on three sides by galleries for women. The ceremony of the consecration took place on April 2, 1873. It was led by Rabbi Landsberg with religious songs and prayers, while the sermon was delivered in German by the Orthodox rabbi of Radom. The first rabbis were usually brought from Bytom or Gliwice to conduct services. Then in 1895, Rabbi Saul Kaatz was engaged to be the rabbi of the community. He later had an assistant named Dr. Rabbi Arthur Victor who passed away in 1934.

The Jewish school of Zabrze on the left and the towers of the synagogue on the right form the Jewish compound of Zabrze

Both Rabbi Kaatz and Rabbi Victor were busy with the Jewish flock of Hindenburg (during World War One, the city of Zabzre asked and received permission to change the name of the city to Hindenburg). Rabbi Kaatz conducted an impressive memorial service at the synagogue on December 8, 1925 where two panels with the names of the 51 fallen Jewish soldiers were added to the memorial wall of the synagogue. All these Jewish oldiers lived in Hindenburg and fell in the battles of World War One defending Imperial Germany. Rabbi Kaatz eulogised the fallen soldiers who gave their lives for the German homeland. He would continue to lead the community until the summer of 1942 when most of the Jews of Zabrze were deported to the death camps, including Rabbi Kaatz.

Benger, Erich	20. 5. 1898	Datum unbek.
Benger, Martin	5. 8. 1896	Datum unbek.
Blandowski, Max	25. 1. 1897	25. 9. 1917
Blandowski, Moritz	4. 11. 1898	16. 10. 1917
		(vermißt)
Böhm, Max	16. 12. 1890	10. 4. 1918
Brauer, Alfred		
Brauer, Max		
Brauer, Artur	19. 10. 1877	9. 8. 1917
Brauer, Salo		
Cohn, Karl	18. 5. 1863	26. 8. 1914
Cohn, Herbert		
Cohn, Siegfried	19. 5. 1899	1. 7. 1918
Daniel, Max	15. 9. 1877	30. 5. 1917
Fabisch, Heinrich		
Fabisch, Max		
Friedländer, Hugo	15. 12. 1876	29. 1. 1916
Gerstel, Alfred	12. 5. 1885	20. 1. 1915
Gerstel, Leo	19. 5. 1898	20. 8. 1918
Gerstel, Wilhelm	21. 7. 1890	20. 1. 1917
Glaser, Ewald	12. 12. 1893	8. 8. 1918
Glaser, Leopold		
Glaser, Max		14. 9. 1915
Glaser, Reinhold		
Grünberg, Salo	15. 12. 1875	26. 10. 1918
Grünwald, Siegfried	5. 10. 1873	17. 8. 1915
Hausderff, Walter		

List of German Jewish soldiers from Zabrze that fell in World War One and some were buried at the Jewish cemetery in Zabrze

Herzko, Max	17. 2. 1896	8. 6. 1917
Jacobi, Berthold	16. 12. 1878	6. 12. 1917
Laband, Manfred	28. 10. 1890	1. 7. 1916
Leschcziner, Ferdinand	14. 10. 1889	21. 11. 1917
Löbinger, Hartwig		
Löbmann, Max		
Malachowski, Alfred	7. 8. 1895	11. 4. 1918
May, Leopold	1. 4. 1889	11. 6. 1918
Notlamann, A.	22. 5. 1897	11. 8. 1915
Perl, Alfred	24. 2. 1884	5. 9. 1914
Pollack, Eugen	11. 2. 1897	10. 4. 1918
Pollack, Ludwig	9. 5. 1895	30. 5. 1918
		(vermißt)
Pollack Samuel	28. 5. 1893	8. 9. 1916
Rinkel ,Alfred		
Sachs, Julius	22. 4. 1891	31. 1. 1918
Seidler, Felix	4. 2. 1882	28. 7. 1917
Silbermann, Arnold	11. 12. 1882	12. 7. 1916
Schlesinger, Fritz		
Schlesinger, Ludwig		
Schutz, Heinrich	1. 12. 1889	19. 5. 1917
Schutz, Wilhelm		
Steinitz, Fritz	30. 4. 1896	24. 5. 1918
Stiebel, Erich	28. 5. 1894	17. 7. 1915
Tichauer, Salo	22. 10. 1883	10. 9. 1917
Totschek, Heinrich	21. 10. 1872	27. 11. 1914

Ferner starben an den Folgen des Krieges folgende jüdische Soldaten aus Hindenburg:

Steinitz, Ernst	4. 2. 1899	18. 8. 1919
Tandesar, Max	15. 9. 1898	29. 9. 1919
Tichauer, Fritz	12. 6. 1889	30. 6. 1919

List of German Jewish soldiers from Zabrze that fell in World War One and some were buried at the Jewish cemetery in Zabrze

The Zabrze community also had the following cantors to serve the community:

    S.Schallamach   A.Landesar

    H. Singermann

Amongst the teachers of the Jewish school we remember:

    J

. Michaelis   D. Malachowski

Dora Kohn   S. Petzal Arthur Wahler

Lamg

Principal M. Strauss

The Jewish community of Zabrze was one of the larger Jewish communities in Upper Silesia. In 1931, the Jewish population reached 1200 people. The president of the Jewish community was attorney Dr. Guthamer, the presiding officer was Mandowsky and the treasurer was Michaelis. Attorney Martin Schindler represented the community to the outside world. The budget for 1931 was 50,000 German marks, which covered the school where 60 children attended classes and another 90 children received religious instruction.

The Jewish community was a vibrant community that had many clubs and associations ranging from a burial society to various sports clubs and social and welfare associations, including the welfare association to help needy people, the women's lodge of Veritas and the men's lodge of Veritas. Bnei Brith was very active as were various Zionist organisations. The largest group in the community was the branch of the Central Union or better known by the initials C.V. This was the largest Jewish organization in Germany that represented Jewish interests in Germany and was at first vehemently opposed to Zionism. As things developed in Germany, the group mellowed its opposition to Zionism and effectively helped Jews leave Germany. The Zionist groups organized orientation courses for people planning to go Palestine, and offered Hebrew courses. Zionist youth clubs such as „Maccabi Hatzair" made great progress amongst the German Jewish youth. Slowly but steadily, the Jews were isolated from the German population. Even the public library was closed to the Jews and the Jews organized their own library.

Jewish children in Zabrze near the aynagogue in the thirties. The children were members of the Zionist youth organisation " Maccabi Hatzair"

The Jews were active in trade, especially grains and cattle. Jews were also in the professions and some had large businesses. Jewish life was very intense and revolved around many social and cultural associations.

Zabrze was officially renamed Hindenburg during World War One in honor of Generalfeldmarschall Paul von Hindenburg. The name change was approved by King Wilhelm II on 21 February 1915. Following the war, the area of Hindenburg was disputed between Poland and Germany. Both countries insisted on taking possession of the area including the city of Hindenburg. The League of Nations ordered a plebiscite to be held. ' 21,333 inhabitants (59%) of the Hindenburg community voted to remain in Germany, while 14,873 (41%) voted for incorporation to Poland. In May 1921 the Third Silesian Uprising broke out and Hindenburg was captured by Polish insurgents, who held it until the end of the uprising. When Upper Silesia was divided between Poland and Germany in 1921, the Hindenburg community remained in Germany. It received its city charter in 1922. Just five years after it's founding, Hindenburg became the biggest city in German Upper Silesia and the second biggest City in German Silesia after Breslau.

At first, the wave of anti-Semitism stoked by the Nazi press across Germany did not affect the Jewish community in Hindenburg. The city was protected by the League of Nations minority charter, which guaranteed the rights of minorities. It was basically designed to protect the large Polish population but also benefited the Jewish residents. But the Nazis were determined to rule the city and slowly imposed their terror tactics on the Jewish population. The other minorities also felt unwanted. The special minority status ended on July 16, 1937. The Nazi terror machine went into full gear in Hindenburg. Some Jews began to leave the city and sought safety in the bigger cities with larger Jewish populations, or tried to go abroad. In Germany, the terror felt by the Jewish population assumed catastrophic proportions. Furthermore, the municipal elections in 1933 gave the Nazi party a victory in Zabrze. The citizens of Zabrze voted for the Nazi politician Max Fillusch who became mayor and remained in the position until 1945. With him started the worsening of the Jewish situation in Zabrze. On November 9, 1938 on the so-called Kristallnacht, the Germans torched the synagogue. The synagogue burned and smoldered for two days, and was reduced to rubble. The adjoining „Mikvah", or ritual bath house, was also destroyed. Two other Jewish buildings in the compound were left standing. One was the old age home and the other was the schol. The area of the synagogue remained desolate until 1998. Then Ernest Shmuel Schindler and the Zabrze municipality erected a memorial plaque on the site where the synagogue stood. Following World War II, the Polish authorities restored the name of Zabrze to the city.

Plaque erected in Zabrze in memory of the destroyed synagogue

The sign reads:

IN MEMORYof the Jewish Community of Zabrze (Hindenburg) that was destroyed by the German Nazis during the Shoah.

On this plot stood the Jewish synagogue that was built in 1872 and destroyed in the "Kristalnacht" pogrom of November 9-10. 1938.

" Remember what Amalek did to you on your way out of Egypt" Deuteronomy chapter...

This memorial was erected due to the efforts of Ernasta Shmuela Schindler and the community of Zabrze in 1998

The Gestapo arrested 350 Jews and kept them in detention. The next day 95 Jews were sent to the Buchenwald concentration camp. The Jewish population of Zabrze declined rapidly and according to a survey in May of 1939, the Jewish population stood at 554 people. Within a few years, the Jewish population shrank by more than 50%.

During World War II there were two major actions aimed at the Jews of Zabrze. According to the testimonies of Jewish survivors of Zabrze, the first action took place on January 1, 1942, where many Jews were rounded up and sent to the death camp of Auschwitz-Birkenau including Rabbi Kaatz . The next action took place in 1943 where the remaining Jews were rounded up and sent to the death camps. By October 1944 there were only 16 Jewish "*mishling*" families where one of the partners was not Jewish. It is not known how many of these families were still in Zabrze when the Soviet army marched into the city in 1945. They became the masters of the city and later handed it over to Poland.

On the right, the Jewish school building in Zabrze remained standing throughout World War II

[Page 24]

Chapter II

Zabrze Following the War
Edited by Phyllis Oster

With the end of the war, the Soviet army ruled Hindenburg but soon handed over the city to the Polish administration in accordance with the Polish-Russian agreement based on the Yalta agreement. The Yalta conference was held in Yalta, Crimea, the Soviet Union. The participants consisted of Joseph Stalin, the Soviet Union; Franklin Delano Roosevelt, the United States; and Winston Churchill, Britain. The conference took place February 4-11, 1945, and was supposed to settle the postwar European border issues. One of the biggest was the frontiers of Poland. The Soviet Union or rather Stalin insisted that the areas that were invaded in 1939 by the Soviet namely the area crisscrossed that included Wilno, Bialystok, and Lwow become part of the Soviet Union. He insisted that Poland be compensated on its western border with Germany namely the area marked with circles that included Gdansk on the Baltic and Wroclaw in Silesia would be attached to Poland... Stalin refused to budge on the issue.

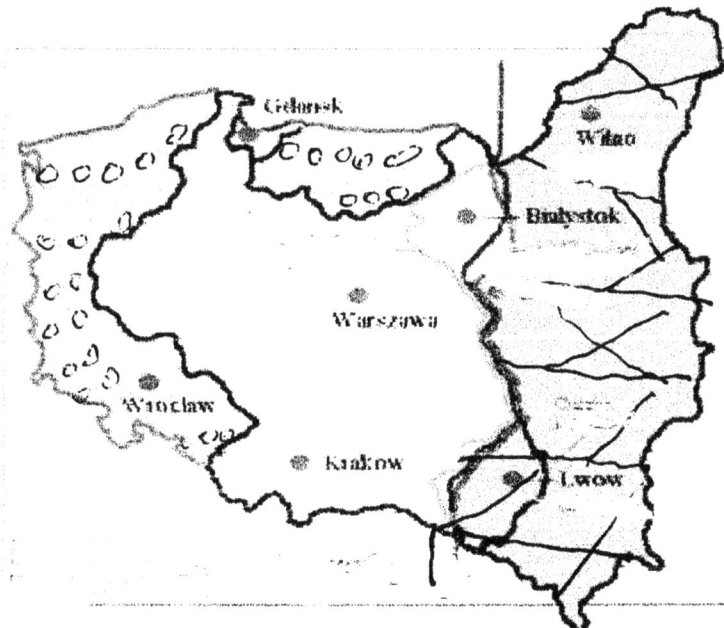

Poland's new borders, 1945 according to the Yalta Conference. The circled areas were given to Poland and the crisscrossed areas were removed from Poland

Roosevelt and Churchill had to accept the Soviet demands since the Soviet army had already liberated most of Poland and was in control of the areas in question. The Polish

Government in exile in London refused to accept the changes but could little to alter the

the situation. Stalin could not care less; he signed an agreement with a Polish committee that he created in the Soviet Union. The committee latter became the provisional government that consented to the new borders and followed the Soviet army into liberated Poland. With the liberation of the city of Lublin, the provisional Polish government began to administer the liberated parts of Poland. The government later moved to Warsaw when the city was liberated.

The Polish-Soviet agreement had an important clause that stated that all Polish residents, even if they were forced to become Soviet citizens, could leave the areas that were given to the Soviet Union and move to Poland. Polish institutions like orphanages or old age homes were also given the same privileges. Of course, the Jews who survived the Shoah in these areas were also given the option of staying or moving to Poland. By the thousands, Poles left the ceded areas; in many instances they were forced to leave and moved to Poland. We have to remember that a majority of the population of the transferred areas were Ukrainians and Byelorussians who could not leave these areas. As a matter of fact, Ukrainians or Byelorussians who lived within Polish areas were also given the option to move to the Soviet Union. There were large Polish populations primarily in the cities such as Lwow or Lemberg but their number in the rural areas was much smaller. The Polish government directed the flow of Polish refugees to the new areas that it just acquired. Transport trains of Poles began to arrive in the new areas. They were joined by many Poles in Poland proper who saw an opportunity to advance themselves economically. The Polish government expelled the German residents of the areas and provided housing, jobs and other financial inducements to the Polish newcomers. The government was determined to " Polonize" the areas as fast as possible.

Many demobilized Polish and Soviet Jewish soldiers settled in the new areas where life was easier than in Poland proper where a wave of anti-Semitism began to spread. The Poles resented the present Communist-dominated Polish government that also happened to include a few Jews such as Jakob Berman, something that would not have occurred prior to World War II. Berman and other influential post holders were also members of the Communist Party. The Polish government in exile in London waged an active campaign against the government in Warsaw and used the Jewish office holders as proof that Jews controlled Poland. Furthermore, the London government claimed that they were not Poles but agents of the Soviet Union sent to rule Poland. The Polish masses bought these lies and the countryside supported the nationalist Polish elements. The government controlled the major cities and the new areas where the residents received many incentives. The Poles resented the loss of territory and the border changes.

Britain and the United States tried to mediate between the two Polish governments and managed to arrange a shaky agreement whereby some members of the London Polish government were assigned posts in the government in Warsaw. Stalin was determined to rule Poland regardless of Polish feelings. The nationalist forces fought the government everywhere; they even used weapons in an attempt to bring down the present Polish government in Poland. Jews were removed from trains and killed. Others were urged to leave their native places or face serious consequences. Many Jews decided to head to the new areas where there were already larger Jews settlements such as Wroclaw or Breslau, Gliwice, Bytom, Walbrzych or Waldenburg and Szczecin or Stettin.

Some small Jewish communities such as Zabrze, were soon reinforced by the mass arrival of Polish residents who had spent the war years in the Soviet Union, According to historian Yehuda Bauer, nearly 250,000 Polish Jews survived the war in the Soviet Union. The bulk of them, 177,000, returned between 1945 and the middle of 1946[1]. Some Polish Jews would continue to arrive in Poland for a number of years.

These repatriated Jews and Poles were Polish citizens who had fled their homes before the advancing German armies in 1939. The Polish government had urged all Poles, civilians and soldiers, to head to Eastern Poland or the area known as Kresy where a defensive line would be established to halt the German advance. Thousands of Polish soldiers and civilians headed to the East of Poland. Of course, these people did not know that the Germans and Soviets had signed a secret pact known as the Molotov-Ribbentrop agreement whereby Poland would be divided between Germany and the Soviet Union. Germany was already in Poland and now the Soviet Union attacked Poland on September 17, 1939, and claimed its share of the spoils. The entire area that Russia took by force was immediately annexed to the Soviet Union. All native residents of the area were automatically converted to Soviet citizenship. All Polish refugees as well as Polish prisoners of war soldiers, were urged to apply for Soviet citizenship. Russia had taken about 230,000 Polish prisoners of war. Most of them refused to surrender their Polish citizenship. People began to disappear, rumors circulated, large security forces were everywhere and fear seized the inhabitants, especially those people who had recently arrived in the area from German-occupied parts of Poland. The Soviet administration tried to force the Polish refugees to change their nationality but had little success.

Then on June 29, 1940, practically all Polish citizens who refused to accept Soviet citizenship were rounded up and escorted to waiting trains and dispersed throughout the Soviet Union, especially Siberia. The National Polish Institute of Remembrance states that about 350.000 Poles were deported to Russia, mainly Siberia and 150,000 of them died there. These numbers did not include the round ups that occurred prior to the massive deportations, which involved the removal of influential elements of society, namely political, intellectual, academic, religious, financial elements and elements hostile to the Soviet Union. There were many Jews among these deportees but the scale was rather limited. The main deportations were massive in the extent of people involved and the limited duration of the entire action.

German and Soviet officers shaking hands following the Polish invasion in 1939

Polish prisoners of war captured by the Red Army during the Soviet invasion of

Poland in 1939

Here is what Awraham Lang, a native of Krosno who escaped the German-occupied city and lived in Lesko, had to say: "I was awakened in the middle of the night and given two hours to pack lightly and was then escorted to the awaiting train by Russian security forces. I was shown into a railroad car with other Polish refuges and the doors were locked. The train soon started to roll. The trip was never ending and took weeks. From the final railway station we still had to walk to get to the special camp, which consisted of wooden barracks. The camp had no name but a number and it was in the area of Novosibirsk. The forest was everywhere but there were no chairs or tables or furniture in the barracks".

"The men and single women were organized into labor battalions and marched to the forest to cut trees and reduce them to logs. These logs were then piled on top of each other and formed sizable triangles of logs. In the spring, the poles that held the triangles in place were removed and the logs rolled down the banks to the river. They floated downstream to a sawmill that converted them to wood products. Some of the branches were chopped into pieces for heating. Mothers, children and old people remained in the camp that was guarded. As a matter of fact, everything was guarded as though someone was going to run away from the forsaken place. Conditions in the camp were terrible; lack of food, lack of medicine and harsh weather caused many people to die. Still the camp organized itself and began to function. Most of the camp officials were former political prisoners who were already free but were forbidden to leave the area. They lived in small poor and desolate villages. They were completely isolated from contact with the Soviet Union except for the official government messengers that the regional offices sent. These inhabitants and the poor captive prisoners were constantly watched and observed by the secret police that was everywhere and instilled fear in everybody, even in these remote areas. I soon learned that there were even harsher camps to which one could be sent if the local authorities took a dislike to someone and a number of people disappeared. The local people used to say: we too hoped that this will be over soon but look at us now, you too will get used to this way of life. Indeed they were hopeless.

"I became a lumberjack and so did the entire working population of the camp. The production was very limited since most of us were city people, hungry, resentful and lacked the basic tools and skills for the job. The work progressed but at a slow pace. I was always looking for food or for clothing as were the other inmates". A black market developed in the camp with the approval of the police. The camp was transformed into a trading post that seemed to engulf the entire country. This situation was aggravated with the news that Germany had attacked Russia.

Awraham Lang erecting a tombstone for his father Chaim Lang in Dzhambul, Kazakhstan in 1943

Władysław Anders and Wladyslaw Sikorski with Joseph Stalin in Russia in 1941

Now everything was in short supply and there was a reason: the war. Everything was needed for the army. Still the German armies advanced rapidly through Russia until the gates of Moscow where they met the Russian's excellent defense system and a very harsh winter. The exhausted Germans came to a standstill. The Soviet government abandoned all slogans and reverted to the national Russian slogan "defend mother Russia." Even in the distant camps of Siberia, films were shown describing the brutality of the German behavior towards the civilian Russian population. Newspapers like *Pravda* began to appear in the camp. I understood the spoken Russian language since it is similar in pronunciation to Polish but the written Russian language was a mystery to most of us since none of us were familiar with the Cyrillic alphabet.

The government tried to enlist the entire population in the war effort, even the so-called Polish enemies of the state. The general feeling eased a bit and people began to make an effort to help the country in the war effort. The Polish citizens in the camp suddenly became partners in the struggle against Germany following the agreement between the Soviet government and Wladyslaw Sikorski, the head of the Polish government in exile in London. Sikorski flew to the Soviet Union and signed the Sikorski-Mayski Agreement on August 17, 1941. The agreement called for the release of all Polish citizens from the prisons camps and "gulags", the formation of a Polish army and the creation of an official Polish administration in the Soviet Union to care for all Polish citizens.

As a good will gesture, the Polish citizens were offered the opportunity to leave the camps for other parts of the Soviet Union where the climate was milder such as Kazakhstan or Uzbekistan. The response was so overwhelming that the government had to organize transports by allocating each camp to a particular city. My camp was assigned the city of Dzhambul in Kazakhstan. The camp was soon filled with Volga Germans, that is to say, people of German origins who had been living in Russia for generations and were distrusted by Stalin. So they were scooped up and sent to these camps that were just deprived of their Polish contingents. I left Siberia with other Polish refugees, mostly Jews, and headed for Dzhambul. Our train rolled and rolled days and nights, nights and days. Stops were frequent since military trains had priority. Each stop became an instant market; people were selling or trading goods for food. This scene would repeat itself throughout the journey. The days were getting warmer and longer and we soon arrived in this huge oriental city. Here the local administration, the Soviet authorities, the Polish Red Cross, and the Polish office of refugees assisted us. Soon other transports began to arrive from the same and different camps. The city's population underwent a radical change in composition. Polish refugees, mostly Jews, were present in large numbers and so were Soviet refugees that were evacuated by the Soviet government before the advancing German armies. Various epidemics started and many people died, especially Polish refugees, due to lack of food, medical facilities and drugs. The food situation was desperate and everybody was hungry. The Polish government later erected a massive monument honoring the Polish citizens who died in the Soviet Union during the war.

**Monument to the Fallen and
Murdered in the East, in Warsaw**
Pomnik Poległym i Pomordowanym na Wschodzie

Soon, help was on the way, American food began to arrive in large amounts as well as packages from relatives in the USA. The American Joint organization managed to obtain lists of names of Polish refugees in the Soviet Union and began to send them food packages. The Joint organized a supply center in Iran that would send relief packages to the Soviet Union. I received some of these packages and they saved my life and kept me going. I sold some of the products such as cigarettes on the black market and bought bread. Then I heard the first good news. The Polish army under the command of General Wladyslaw Anders was permitted to leave the Soviet Union for Iran. The army consisted of 88,000 soldiers and thousands of Polish civilians and orphans. There were very few Jews among the exodus. The Polish military authorities rejected many Jews who volunteered to fight the Germans.

"As the Soviet armies began to drive the Germans out of the Soviet Union, the food situation began to improve. So did the hope that the war would soon end and the refugees would be sent home. Nobody had any illusions about conditions back home but still nobody wanted to believe the rumors that were rife that large parts of Polish Jewry were destroyed. Everybody was certain that these rumors exaggerated the situation.

The Soviet armies pushed the Germans out of the Soviet Union and the Soviet refugees began to return to their homes. The Polish offices in the Soviet Union began to prepare lists to transport the Polish refuges back home. Slowly the Soviet armies liberated Poland and the first transports began to roll to

Poland. The Polish government directed these transports to the new areas that Poland acquired since it wanted to settle the areas with Poles. It also wanted to direct the transports that contained many Jews to the new areas in order to avoid confrontations between Jews and non-Jews. I was soon contacted and given orders to prepare to head home to Poland. The transport left Dzhambul and headed to Poland. It was directed to Walbrzych. Along the road in Poland, many Poles left the transport and went home, but I and most of the Jewish passengers decided to follow to our destination since we already heard of unpleasant events that happened to Jews returning to Poland. The transport arrived and I was immediately assigned a flat from which the previous Germans occupants were simply expelled, escorted to trains and forced to board them. These transports headed to Germany.

It is estimated that 3.3 million Jews lived in Poland in September 1939. When the war ended in May 1945, only 42,662 Jews remained in Poland. Soon, starving survivors from the labor camps and concentrations camps returned home and increased the number of Jews to 80,000. By January 1946 the numbers increased to 106,492 with the discharge of Jewish soldiers from the Polish and Soviet armies. Many Polish citizens in the Soviet Union had been drafted into the Soviet armies. With the massive arrival of repatriated Polish Jews from the Soviet Union, the number of Polish Jews swelled to 240,489, still a small fraction in comparison with the prewar Polish Jewish population. Most of the Jewish population now lived in the new Polish areas. The Jewish population shifted from the eastern and central areas of Poland to those in the west. The new Jewish communities like Zabrze benefited by the shift of Jewish population.

CENTRALNY KOMITET ZYDOW POLSKICH
Warszawa-Praga Szeroka 5
Wydział Ewidencji i Statystyki.   Komitet w Zabrzu
                                                   woj. Śląskie

                        Podajemy odpis ankiety wypełnionej przez Komitet w
                        Zabrzu. Kwestionariusz niniejszy odzwierciadla warunki
                        życia i potrzeby społeczenstwa żydowskiego w Zabrzu.

                              A N K I E T A.

    I. Istniejące instytucje i placówki żydowskie oraz osoby, stojące na ich
        czele;

        1/ Komitet Żydowski w Zabrzu,   Jakub Wieselberg,   przewodniczący,
        2/ Dom Starców   dr. Necha Geller   "
        3/ Dom Dziecka   dr. Necha Geller   "
        4/ Internat   Zofia Kacowa   "
        5/ Zrzeszenie Religijne   Jakub Wieselberg   "

   II. Ilość osób zarejestrowanych w Komitecie   432
        a/ dzieci do lat 14   58
        b/ repatriantów z Z.S.R.R.   326

  III. Ilość osób korzystających z opieki
        a/ Komitetu   432

   IV. Opisać możliwości życia i pracy w danej miejscowości/uwzględnić
        stopień zniszczeń wojennych miasta/
        Miasto niezniszczone, możliwości pracy w kopalniach i hutach.

    V. Potrzeby kulturalne i materiałne ludności;
        / Szkoła Żydowska.

        Zabrze w lutym 1946 r.

Below is a loose translation of the document.

The document dated March 1946 in Zabrze, Slansk region and directed to the Central Committee of Polish Jews at 5 Szeroka Street, Warszawa-Praga, Statistical division.

We are complying with your requests and answering your questions to the best of our ability.

I List of institutions, their leaders and titles;
     1 Jewish Committee in Zabrze, Jakub Wieselberg, president
     2 Old age home, dr. Necha Geller, chairman
     3 The Orphanage, dr. Necha Geller, chairman
     4 The home for youngsters, Zofia Kacowa, chairman
     5 Religious slaughterer, Jakub Wieselberg, chairman
II Number of people registered with the committee – 432
     1 Children to the age of 14 years – 58
     2 Jews that returned from the Soviet Union – 326
     3 Number of Jews that are helped by the committee of Zabrze – 432
III The city is basically a military city
IV The city is surrounded by mines and melting factories
V   The Jewish population needs more cultural activities.
VI The city needs a Jewish school

The above document also had an attachment that listed all the Jews that registered with the Zabzre Jewish Committee. The extensive list is attached at the end of the book. According to the list of Zabrze residents four Jews of Zabrze who survived the Shoah and were residents in Zabrze in 1946. Their names were[2];

    Sarita Nizinska born 1926 in Zabrze
    Willi Ofner born in 1906 in Zabrze
    Arthur Orenstein born 1887 in Zabrze
    Hilda Offenberg born 1888 in Zabrze

Of course, there were also some "mischling" or descendants of mixed parentage, namely Jews who married Christians and vice-versa, that were not added to the list. It is also possible that some Jews in Zabrze still lived under assumed names and refused to be identified as Jews. A list of all registered Jewish residents of Zabrze can be found at the end of this book.

The needs of the Shoah survivors and the repatriated Jews from the Soviet Union were immense. The Zabrze Committee like similar other committees submitted their requests to the Central Committee of Polish Jews in Warsaw that in turn assembled all the requests and submitted them to the Polish government. The Central Committee of Polish Jews, also referred to as the Central Committee of Jews in Poland and abbreviated CKZP, (Polish: Centralny Komitet Żydów w Polsce, Yiddish: פוילן אין יידן די פון קאמיטעט צענטראל was a state-sponsored political representation of Jews in Poland at the end of World War II. The creation of the Committee was approved on November 12, 1944, by the Provisional Polish Government. The Zionist Emil Sommerstein was appointed head of the Central Jewish Committee of Polish Jews.

Emil Sommerstein

Emil Sommerstein, born in the village of Chleszczewa near Lwow, was an attorney but devoted himself to Zionism and politics. A Zionist leader, Sommerstein was elected to the Polish senate in 1922-1927 and again in 1929-1934. He was also a member of several important commissions. In 1939 Sommerstein was arrested by the Soviet authorities and sent from gulag to gulag on various charges. But, because the Soviets wanted to legitimize their puppet Polish government to usurp any power from the Polish Government in Exile in London, they decided to rehabilitate former well-known Polish political figures like Sommerstein.

In 1944, the Soviets first flew Sommerstein, sick and a shadow of himself, to Moscow, where he was appointed a member of the Polish government. Sommerstein was appointed to the cabinet and urged to organize the Committee for Polish Jews. He hoped to reestablish the Jewish community in Poland. But Sommerstein was also a Zionist, a leader of the Ichud Zionist party or the Democratic Zionist center party. He believed that those Jews who wanted to leave for Palestine should be able to do so. But, he was certain that many Polish Jews would remain in Poland and would need all the help they could get from the Polish government. Sommerstein also published the Yiddish newspaper entitled "Dos Naje Leben" or The New Life.

As a Zionist leader, Sommerstein participated at a meeting of Zionist leaders in London in 1945. He described the conditions of the Jews in postwar Poland and appealed for help to revive the Jewish community.

Zionist Convention London, 1945. Some of the Polish Zionists

Top row, left to right : **Abba Hillel Silver, Moshe Kleinbaum–Sneh, Yitshak Grunbaum**
Middle row, left to right: **unidentified, Moshe Sharett, Nahum Goldman**
Bottom row, left to right: **Yitzak Zuckerman, Haykah Grossman, Emil Sommerstein with beard, Leib Salpeter, and Meler**

The Central Committee of Polish Jews consisted of six members of the Communist Party that called itself the Polish Workers' Party, four Bund representatives, four representatives of Ihud Zionist, three representatives of Poale Zion Left (leftist faction of Workers of Zion), three representatives of Poale Zion Right and one representative of *Hashomer Hatzair*. There were no religious representatives or right wing representatives. The presiding officer was Emil Sommerstein. The communist influence within the committee was obvious but Sommerstein wanted to get all the aid of the government for the needy Jewish survivors. The Polish government dealt only with this committee which had several district offices throughout liberated Poland, and all Jewish community requests were directed to it before being considered by the government. The Polish government granted most of the requests but it must be remembered that Poland was a devastated country after the war and its resources were limited.

Sommerstein also wanted to revive Jewish religious life in Poland. The Central Committee was not keen on the idea but the Polish government or rather the Soviet government liked the idea. The Russians were willing to do anything to score international political points in the fight against the London based government. Sommerstein obtained approval to bring Rabbi David Kahane to Lublin. He was one of the few rabbis in Poland to survive the Holocaust and later became Chief Rabbi of the Israeli Air Force and then Chief Rabbi of Buenos Aires, Argentina.

David Kahane was born March 15, 1903 in the village of Grzimalow in the Tarnopol region, Eastern Galicia. He was ordained as a Rabbi in 1929 in Vienna where he also received his Ph.D. After his studies, Kahane settled in Lwow (Lemberg), Poland, and became the Rabbi of the Sistoska synagogue. He held that position until the Nazi invasion of Poland in September 1939. In his memoir "Lwow Ghetto Diary," Rabbi Kahane describes how he survived the war by playing cat and mouse with the Nazi troops searching the city for Jews, including being shot at when one of his hiding places was uncovered. Nevertheless, Kahane was soon captured and moved with the other Jews of Lwow to the Jewish ghetto built by the Nazis. Eventually he was deported from the ghetto and wound up in the Janowska labor camp outside the city of Lwow. Janowska was also a transit camp. From there Jews unfit to work were sent to the death camp of Belzec. According to Rabbi Kahane, conditions in the camp were so horrible they defied description. The rabbi escaped the Janowska camp and begged for refuge in the palace of Lwow's Ukrainian Metropolitan Archbishop Andreas Sheptytsky. During the war Sheptytsky harbored hundreds of Jews in his residence and in Greek Catholic monasteries. He also issued the now famous pastoral letter, "Thou Shalt Not Kill," to protest Nazi atrocities. Rabbi Kahane arranged with the Archbishop to place his own daughter in a convent. She survived the Holocaust as did Kahane's wife, who was admitted to a Uniate institution under orders of Sheptytsky. Archbishop Sheptytsky also issued orders to the Uniate convents of the Studite order in Eastern Galicia to accept Jewish children and hide them. The Archbishop died in 1944 and is buried in St. George's Cathedral in Lwow.

Rabbi Kahane's experience led him to a deep understanding of the complexities the Jewish community faced following the war. Having survived with his family due to the good offices of the Christian community, he respected any Christian family or institution that harbored Jews during the Nazi terrorist rule.

Rabbi Doctor Major David Kahane, chief Jewish chaplain of the Polish army

With the liberation, Lwow became Soviet territory. Rabbi Kahane began the uphill battle of reviving the decimated Jewish community of the city. One day Kahane was surprised to receive an invitation to come to Lublin where the Polish government had established its administration. He met Sommerstein and together they met the Polish Minister of Defense, General Rola-Zymiersky, who offered Rabbi Kahane the job of Chief Rabbi of the Polish Army with the rank of major. The Rabbi graciously accepted the post but only after requesting, and receiving permission to open a bureau to restore the destroyed Jewish religious communities throughout liberated Poland.

Rabbi Doctor Major David Kahane (in his military uniform) with family

Sommerstein and Kahane were familiar with Soviet political tactics and knew full well that they were being used for propaganda purposes. They decided to use the opportunity to obtain as many benefits as possible for the Jewish survivors who needed all the help they could get.

Rabbi Kahane immediately began to tend to the needs of the 15,000 Jewish Polish soldiers. He also began to help restore Jewish religious communities in liberated Poland. The job was immense so he enlisted the help of a military chaplain named Aaron Becker. Kahane also tried to enlist the services of Private Yeshayahu Drucker. Drucker was active within the Polish army on behalf of Jewish spiritual matters, organizing a "seder meal for Jewish soldiers." Kahane saw in Drucker a man who could help him restore Jewish religious life in Poland.

Captain Yeshayahu Drucker

Yeshayahu Drucker was born in 1914 to Israel and Rachel Drucker. The family lived in Jordanow, a small town near the large Galician town of Krakow where the father was a watchmaker and was very active in the religious Zionist movement "Mizrahi." Young Drucker studied in various heders, traditional Hebrew schools, and then entered the Hebrew high school. On completing high school, he enrolled at the well-known teacher seminary "Poznansky" in Warsaw. He graduated from the institution with a teaching certificate in Jewish studies in 1939.

With the German advance in Poland, Drucker fled east. Arrested by the Soviets, he and his brother Aaron were sent to a gulag or labor camp in Siberia. Following the Polish-Soviet agreement in 1941, the brothers decided to join the Polish Army in the Soviet Union headed by General Wladyslaw Anders. Both were rejected as being Jewish. They tried to join later and were accepted in the new Polish Army headed by General Zygmunt Berling.

Both brothers fought their way to Germany. Both helped Jews along the way, especially Yeshayahu who petitioned the Polish Army command to provide the Jewish soldiers with the same spiritual assistance that was granted to Polish Catholic soldiers.

Yeshayahu's army unit was chosen to parade in Berlin following the defeat of Germany. Yeshayahu was then posted to the Polish city of Siedlice. This is where Rabbi Kahane met him and signed him up as a religious officer with the rank of captain in the Polish Army. Drucker was given the job of restoring Jewish religious communal life in Poland. He immersed himself in his work together with Rabbi Aaron Becker. Both rabbis visited newly established Jewish communities in liberated Poland and helped organize Jewish religious life. Everywhere, they tried to organize a local Jewish religious association that would provide the basic religious needs of the local Jews. All religious items such as prayer books or prayer shawls were in great demand. Drucker and Becker took the demands back to Warsaw and presented them to Rabbi Kahane. Kahane began to write letters of appeal for help to the various Jewish communities in Palestine, Britain and the United States. The response was overwhelming. Religious materials and money began to flow to the offices of Rabbi Kahane. He distributed the items to the various Jewish communities.

Drucker took some religious materials to the Jewish community of Zabrze, where he saw the Jewish compound with several buildings standing empty. He reported his findings to Rabbi Kahane who was looking for a Jewish home for orphans where rescued children would get a general and Jewish education, something that the Central Committee orphanages did not provide. With the liberation of Lublin in 1944, the Central Committee of Polish Jews established a Jewish children's home to cope with the young Jewish survivors. Other Jewish homes were soon established in Otwock near Warsaw, in Helenowek near Lodz, in Krakow, in Zakopane under the leadership of Lena Kichler, and other places. Usually it was Jewish individuals who had survived the war who established these homes, but eventually most of them came under the control of the Central Committee of Polish Jews or the local branch of the organization. Being an official institution of the Polish government, the Committee received building facilities, supplies and some financial assistance. At the end of 1945 there were already 11 Jewish foster homes. The homes were maintained by the Education Department of the Central Committee headed by Shlomo Herszenhorn, a Bund leader. These homes taught curriculum established by the Committee that followed newly created Polish educational curriculum. The emphasis was on Polish culture and language with a smattering of Yiddish culture and the Yiddish language. Rabbi Kahane and Captain Yeshayahu Drucker did not approve of the curriculum.

‫ו' שבת תש"ז.‬

‫לכבוד‬
‫ידידנו הנכבד הקפיטן דרוקר,‬
‫ואַרשה.‬
‫ר.פ.ל.‬

‫הרינו מצרפים לו בזה רשימה‬
‫של ילדים הנמצאים בידי נכרים, או מקרים‬
‫אחרים בפולין. קרוביהם בארץ פנו אלינו‬
‫בבקשה להצילם, או למחות להעבירם לידי‬
‫מוסדות יהודים בפולין. נבקר לו תודה‬
‫תודה, אם יואיל לטפל בכל המקרים האלה‬
‫ולהודיענו בפירושים את התוצאות.‬

‫נשמח מאד לעמוד אתו בקשר מכתבים‬
‫הדוק.‬

‫בכבוד רב‬
‫ובברכת התורה והארץ,‬

‫יעקב הרצוג.‬

**Letter sent by Yaacov Herzog to Captain Drucker, dated December 29, 1946.
"Enclosed is a list of Jewish children who survived the war hidden by non–
Jewish families in Poland. Their families in Israel asked us to help them recover
the children or at least to place them in Jewish institutions in Poland. We would
appreciate if you could follow all these cases. Please let us know of the results.
Please keep up written contact.
Yours, with blessings from the Torah and the land of Israel."**
(Freely translated by William Leibner)

Yaacov Herzog was Rabbi Itzhak Herzog's son and secretary

Members of the Association of Religious Jewish Communities (ARJC) in Poland began reporting to the main office that Jewish children remained hidden with Christian families and asked for help to restore these children to their Jewish families. Meanwhile letters, pleas and appeals were being sent steadily to Rabbi Itzhak Halevy Herzog, chief rabbi of Mandate Palestine, to help locate Jewish children who had survived the war hidden with Christian families or institutions in Poland. Many of the saviors refused for one reason or another to restore the children to their Jewish families. Children who no longer had living relatives in Poland or no surviving family at all, presented special difficulties. Legally, no action could be instituted for the return of these children. Families who had fled Poland and were now living abroad were pleading for Rabbi Herzog to help.

Rabbi Itzhak Halevi Herzog, chief rabbi of Mandate Palestine and later chief rabbi of the state of Israel

Rabbi Herzog saw but one way to help all these Jewish families: the children must be redeemed in accordance with the old Jewish tradition of "Pidyon Shvuyim" or redemption of the Jewish prisoners by paying ransom. Herzog and Kahane now decided to apply this ancient tradition in Poland to restore the Jewish children to their families and community. They knew that large sums of money would have to be raised to implement the program.

Rabbi Kahane had the right man to implement the task: Captain Yeshayahu Drucker who spoke Polish fluently and had a Polish appearance. Drucker soon began to receive letters and lists of children that were supposedly hidden in Poland during the war years. Above is a letter addressed by Rabbi Herzog's son Yaakov to Drucker. Rabbi Kahane and Captain Drucker decided to open an orphanage for the rescued Jewish children. The Polish army actually had a tradition of caring for orphanages as General Anders removed his troops from the Soviet Union. Several Polish orphanages had followed the Polish army. So Kahane used all his connections within the Polish Army and received permission to open the Zabrze orphanage. All the permits were obtained in the name of the AJRC of Zabrze. The main building would be the orphanage except for the top floor, which was reserved for an old age home. The orphanage would also use the elementary school building that had been closed for many years.

The Zabrze Jewish orphanage, previously an old age home

There was one other building in the compound that was given to the Ichud Zionist organization where their kibbutzim or collective youth groups would train prior to leaving for Palestine. These groups were Zionist pioneers and were determined to head to Palestine. The kibbutzim were organized along political Zionist line and consisted of members of Maccabi Ha-tsa'ir and Gordonia. Gordonia was founded in Poland in 1925 had been very active prior to World War II and started up its activities immediately in liberated Poland after the war.

Members of a kibbutz (Zionist pioneering communal group) in Zabrze, named for Meir Zarchi

The kibbutz was made up of Holocaust survivors belonging to the Zionist youth movements Gordonia and Maccabi Ha –Tsa'ir
In the photo: **Ichezkel Flekier (Yechezkel Fleker) – (middle row, fourth from the left)and his wife Elka, nee Popok (to the right of Ichezkel)**
Photographed on October 1, 1946

The first group soon left Poland and headed to Germany to a D.P. CAMP. The group would continue to move until it reached the shores of Italy or France and head illegally to Palestine. Another kibbutz would then take its place.

The Jewish community of Zabrze helped these institutions since they contributed greatly to the growth of Jewish life in the city.

The team that managed the Zabrze home

Seated from left to right: **Dawid Hubel, headmaster; Dr. Nechema Geller, administrator of the Zabrze orphanage; Captain and later Major Yeshayahu Drucker dressed in his military officer uniform**
Standing left to right: **1 Unknown; 2 Unknown; 3 Randolf Wittenberg, gym teacher and security officer; Mrs. Olnicka; Mrs, Englard, a teacher**

The school building of the Zabrze home

Dr. Nechema Geller, administrator of the Zabrze orphanage

Rabbi Kahane speedily proceeded to assemble a staff for the orphanage. He appointed Dr. Nechema Geller, a Shoah survivor, as headmistress of the orphanage and school. Her husband was also involved in the Jewish community of Zabrze and nearby Katowice

David Hubel was the headmaster of the orphanage and the father figure. He survived the Shoah and was the official Hebrew teacher at the orphanage

Rudolf Wattenberg, gym teacher and security officer. With existing conditions in Poland, security was needed especially around Jewish institutions

A picture of the enlarged staff at the Zabrze orphanage

Seated from left to right: **Mrs. Schapiro; Dr. Nechema Geller and her husband Dr. Geller, active in the Jewish community of Katowice; Mr. Gotlieb, secretary of Nechema Geller; dentist of the Zabrze home**
Standing from left to right: **Unknown; Mr.Gotzed; Unkown; David Hubel; Unknown; Unknown**

With the staff completed, the orphanage of Zabrze was ready to receive the first Jewish orphans in post war Poland. Rabbi Kahane wrote to the JDC in Poland to help run the orphanage. The plea was received by David Guzik, director of the Joint Distribution Committee's operations in Poland.

David Guzik was born in Warsaw, Poland. He joined the JDC Warsaw office as an accountant in 1918. During the course of World War II, he became a central figure in JDC Warsaw. Using his skills to raise funds by legal or illegal means, he helped finance welfare services, medical help, and cultural and underground activities in the ghetto including the Oneg Shabbat project and the Warsaw Ghetto Uprising. He survived the war in hiding on the "Aryan" side. In 1945, he was appointed Director of JDC Operations in liberated Poland. David Guzik was killed in a plane crash in Prague in 1946 while returning from a conference in Paris, France. He had gone to Paris for consultations and met Dr. Joseph Schwartz, head of JDC operations in Europe.

David Guzik

Dr. Joseph Schwartz was a brilliant and exceptional man. Known as Packy to those close to him, he was born in Ukraine and moved to Baltimore at an early age. A distinguished educator and scholar and an authority on Semitics and Semitic Literature, Dr. Schwartz received his doctorate from Yale, following his graduation from the Rabbi Isaac Elchanan Seminary of Yeshiva University. Dr. Schwartz taught at the American University in Cairo and at Long Island University and then served as Director of the Federation of Jewish Charities in Brooklyn. He served the JDC from 1939-1950/1, and then went on to become the Executive Vice Chairman of the United Jewish Appeal and later the Vice President of Israel Bonds. He passed away in 1975, leaving behind a legacy of countless good deeds.

Following World War II, Dr. Schwartz organized a massive organization that helped thousands of Shoah survivors and enabled them to regain their human composure. The Joint Distribution Committee not only provided food, medicine and financial help but also provided hope. Schwartz was especially concerned with the Jewish infants who had survived the war. Orphanages and Jewish youth centers were on top of his list. He of course endorsed the support for the Zabrze orphanage. With aid from JDC the Zabrze orphanage began to provide a loving home for rescued Jewish children.

Partial JDC Archives List of Children's Homes. Notice Zabrze is listed as a religious congregation

Institution	Address	Number of children
TOZ, Jewish Health Assoc.	Otwock, Olin	40 Sanatorium
	Glussyoe	80 Preventorium
	Srodborow Cleszynska	70
Religious Organizations	Krakow Dreitele	29
Agudas Israel	Dzierszew	50
	Lodz	10
Children Home	Dzierzoniow, Browarna 12	30
	Lodz, Zachodnia 66	10
Religious Congregation	Zabrze, Karlowicza 10	31
Vaad Hatzala	Bytom, Smolenska 15	70
Zionist Organizations	Headquarters, Lodz	
	Poludniowa	26
Mizrachi	Krakow, Miodova 26	25
Mizrachi	Sosnowiec	39
Coordination of Zionist	Lodz, Zawadzka 17	93
Hashomer Hazair	Srodmiejska 4	49
Poale Zion	Bielawa	52
Central Jewish home	Committee Legnica, Piastowska 6	60
Central Jewish home	Piotrolesie, Ogrodowa 10	88
Central Jewish home	Chorsow, Katowicka 2	80
Central Jewish home	Otwock, Bolesl. Pruss 11	80
Central Jewish home	Srodborow, Cieszynska	75
Central Jewish home	Bielsko, Mickiewicza 22	56
Central Jewish home	Srodborow, Literacka	2
Central Jewish home	Srodborowianka"	104
Central Jewish home	Helenowek	117
Central Jewish home	Krakow, Augustyuska Boczna 8	66
Central Jewish home	Czestochowa, Jasnogorska	32

This is a translation of the original Hebrew list of Jewish homes into English. The first column on the left gives the name of the organization of the home. The word central indicates that the home was under the control of the Central Committee of Polish Jews. The second column gives the address of the home and the last column indicates the number of children at the time of the visit of the inspectors of the Joint Distribution Committee. The number of children in the central homes remained relatively steady while the Zionist or Agudah homes constantly shipped children out of Poland.

Dr. Joseph Schwartz in his military uniform

**Original partial list of the orphanages that the Joint Distribution
Committee supported in Poland**

Footnotes

1 Dobroszycki, Lucjan. "Survival of the Holocaust in Poland- A Portrait based on Jewish
        Committee Records 1944-1947". Armonk, New York, M.E. Sharpe, US, p.10
United States Holocaust Memorial Museum, Washington D.C. USA

[Page 55]

Chapter III

The Children of Zabrze
Translated from Hebrew by William Leibner
Edited by Phyllis Oster

David Danieli

**David Danieli, formerly Daniel Danielski,
at the orphanage in Zabrze in 1946**

David Danielski (surname later changed to Danieli) was born in 1932 in the hamlet of Pszczyna. His father, Max or Maximilian, was a pastry baker. The family soon moved to the bigger township of Rybnik in Silesia where Max opened a bakery in the center of the city. The bakery was very successful and the family flourished. They had a maid and their apartment was well furnished including a piano, and many antiques which David's mother, Hannah, collected. David's older brother Sasha had died in 1928 so the younger boy received a great deal of attention from Max and Hannah. But his parents insisted that David be independent and able to defend himself when the need arose.

David does not remember much about the family or their friends. He does remember playing with other children in the courtyard of their apartment building. The family was not very religious although they belonged to the Jewish Community Center. He recalls attending very crowded services on a few occasions at the main synagogue, and his mother giving him a flag crowned with an apple to take with him to synagogue in celebration of Simchat Torah.

The new order in Germany appointed a German supervisor over the bakery, who was in essence the owner. Max Danielski was permitted to stay on at the bakery but only as a worker. Then the family was forced to move to a poorer section of the town, where other Jews were also forced to live. The new flat consisted of one room into which everything possible was moved. David's mother started to sell items from their home to provide food for the family since her husband's income became smaller with time. While selling her household items, Hannah Danielski met a German Silesian woman, Martha Kapitza, who was also involved in buying and selling goods. The transactions were highly illegal, but Hannah was able to trade her valuables for food.

Max learned from a friendly policeman that anti–Jewish actions were being planned and started to make arrangements for his son's disappearance. He contacted a Polish farmer who lived in Babia Gora and was willing to take David for a time. Hannah packed a small suitcase, gave him some pocket money and bought him a train ticket. He traveled alone to the farm. He remained with the farmer and his family for some time helping with various farm chores. On a cold night in February of 1942 the farmer took David to the station and sent him home to Rybnik. He headed home and found the apartment dark with no lights in the window. The Gestapo had posted an order on the door forbidding admittance to the premises. He had no idea what had happened to his parents and did not know what to do next having no other family in the city.

David decided to cross the street and approach the neighbor, Martha Kapitza, who had become friendly with his mother. She offered him a place to stay until things settled down. Through her David learned that all the Jews of Rybnik including his parents were rounded up and shipped to an unknown destination. Nobody knew what happened to them. He snuck into his parents' flat through a window and found that the police had ransacked the place and made a shambles. He made two trips to his former home, carrying away as much as he could and never returned. .

Anton Kapitza, the husband of Martha Kapitza, was an out of work, disabled coal miner of Polish Silesian origin. Martha was a native of Zabrze or Hindenburg, and provided for her family by selling luxury goods in exchange for food which she then resold. The market for these goods was excellent since there was a scarcity of finer goods in Germany during the war years. Hannah Danielski traded regularly with Martha Kapitza before she was deported and they had become good friends. Mrs. Kapitza had five children: Elizabeth who was a mute; Ernest, a soldier; Gertrude who delivered papers; Ludwig who worked in the building trades and was a bit slow; and the youngest Zigmund, born in 1933. David and Zigmund were close in age and got along pretty well. Gertrude, the oldest, born in 1923, assisted her mother in running the house and contributed financially. David did chores and errands at the direction of Martha or Gertrude Kapitza and adjusted to the situation as best he could. He knew that he was Jewish but that was about all he knew about Judaism.

Time went by and suddenly the Gestapo started searching and questioning people in the area. Apparently, someone either reported David or he heard the authorities were looking for him. Mrs. Kapitza packed a few items of clothing, gave him some money and the address of a farm supervisor in Striegau, Germany, who was originally a Polish police official. David left the house and headed for the train station just before the Gestapo arrived at the Kapitza home asking questions about his whereabouts. Gertrude later told him that her mother stated that he had left the house after stealing money. Mrs. Kapitza was even questioned at headquarters about the case but eventually the matter was dropped since she insisted that she had no knowledge of his whereabouts. Gertrude also revealed to him that her mother had promised Mrs. Danielski to help protect her son.

Meanwhile David remained with the farm supervisor helping with the chores. He started school, immediately proceeded to third grade and joined the "Hitler Jugend" or Hitler Youth, as every child belonged to the organization. He remembers collecting all kinds of materials for the war effort. One day, on the way to school, he saw for the first time people in striped pajamas who were inmates of the Gross Rosen concentration camp. He was reminded of his Jewish heritage and very worried about his parents. He would find out later that Mrs. Kapitza sent food to the Danielski's with a German who had worked with Max near Rybnik. Max died about June 16, 1942 and Mrs. Danielski was killed in Auschwitz in December 1943 at the age of 43.

By June 1942 David had returned to the Kapitza household and taken over the newspaper route since Gertrude had married and left the house. Mrs. Kapitza managed to obtain a baptismal certificate for David and he began to attend school. He was frequently late due to the newspaper deliveries that steadily declined as the war went against Germany. Conditions in Germany worsened by the day although there was still enough food. The school building was soon converted into a military installation and classes ceased. The Russians were advancing on Germany. Being sent to the Eastern front was considered a death sentence. The Russians reached Rybnik in the winter of 1945, where they expelled the entire German population. The Kapitza family made the 40 mile trek to Zabrze where Martha's sister lived. Then the hardships really began. Anton Kapitza and David decided to head back to Rybnik and found the Kapitza home ransacked. The Russians had cleaned the place out including the basement where some food was well hidden.

Conditions were very bad The family made cookies and sold them to buy food. While dealing in the Rybnik market, David was approached by a Jewish man, Mr. Gold, who asked if he was Jewish and offered to help him return to Judaism. David felt an obligation to talk to Anton Kapitza first who saw no problem in David's learning about Judaism, Mr. Gold, who resided in Bytom, invited David to live in his home. Gold was in the process of preparing to take his family to America and asked David to join them. He agreed.

Gold also told David about the orphanage in Zabrze where he could learn about Judaism. David was sent to the orphanage, where the head teacher, David Hubel, had a great impression on him. David became an ardent Zionist, and was no longer interested in emigrating to the United States. Instead David wanted to go to Palestine, and became very active in Zionist activities at the orphanage. The Gold family was disappointed by the decision since they really wanted to take David to the United States. They parted and never met again.

David enjoyed his stay at the orphanage where he learned the basic tenets of Judaism, Jewish history and the Hebrew language. He also attended the regular Polish school in accordance with Polish educational requirements. But David really did not devote himself to those studies since he wanted to go to Palestine. Then rumors started in the orphanage that Rabbi Herzog was coming to take all the children to Palestine.

Rabbi Itzhak Eisik Halevi Herzog, chief rabbi of the British Mandate of Palestine, received a promise from the British administration in Palestine to give entrance certificates to 500 Jewish orphans who had survived the war in Poland in monasteries, Christian homes, forests and caves. There was great excitement at the Zabrze Jewish orphanage on Karlowica Street Number 10, Zabrze, Upper Silesia, Poland, with the news of imminent departure for Palestine. Rumors chased rumors but then the children were ordered to pack. Every child began to pack their few belongings; some had smaller, others bigger suitcases. The Zabrze contingent consisted of complete orphans, partial orphans, children with one parent, children with one parent aboard the transport, and children who had returned from Russia.

The following is a list of some of the Zabrze children that David Danielski could remember. In some instances the children were known merely by their nicknames.

Shlomo Korn	Hannah Hoffman
Tzvi Shpigler	Rivka Motil
Shlomo Shpigler	Fela Kozoch
Yehuda Tzvi Sobol	Sonia Mayer
Riwka Brender	Heniek Mayer
Tzvi Brender	Arieh
Yeizik Peitznik	Charlotka. Brother and sister
David Fridman	Yehudit Wilczenski

Mrs. Wilczenski	Ella
Renka	Roma
Her sister	Dwora Ditman
And mother	Shmulek
Naomi Agrabska	Batia Sheinfeld
Esther Kastenberg	David Danieli
Emil and mother	Raya, the group leader
Big Eva	

Some children remained at the Zabrze home with a staff headed by principal Dr. Nehema Geler and head teacher David Hubel.

David left the Zabrze home on Thursday afternoon the 22nd of August 1946. The Zabrze group first headed by tramway to the nearby town of Katowice where a train was standing on a sideline with hundreds of children, group leaders and teachers. They came from many orphanages in Poland: Lodz, Krakow, Warsaw and Katowice. The greetings, shouts and tears were beyond description. Order was soon established and the Zabrze group boarded its assigned car. Captain Yeshayahu Drucker, dressed in his military uniform, was there as was Rabbi Aaron Becker. Both military chaplains had their hands full with all the logistical problems. Soon, the Chief Rabbi of Mandate Palestine, Rabbi Itzhak Eisik Halevy Herzog and his son Yaakov Herzog arrived and boarded the train. They came specifically to escort the train out of Poland. Late that evening, the Herzog transport of children started to roll in a westerly direction toward the Czech border. The trip was slow moving and frequent stops occurred, especially on the border between Poland and Czechoslovakia. Rabbi Drucker and Rabbi Becker said goodbye to the children and headed back to Warsaw to report to the Chief Military Chaplain of the Polish Army Rabbi David Kahane. A day later, on the afternoon of August 23, 1946, the train crossed the border and arrived at a big industrial Czech town, Moravska Ostrava. Arrangements were made for lodging and feeding the children and Rabbi Herzog's entourage at a local hotel, the "Moravska," where they stayed until Sunday when the trip continued to Prague.

The situation at the hotel was quite chaotic until each child was assigned a room and Shabbat set in. The transport included religious youth from Hapoel Hamizrahi and Agudath Israel, who tended to religious services presided over by Rabbi Herzog. The hotel was nicely furnished and included such novelties as elevators, telephones and venetian blinds which were all a great source of entertainment for the children. .

On arriving in Prague, the children disembarked and were taken to the Repatrianski Tabor Dablice refugee camp located in the northern part of the city. The camp was huge, with Jews from many different places, and absorbed the transport easily. It is unclear why the children were taken to the camp, but they remained there for five weeks. His stay in the camp had a great impact on David, both because he was immersed in Judaism, and had the opportunity to learn about Prague, which he came to love. To keep the children busy, city tours and lectures were organized. Most of the children were exposed for the first time to the wonders of an important cultural metropolis.

The High Holidays arrived and on the first day of Rosh Hashanah, the children walked from the camp to the Maharal synagogue, better known as the "Alte Neu Shul." There David heard the story of the "Golem" for the first time. He was very impressed with Prague, its streets, its bridges and squares. The Charles Bridge with the huge cross and the Hebrew words "Kadosh, Kadosh, Kadosh!" (Holy) written on it particularly caught his attention. Here was a city that respected Jewish letters in Europe.

With the end of Rosh Hashanah, the children boarded a train headed south to Bratislava along the Danube River, crossing the German border near Munich, Bavaria, then continuing west across the Rhine River to Strasbourg, France. Here for all practical purposes ended the Herzog transport of children. Despite all efforts, the British refused to grant entrance certificates to the children. Rabbi Herzog was aware of the situation but could do little except make arrangements for each political group to care for its contingent in the transport. At the beginning of their journey in Katowice, the Zabrze contingent had been absorbed into the Lodz and Krakow group under the auspices of the Hapoel Hamizrahi movement, a moderate religious Zionist group.

On arrival in Strasburg, the Bnei Akiva youth organization, part of the Hapoel Hamizrahi movement, welcomed the children and saw to their needs. Their actual host was the well to do Bloch family who first lodged the children at the university and within a few days moved them to a large home at 23 Rue de Selenic in a nice residential neighborhood. The house was big but not large enough to comfortably accommodate the group of about 250 people, including children, parents and staff. The noise, the commotion and constant activities soon attracted the attention of neighbors who began to refer to the house as " la maison de fous" or crazy house. It quickly became a problem and the Bloch family moved the smaller children to a large estate in Schirmeck with plenty of land. The Schirmeck home was headed by Mr. Spiner, who came from Krakow. The older children lived at a home in Strasburg run by Meir Weissblum with whom David still maintains contact.

The older youth were anxious to leave for Palestine and became frustrated. Soon a group of about17 youngsters formed a small unit that worked to secure passage. David was chosen to write a letter to David Hubel asking his help. The letter worked and the group was told to leave for Marseilles, one of the assembly points for illegal immigration to Palestine. The group left Strasburg in March 1947 and shortly thereafter boarded the illegal refugee ship named "Exit Europe 1947" better known as the *Exodus* ship".

The story of the passengers experience on the *Exodus* is well known. David still vividly remembers the Rosh Hashanah that he celebrated on a British detention ship in the port of Gibraltar on the way to a detention camp in the

British sector of Germany. He quickly left the British detention camp and began to move in the direction of France. Luckily he was able to cross the border to France and rejoin the orphanage that he had left earlier that year. The home was now closed but the orphanage had moved to the castle named "Chateau Raye" in the village of Le Vauson near Paris.

Then the State of Israel was proclaimed in 1948. After having left Zabrze, Poland on August 22, 1946, David, and other Herzog transport youngsters arrived at the port of Haifa on August 16, 1948.

David is presently retired and has made several trips to Zabrze where he met Gertrude Kapitza, the only surviving member of the Kapitza family.

Shlomo Koren

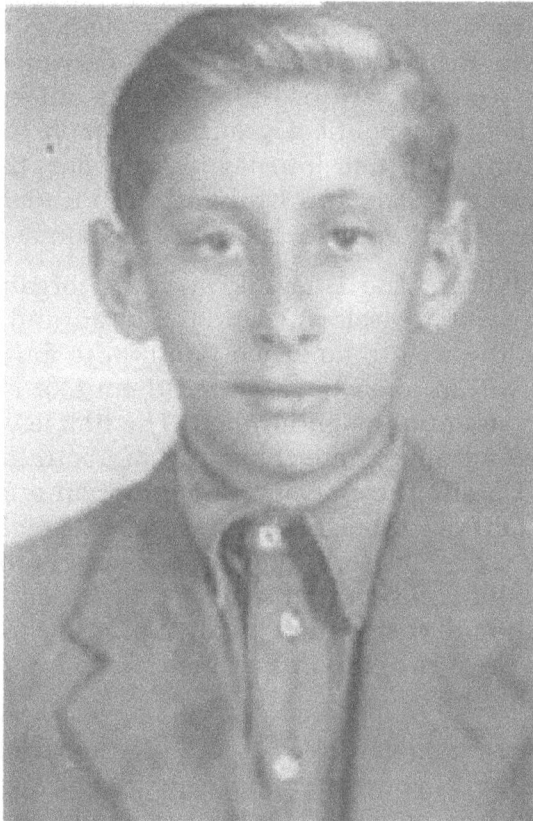

Shlomo Koren at Zabrze
Shlomo Koren is a friend of David Danieli. They started their friendship at Zabrze and maintain it to this day. Shlomo was kind enough to write his life story for us in Hebrew and we translated it to English.
The above picture was provided by the museum of "Lochamei Hagetaot".

I, Shlomo Koren was born in Nowy Sacz, Galicia, Poland and survived World War II in Russia, returning to Poland following the war in 1946. My family settled in Katowice, Poland, where I was registered in a city public school but did not attend classes. I barely spoke Polish. I met David Danieli (Danielski) in Katowice. He told me that he was attending a Jewish school in Zabrze, about a half hour away, and invited me to visit him. I visited the Zabrze home on several occasions and was pleased by the ambience of the place. I liked the home, especially the individual attention that the place gave the children. I discussed the situation with my mother and sisters. I had no father. The family had difficulty controlling me and I often roamed the streets of Katowice, so they consented to my moving to the home. The orphanage readily accepted me, for the institution was specifically created for children like me.

At Zabrze, I was in a room with two other boys; one of them named Morin Landau. Each of us had experienced horrible events that we tried to forget. Some of the girls at the home spoke only Polish and continued to pray and cross themselves, refusing to admit that they were Jewish. The teachers and supervisors had a difficult time reaching some of the children but with time managed to win their confidence and provide them with a basic education and a bit of self–confidence. Jewish religious education was introduced in moderation so as not to antagonize the children who were ill at ease if not hostile to anything Jewish. The boys were taught how to pray, put on phylacteries, the girls were taught about lighting candles and all children were exposed to Jewish holidays and a bit of a Jewish atmosphere. Hebrew, Jewish history, and Zionism were stressed at the home.

Within the compound of the Jewish community at Zabrze near the orphanage, there was also a building where a group of young pioneers were preparing themselves to move to Palestine and work the land. The group or kibbutz belonged to the Ichud Zionist movement. We watched the youngsters frequently dancing "horas" and other folk dances in the yard of the compound and were impressed. Their enthusiasm inspired us to become more fervent Zionists. After four months of ideal life at the home, we heard that Rabbi Herzog was coming to take us to Palestine. I began to beg my mother and sisters to permit me to leave Poland with the others. They were not opposed to Palestine but feared the distance and the unknown. Slowly and persistently I managed to convince them that I must go to Palestine. Mother bought me a new jacket, shoes and stitched some dollars into my pants in case of an emergency.

Time flew and we left the home and headed to Katowice, Poland, where we boarded a train with other youngsters. The train waited for the arrival of Rabbi Herzog and his entourage. He arrived late in the evening and the train started to roll to the Czech border. The next day was Friday, the train stopped and we spent Shabbat at a hotel in Moravski–Ostrava. There was a bit of chaos at the hotel since the children made great use of the hotel telephones, elevators and borrowed items that were never returned.

On Sunday the train resumed the journey to Prague where we disembarked and were taken to a refugee camp named Repatrianski Tabor Dablice to await entrance visas to France. We would remain in this camp for about six weeks. Our Zabrze group became part of the Hapoel Hamizrahi group. The group leaders were not well disposed to our Zabrze contingent since we spoke primarily Polish and were less familiar with Jewish customs than the Mizrahi group. A certain distance existed between the groups. The Zabrze group was very sensitive and received a great deal of attention at the home due to our origins and experiences while the regular Mizrahi youths were familiar with Jewish life. The Mizrahi youth leaders also lacked the necessary educational tools to handle the sensitive Zabrze contingent. Still, a routine was established at the refugee camp and we youngsters had to abide by it.

Some of us boys, including David Danieli, soon formed a group that would travel to Prague and spend time in the city. I sold my stamp collection in Prague in order to have spending money. We went to the movies and saw many city attractions in Prague. I was displeased with our group leader and joined a group of boys that raided the youth warehouse following dinner on the first night of Rosh Hashanah. We took clothing and food and gave it all out to the children, who appeared at services the next day at in brand new outfits. The group leaders could do little about our antics.

The French visas arrived a day after Rosh Hashanah. We headed to the railway station, boarded a train and traveled for the next two days across Germany until we reached Strasbourg, France. We were taken to the Strasbourg Jewish community service center, where we spent the holidays. We were then moved to a three–story house on Rue Selenic in the center of Strasbourg that belonged to the Jewish community. The main floor had halls that were converted into a synagogue, dining room and study centers. The second floor consisted of dorms and the third floor had small rooms for the staffers and their families. The place was crowded and disorganized. The group leaders became a bit more tyrannical in their behavior toward us. Discipline was strictly enforced and offenders were given cleaning chores as punishment. Soon the younger children were removed to a home in Schirmeck, making life at the home a bit easier.

Some of us were not pleased with the management at the home and expressed it openly. The administration then made arrangements to move nine of us to the Jewish orphanage of Strasbourg administered by Mr. and Mrs. Blum. The Blum's gave us a warm reception with plenty of tasty food, some clothing, bed sheets and transportation passes. We were assigned to an American ORT program where we were taught various trades. I selected courses in metal work. The instruction was primarily in German but I also received instruction in French. All children had to attend services at the synagogue of Rabbi Deutch of Strasbourg.

I had ample time to enjoy the city and meet with my friends who remained at the home in Rue Selenic. But I was restless and anxious to head to Palestine. I started to talk to the other boys of the transport and we soon formed a group that was determined to make aliyah. We approached the children from the home on Selenic with our plan and some youngsters joined us, including David Danieli. We had neither the money nor the connections to carry out our plan. David decided to write a letter to his friend, David Hubel, the headmaster in Zabrze, explaining our problem and asking for help.

The answer soon came in the form of train tickets and a date of departure to Marseilles, France. We packed and bid farewell to our temporary homes. The Selenic Street home threw a party in our honor and we left for Marseilles where an emissary met us and took us to an isolated and empty house. We remained there until Passover and then moved to another camp facing the sea. Here preparations were being made for the departure of the next illegal ship. Hundreds of boarding passes were forged with the South American country of Columbia as the destination. Then one night, Jewish refugees began to arrive en masse and were organized in groups and sent to board the *Exodus* ship. Our group was one of the last to board the very crowded ship.

On July 11, 1947, the ship managed to leave the docking berth without a pilot and headed out to sea. The British navy followed the ship and then rammed the boat on the high seas. Fights ensued between the British boarding parties and the immigrants resulting in the death of three civilians, among them an American sailor, and dozens of seriously wounded passengers. The illegal ship was brought to Haifa where all passengers were transferred to three prison ships and started their voyage back to France.

The French refused to force the passengers off the boats and eventually the ships sailed to Hamburg where we docked on September 6, 1947. Our ship, the "*Empire Rival*", was the last ship to dock and we were immediately placed aboard a train and transported to Lubeck where trucks took us to the camp called Amstau. We were later transferred to another camp named Pependorf where there were more youngsters. Here we participated in various activities and also studied Hebrew. Soon we began to travel in the direction of France under the leadership of "Bricha" agents and eventually made it back to Strasbourg. The home at Rue Selenic was closed and Mr. Blum was happy to see the group. I continued my train trip to Marseilles where I entered a huge refugee camp named "Grand Arnas."

The camp contained many nationalities including Jews waiting for visas for America or residence papers to stay in France. Within a week we were transferred to the Jewish Agency camp "Villa Gabi," a beautiful place overlooking the sea. Here we awaited an illegal ship that would take us to Palestine. Then came the order that only volunteers for the Israeli Army would be sent to Israel. I was informed that I would be sent back to the Rue Selenic orphanage that had now moved to the Chateau Voisin near Paris. I refused to go back to the home and joined a Hagana training camp in the vicinity of

Marseilles. I lied about my age, told them I was 18 and was accepted for military training. I then boarded a ship with Canadian volunteers and landed in Haifa toward the end of May 1948. I was immediately sent to the "Yona" military base near Beit Lid and within a few days, I was ordered to assemble with the other soldiers. I must have looked younger than the other soldiers because when the commander saw me, he told me to return my weapon and wait for him. Following the formation, he dropped me off at the immigrant hostel in Raanana on his way to visit his parents. Thus ended my wanderings from 1939 to 1948.

Numbered certificate issued to the passengers of the famous "*Exodus*" ship.

Batia (nee Akselrad) Eisenstein

Batia Akselrad in 1946 in France
Batia Akselrad was another resident at the Zabrze orphanage.
She has graciously written her life story for us.

I, Batia Akselrad Eisenstein, was born on May 5, 1932, in Krosno, Galicia, Poland. My parents were Bendet and Cila (nee Freifeld) Akselrad. My father owned a sawmill and was the head of the Jewish communities of Korczyna and Krosno. I had five older brothers. The oldest Shmuel, was born in 1909, married to Klara Rosenberg from Debice and had a daughter named Irenka, born in 1935. My second brother was Shalom, born in 1911, followed by Avraham in 1922, Yehuda in 1924 and Levy in 1930.

Bendet Akselrad

Cila Freifeld–Akselrad

My family revolved about my father who was devoted to the Jewish community. He was a gentle person who had a great deal of patience and listened to everybody who came to the house with a problem and the Jews of Krosno and Korczyna had many problems, mainly survival problems, in a sea of anti–Semitism. To this day, people who knew my father praise him for his patience, understanding and assistance in solving problems. These people describe to me in great detail his deeds that were unknown to me at the time, and make me feel proud of my parents and family.

As a child I loved the Jewish holidays of Purim, Passover and Friday nights. My father always brought home dinner guests from the synagogue who joined us at the table and shared our meals. Dinners were always interlaced with conversations and discussions. Father devoted most of his time to the community and considered this task to be his "raison d'etre" or essence of life. Mother also helped my father since she received the people who came to the house while father was not at home. She spoke to the visitors and made notes that were relayed to father on his arrival. My brother and I also had important jobs for we ran to open the door whenever the bell rang. Many of the family discussions revolved around the impending war and my parents and older brothers were very perturbed by the news events of the day. I was terrified and expected the worst, especially when I heard the rantings of Hitler on the radio. I had bad feelings but did not really understand what was happening

Many influential Polish gentiles visited our home and discussed ways and means to avoid or smooth sore spots within the Krosno community among Jews and Christians. The Polish population was very anti–Semitic and the slightest incident could turn into a major riot or a pogrom as often happened in the country. The Jews wanted to avoid confrontations at any cost and merely desired to continue with their lives.

My father left his various businesses in Krosno to his older sons while he devoted himself to the needs of the Jewish population. Shmuel and Shalom graduated from the school of commerce and administration, where my father had also graduated. Schooling was very limited to Jews and some trades or professions were closed to Jewish students. In some instances a few Jewish students were admitted as tokens. Even gifted Jewish youth could only dream about positions or jobs in governmental or public offices.

The Polish–German war started in September 1939 and my brother Shalom was immediately drafted at night and I was unable to say goodbye to him. Time passed and we heard nothing from Shalom. Then a Pole came to our house and told the family that my brother was seriously injured and being treated at a hospital in Stanislawow, Eastern Galicia. Of course, he received a nice reward for the information. My father, Avraham and Yehuda, went to Stanislawow where Shalom was supposedly convalescing. They soon discovered the whole thing was a hoax. Shalom was not there. They did meet many Jews from Krosno who had fled to this area prior to the arrival of the

Germans. My father and brothers had a difficult time returning home because Russian forces now occupied Stanislawow as part of the partition of Poland by Germany and Russia. When they managed to reach Krosno, a post card was waiting from Shalom saying he was a prisoner of war in a German camp. Shalom continued to send post cards and in one of them he let us know that he would soon be sent home. Our joy was boundless.

By then father was very busy with the community, assisted by his elder sons. The city of Krosno had received Jewish refugees from many places who needed help and temporary lodgings. The Jewish economic situation in the city was very bad, many Jewish businesses were confiscated and Jews were not permitted to circulate freely in the city. Each day was worse, a white armband with a Star of David had to be worn, new anti–Jewish rules and regulations appeared regularly. The situation assumed alarming proportions and my father and brothers barely coped with the situation and found it difficult to provide all the help needed.

The fact that father and my brothers spoke German fluently — since the family had lived for many years in Vienna and had Austrian citizenship —gave them the ability to use the language to help the Jews of Krosno. The Germans refused to deal with Jews and especially those who did not speak German. Every demand had to be written and submitted to the Germans in their language. Requests were constantly drafted on behalf of the Jews of Krosno. Then each had to be followed up. These missions were mostly met with negative answers, which reflected on my father's face when he returned home. Although I was small, I began to hear strange and meaningless but frightening words like concentration camps, ghetto, searches and Gestapo. I did not understand these words but feared them for they were uttered in fright. I began to mature rapidly as children do in such special circumstances.

One evening father came home and I saw the sadness in his eyes. Mother told me that they wanted to talk to me privately. Father told me that he had found a special place for me with a fine Polish family that wanted me to live with them. He told me that this family would like me very much. I listened seriously but did not really understand what was taking place. Mother packed a bag with clothing. The next evening, my brother Shalom took me to the home of the Krukierek family. We were well acquainted with the Krukierek's because the sons worked at our sawmill in Krosno.

During the walk he explained to me how to behave in the new home and to be a good and obedient girl. He instructed me to listen and fulfill all the commands of the new family. He also told me that I now had a new name that I must use. Furthermore, he said, I must not cry or ask to return home, my family would visit when they could. Parting was very sad, I saw the tears in my brother's eyes and I barely restrained myself from crying.

The Krukierak family consisted of the grandmother, Weronika, the grandfather, their married daughter Jozefa and her husband. The new family named me Basia (a typical Polish Christian name). I cried the entire first night and was unable to fall asleep. I had a hard time adjusting to the idea that I was left alone with a new and strange family. No longer would I be able to rejoin my dear and beloved family. I rose early in the morning and went to the yard. I approached the gate and looked at the path that we used the previous night, but nobody was in sight.

I stood there and cried, hoping to see a familiar face, but no one appeared. I stayed there for hours each day in the hope of seeing someone from the family, but in vain. I was depressed and entered the home only when grandfather called me to eat, but I had no appetite. Grandmother understood the situation and tried to alleviate my fears by saying that my old family would probably visit me soon. This of course did not help but it did show me that someone cared. Needless to say, I was very happy when a member of the family visited and brought a gift from my old home. They made promises to visit often to cheer me up, for they saw my red and swollen eyes. They all did try to visit often except my brother Avraham. One day he went to buy bread and had disappeared. Our visits always ended in sadness for I was left alone again.

These visits continued and then suddenly stopped. At that point I was 11 years old. Although I didn't know it then, in one year most of my family was taken and murdered by the Nazis. My mother Cila Akselrad was caught and shot in 1943 in Korczyna. My father Bendet Akselrad was shot on July 15, 1943, in the concentration camp of Szebnie. My brother Shmuel, his wife Clara, their daughter Irenka, and Shalom Akselrad were caught in Warsaw with false Aryan papers and killed. My brother Yehuda joined the partisans and fought with them until 1943 when he was killed in the vicinity of Warsaw. My brother Levy was killed in Krosno in 1943. Only Avraham Akselrad survived the concentration camps and managed to reach New York where he passed away in 1991 after a lengthy illness. He never married. Thus, I was the sole survivor of the family in Krosno and continued to live with the Polish family.

I missed my parents and brothers and kept dreaming about them. I saw them almost every night in my dreams and was very happy, only to awaken to the bitter reality that I was alone. I remained in the house with grandfather and grandmother, while the couple went to work, and helped in the house with everything that I could since I was always afraid that I might be kicked out. This fear lingered on and frequently prevented me from sleeping. I slowly became attached to the new family and became more familiar with them. They worried about me and were constantly fearful that an informer might reveal my existence to the Germans. The home of the new family was located in a rural area in the vicinity of the airport of Krosno. Still there was fear that someone might spot this young girl in the courtyard. The Krukierek family decided that the risks of being exposed were serious and began to shift my hiding places. Sometimes I slept hidden in a straw bed in the attic. Others times I was hidden in dark places that affected my vision on seeing light.

On nice evenings, I would emerge and play a bit in the wheat field. Some evenings, grandmother would give me a basket and send me to pick potatoes. I dug the potatoes by hand in the dark so that no one would see me. I picked the big ones and left the small ones in the ground so that they would continue to grow, as grandmother Weronika instructed me to do. I would return with a basket full of potatoes and then clean them before entering the kitchen. I spent a lot of time peeling potatoes, and was very busy doing household chores, for grandfather had a leg injury and limped, and grandmother was weak and tired easily. When Grandfather was pleased with the work, he would say that I had earned my keep for the day and give me an extra heavy slice of bread. Grandfather was rather economical with his compliments; thus I relished them when I received one.

Potatoes and cabbage was the standard food for the family. Sunday was a special meal that consisted of potatoes, cabbage and rabbit meat. The rabbits were raised on the farm next to the cows and roosters. At night I picked potatoes and during the day I tended to the daily house chores. I did all the chores with devotion for I craved attention and very much wanted to be accepted.

In addition to the regular house chores, I also mended clothing, helped prepare the feed for the cows and did many other kinds of work in the house. Of course, there was less work during the winter when the weather was freezing and the fields were covered with snow. I spent my time hiding in the cowshed, talking to the rabbits and roosters. It seemed to me that they answered but I was not sure if I heard them. I was very lonely and continued to talk to the small animals for I had no friends.

This was a difficult period, for the Germans increased the intensity of their searches. My adopted family was seriously frightened and even considered throwing me out. I was terrified and could not fall asleep for fear of winding up in the street. Grandmother cared a great deal for me and told the others she would assume full responsibility for my protection. She also said that she would leave the house if I were thrown out. Grandmother's threats worked and she saved me. She then asked her son Kazek to hide me at the mill where he was a guard. The sawmill had belonged to our family prior to the war, but was now owned by a German named Schmidt, and Kazek watched the place. He built a hiding place and one night took me from the house in a bag of sawdust.

The hiding place was under a wooden floor amid sawdust. Kazek's brothers also worked at the mill. Kazek brought me to the hiding place and gave me instructions on how to behave during the day when the Polish workers tended to their jobs. He also showed me how to position myself in the hiding place so as not to arouse suspicion. I could not sit, move or turn in the dark hiding place. During the day it was still bearable but at night it was frightening. I kept dreaming about my parents and brothers. I had the premonition that they were all killed. I did not want to dream but could not help myself. Rats occasionally ran over my body and I could not stop them because there was no room to move my hands. It was horrible.

For several months I continued to sleep in sawdust under the wooden floor. Autumn was approaching and with it came the rains. Everything was cold, wet and dreary. Still I had to stay in hiding during the day for fear of being spotted by a worker or by a customer who came to buy wood. Only at night could I slowly venture out. As a result of my hiding position, I could barely walk. I was depressed and often thought of ending my life, but I was a coward. I did not divulge these thoughts to Kazek for fear of embarrassing him after all his efforts on my behalf.

Winter approached and the family decided to return me to the house. They still hid me but within the house for it was bitter cold outside. I also became accustomed to Catholic traditions and realized then that I would never return to Judaism. I no longer wanted to belong to the persecuted and humiliated Jewish people. Grandfather often told me that the Jewish people had been persecuted throughout history. Even the Arabs were killing Jews in Palestine. I heard and saw all these things. I saw how Jews were being persecuted while the Christian children played and had fun. I felt jealous and felt ashamed at having been born a Jew.

These thoughts persisted and became stronger as time passed. Suddenly, the roar of shells shook the entire area for we were near the Krosno airport. The Russians shelled the entire area prior to their advance and for several days the cannon fire could be heard and then silence. The area was liberated but nobody came to take me home. I started school for the first time in 1945 and was registered as a Christian student. I excelled in my studies since I devoted myself wholeheartedly to schoolwork. I was a very good student and easily made friends. I felt a certain compensation for all the years spent in terrible deprivation. I also decided to convert to Catholicism; which pleased the family and gave me further security at home.

I went to the priest in Krosno and asked to be baptized. He was very surprised and told me that he knew my father. He asked whether there were any survivors in the family and I replied that I was the sole survivor. The priest baptized me on September 5, 1945, and the same month I started school for the first time. I was admitted to the seventh grade in the elementary school for which I was prepared by a private teacher since I had to make up a great deal of schooling. I was a very diligent student and loved to go to school and to study. I made many friends and wanted to be accepted. I tried to make up for all the lost time that I was locked up. I finished elementary school and received a certificate. I was registered to continue schooling the next year and meanwhile I enjoyed the summer recess during which time I met my friends and took trips with them.

My brother Avraham Akselrad had survived the camps and slowly recovered from his poor medical condition. He returned to Krosno and came to the Krukierek family to look for me. Avraham tried to take me away from the

Krukierek family but saw that he was getting nowhere and was too weak to fight. He spoke to me about traveling to the Jewish orphanage in Zabrze but I refused. I was determined to stay with the family. I even refused to talk to him. I left the house and hid in the bushes until I was certain that he had left the house. Then I returned home and was furious at my brother for trying to separate me from my new family. He decided to seek legal redress and contacted the office of Rabbi Kahane to plead for help. Yeshayahu Drucker was assigned to the case. Drucker took the case to court since I was a minor. The court heard the case and forced me to stay with my brother at the orphanage in Zabrze for a period of two weeks. The family presented a huge bill of expenses for my upkeep during the war years. The bill had to be paid to the court as a deposit in case I did not return to the family. My brother did not have the necessary cash but he assigned his share of the family property to the Krukierek family if I did not return to their house. My share was untouched since I was a minor. Then the court began to implement the decision.

I was very homesick and wrote letters to my adoptive family but never received a reply. They evidently wrote to me but I never received the letters. The orphanage knew that my adopted Polish family could kidnap me, so the Zabrze home stopped all my correspondence. Shortly thereafter, I was sent to France with a transport of Polish Jewish children. I remained in Perigueux, France, for two years and then I went to Israel in 1948. I was sent to the agricultural school "Mikveh Israel" and in 1950 joined the army. By 1953 I had married and was raising a family, including two sons and 4 grandchildren. I live in a private home at Kiriat Ono and spend my time tending to my garden, attending lectures and reading books.

I continued to write to the Krukierek family after I went to Israel. Jozefa Krukierek, the woman that kept me hidden during the war years, died in 2002 at the age of 92. I even maintain correspondence with the grandchildren and the great grandchildren of the family who never met me. But it is important for me to maintain contact with my past.

Zabrze orphanage children dressed in their best in the city of Zabrze

[Page 90]

Chapter IV

More Children

Michal Heffer, formerly Hinda Zurkowska, was another child redeemed by Captain Yeshayahu Drucker.

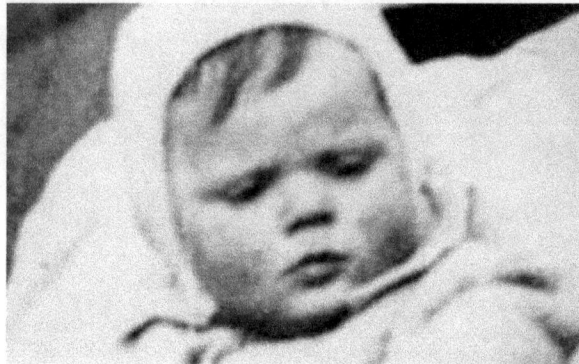

Michal Heffer (Hinda Zurkowska) as an infant

Michal was the only member of her family who survived the Nazis. She was smuggled out of the Warsaw Ghetto and made her way to a church nearly 200 kilometers from Warsaw. She was taken in by the local priest, given chores and for a year became a farmhand, tending to the cows and helping out around the church, even singing in the church choir. One day, returning from the fields with the cows, she saw a crowd gathered in front of the church. A big official Polish military car was there, and everyone was staring at it. The priest rushed her into the church where she was confronted by a tall, blond Polish military officer and an American in a U.S. Army uniform. She remembers that "The American smiled at me and spoke to me in Polish, reaching into his pocket and showing me photographs of my family, my grandfather, whose picture I imagined I'd seen on the church wall, my mother and others of the family. He said he was my cousin Yehuda Elberg. Then I remembered him; I used to sit on his knee in Warsaw. He had moved to the U.S. a few years before the war started."

Michal Heffer with her father and brother prior to World War II

At the time Elberg, a journalist, was attached to the U.S. Army's press corps. "The Polish officer produced papers from the court saying that cousin Elberg was my legal guardian. The priest was a little afraid of the Polish officer and the official paper and didn't argue. I gathered up my few things, and got in the big army car." The Polish officer was Yeshayahu Drucker. As was his custom, Drucker left money with the priest for caring for me and risking his life in the process. "We left the house. The village people stared after us. The drive was pleasant but tense in the military car. I was sad on leaving the place where I had spent so much time and become so attached. I wondered where I was heading and what the future held in store for me. Then, suddenly, the car stopped at a roadblock outside Pilczyka, not far from Kielce. We were all forced at gunpoint to step out of the car. "

Michal Heffer's mother

The men with weapons were part of the anti–Communist "Army Krajowa" (home army), the largest para–military underground organization in Poland during the war. The group was extremely nationalistic and anti–Semitic. Jews who joined with them during the war hid their Jewish identity. When the war ended, the Army Krajowa did not stop its para–military activities but continued to harass both the Polish government and any Jewish survivors it came across. This militia considered the communists the enemy of Poland, and the Jews part of the communist plan to take over the country. Anti–Semitism was rampant in the region around Kielce, and Jews were not safe on the roads. Yeshayahu Drucker, in a Polish Army uniform, was in double jeopardy. First, he was part of the Polish army that was an arm of the communist–run government. Second, he was a Jew.

Batia Akselrod Eisenstein (left) Michal Heffer (right) at Zabrze

A militia soldier approached Drucker, and in a friendly tone asked who he was and why he had a little girl in a Polish military vehicle. Michal Heffer said Drucker then made a nearly fatal mistake. "She's a Jewish girl, we're taking her back to Warsaw." The militia soldier went back to the commander, who was still at the roadblock, and conferred with him. The soldier came back, pushed Drucker to the side, pulled back the breach of his rifle and was ready to take aim. Drucker realized he was in serious trouble and started talking fast. "You see that guy over there? He's an American officer. A journalist. You shoot me, he'll have it in every newspaper in America. So you'll have to shoot him, too. You ready to do that?" Confused, the soldier went back to the commander. Another conference ensued. Then the soldier returned, jerked his rifle in the direction of the car. Michal said she and Drucker and Elberg got in, and drove away, fast.

"I thought I was going home with Elberg, but he explained he couldn't take care of me. Rather I was going to Zabrze, to the Jewish orphanage. And that's where I went with Uncle Elberg and Pan Capitan."

Drucker visited her at Zabzre, stopping by to say hello when he'd drop off another child, or just come out on a Sunday. According to Michal many of the children at the Zabrze home considered themselves Christians and even attended church services on Sundays.

Michal Heffer

In nearly every case, removing Jewish children from non–Jewish homes was a very tedious, delicate, and dangerous situation.

President Ezer Weitzman awards prize to Michal Heffer

Michal went with the second children's transport from Zabrze, Poland to France where she remained for about two years at Perigueux, France and then arrived in Israel. She served in the army, married and raised a family. She lives at her Kfar Vitkin home. Michal is a published author and recognized artist in Israel. She received an award from the state.

Edzio Rosenblatt

Seated from left to right; Dr. Nechema Geller with pocketbook at her feet, and David Hubel.
One of the children at this celebration was Edzio Rosenblatt

The toddler section of the Zabrze home is shown in this picture, taken during one of the festivals organized to acquaint the children with their Jewish heritage.

Chaya Garn was born in Radomysl in 1921 to Chaim Leib Garn, the son of Benyamin Garn of Wielki Most in the Mielec district near Rzeszow. The Garn family were successful merchants. Chaya was one of six daughters. Two of her sisters left Poland for France prior to World War II.

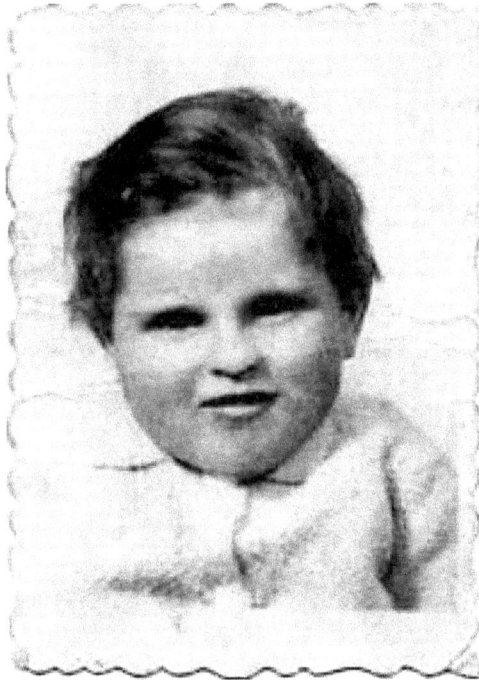

Edzio Rosenblatt
Edzio (Stanislaw) Rosenblatt, Krakow, Poland 1946
The picture was dated December 17, 1946.

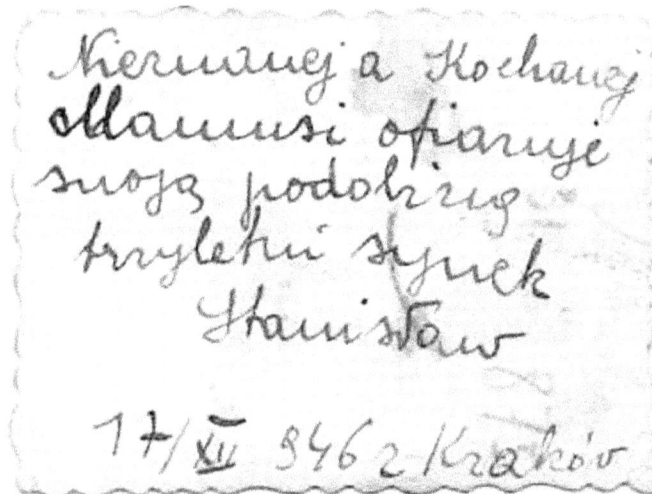

An inscription was written on the back, reading
"I do not know you, dear mother, who sacrificed herself so much for me, your son."
It was signed, "Stanislaw and written in Polish."

On September 8, 1939, following weak Polish military resistance, German soldiers entered Radomysl. They immediately began to harass Jews, especially Jewish men who were forced into work details or sent to the Pustkow labor camp near Debice, helping build a new S.S. military training base. Some Jews managed to escape Pustkow but most died there. The Germans also carried out house–to–house searches ostensibly looking for weapons, but in reality using the searches as an excuse to loot Jewish apartments. The German authorities installed a "Judenrat," or a council of Jewish leaders in Radomysl mainly to carry out the Gestapo's orders to provide cheap Jewish labor to Pustkow. In one action in November 1940, 700 Jews of Radomysl were rounded up and sent to Pustkow. Before long, just breathing the word "Pustkow" terrified any Jew within earshot.

Awraham Rosenblatt, originally from the town of Oswiecim (Auschwitz), came to Radomysl where he heard life was relatively better than in other Polish towns. He met and married Chaya Garn. But in July 1942, a few weeks after Awraham and Chaya were married, the Germans ordered the registration of the entire Jewish population of Radomysl. Special identity cards were issued to young skilled workers, among them the young Rosenblatt couple. Supposedly these cards carried with them some measure of protection from being shipped off to Pustkow. Awraham and Chaya were smart enough not to trust the Germans. The young couple made arrangements for themselves and Chaya's parents to hide outside the city in the house of a Polish farmer.

One Saturday night they all snuck quietly out of Radomysl, reaching the house of Tomas Szczurek in the village of Dulcza Wielka. It was a lucky move. The next day, while they hid out in Szczurek's farm, the Jews of Radomysl were all rounded up, faced the dreaded "selection" process and were deported to concentration camps.

The next day was a Sunday and Szczurek's wife was in church where she heard rumors the Germans were searching for Jews. She rushed home terrified, knowing that hiding Jews carried the death penalty. She immediately ordered the Rosenblatt's out of the house, but relented slightly when they begged for a few more hours. That night the Rosenblatt's slipped off into the fields, heading for nearby Dombrowa. In exchange for the risks they took, the Szczurek's kept most of the Rosenblatt's belongings.

Jews could not use the main road for fear of discovery and arrest, so Awraham and Chaya and her parents stumbled over difficult paths, uneven fields and undulating meadows. The fields were beautiful in the sunlight with the light, refreshing breeze, but torture for these city folks plodding through mud and rocky cowpats.

The group finally reached Dombrowa where they sought shelter and a much needed rest. But the Nazi "actions," shootings and searches forced them to keep moving. But where to? Which direction? Danger lurked around every bend in the road.

Chaya turned to a Polish friend, a bureaucrat with the Polish government who worked in Mielec. In Dombrowa she used a phone in a Polish stranger's home and called her friend who said he would send a truck to pick her up the next day. When she hung up the phone her Polish benefactor, who had overheard the conversation, warned her that staying in Dombrowa was impossible. The Nazis were planning an anti–Jewish "action the next day, probably before the truck would arrive."

The family hired a trusted guide and reluctantly left Dombrowa, looking over their shoulders. They snuck into the Jewish ghetto in Tarnow, where they found a place to stay and some work. But the Nazis began rounding up Jews in Tarnow and the Rosenblatt's were forced to flee to the forest. Fugitives, they hid in the woods, living in caves, risking their lives when they snuck into a farmer's yard to buy food.

Winter was fast approaching, the leaves had turned yellow and some of the trees were already barren. When the chill wind blew, it carried a hint of the harsh winter close behind. And Chaya discovered she was pregnant. It was one thing to be pregnant in a city or even village, where a hospital or midwife could help with the birth. But they were in hiding, dodging the Nazis who still roamed the area, constantly exposed to danger. Even if the baby were delivered successfully and both mother and child were healthy, what then? Who would take care of the infant? Chaya, undernourished, weak and sick, was in no position to nurse a child or even care for one.

They found shelter with a family named Kokoszka. But when their hosts discovered Chaya was pregnant they were evicted. A pregnant woman could not sprint away and hide from Nazis if they showed up to search the house. Again the Rosenblatt's were reduced to begging for their own lives and for that of the unborn child.

The Kokoszka's were not bad people. They had already risked their lives allowing the Rosenblatt's to stay in the drafty, cold attic. They then mercifully took an even bigger risk: they allowed the Rosenblatt's to remain at their farm temporarily. On the evening of January 4, 1944, Chaya was lowered from the attic and taken to the stable. The next day, on a blanket covering a thin layer of straw, Chaya, perhaps because of her weakened condition, strained terribly but still gave birth to a healthy baby boy. After the birth she lost consciousness and was carried delirious back to the attic. She did not waken for several days.

During that time both the Rosenblatt's and the Kokoszka's knew that only drastic measures would save the child. The infant was cleansed, swaddled, and wrapped in a blanket. They hung a note from the baby's wrist stating falsely that his name was Edzio and that he had been baptized. Then they placed the infant placed on the windowsill of a Polish farmer named Jozef Balczyniak.

That night in January was bitter cold. Balczyniak's wife thought she heard the house cats meowing at the door begging to come in from the freezing outdoors. She told her husband to open the door and let the poor cat into the house. He spotted a bundle on one of the windowsills, and realized immediately it was a baby. Their ten–year old daughter thought the baby adorable, even if he was crying. Balczyniak's wife was suspicious. She pointed angrily at her husband accusing him of being the father. At the time farm girls were known to abandon a baby they couldn't care for. But Balczyniak denied any connection to the baby. Then they discovered the note, with the child's name and that he'd been baptized.

The Balcyzyniak's decided to wait until morning before making any decisions. The hungry infant wailed through the night. While the Balcyzyniak's had milk in the cupboard they had no bottle to feed the child. But maternal instincts run strong. Mrs. Balcyzyniak cuddled theinfant, trying to sooth him to sleep. In the morning the Balcyzyniak's went to the local police station and told the police they had found a baby on their windowsill. "Keep him or get rid of him," the policeman told them. "I don't care. This isn't a matter for the police." The Balcyzyniak's brought the baby home.

Mrs. Balcyzyniak took pity on the child. She'd found a bottle and fed the child properly and decided to keep him. Not sure of his baptism, they had him baptized formally and legally adopted the child. They officially registered him as Stanislaw Dulecki, in honor of the town's mayor. But they continued to call him Edzio, the name that was on the note attached to his wrist when they found him, the name his birth parents knew him by.

As an example of how life can change minute by minute, from smiles to tears, Chaya Rosenblatt finally regained consciousness, weak and feverish, wanting to see her baby. How do you tell a woman that her baby was no longer there? "No longer there," she asked, shocked.

Groggy. Was the baby dead?

No, not dead. Gone.

Gone? Gone? Yes, gone. Safe. Well–fed. Cared for. But gone.

Minutes passed slowly as Chaya accepted the harsh reality: she no longer had a baby.

A few days later, their host, Mr. Kokoszka, came back from town with bad news. Kokoszka's son had received an order from the Germans in charge of the area that he was to leave immediately for Germany where he was needed as a laborer. But Kokoszka's son decided to ignore the orders, dangerously defying the Germans. Kokoszka was wise enough to know that this defiance would incite the Germans to search for his son and punish him. Through his act of rebellion, Kokoszka's son had invited the wrath of the German authorities down on the village and all who lived there.

Even though Chaya was running a high fever and there were few options, the Rosenblatt's decided they had to leave. Knowing Jews were already hiding in the forest, Kokoszka volunteered to help. He backed his old mare into the carriage he used to carry supplies to town and laid Chaya tenderly on the cracked, thinly padded seat of the carriage, helping the Rosenblatt's flee to the forest.

Over the summer of 1944 the Red Army made significant advances, liberating the towns of Mielec, Radomysl and even half of Dulcze. But the Germans beat them back. With snow already on the ground, large contingents of German troops poured into the forest with orders to capture or shoot whoever they found, especially partisans who had fought against them, and Jews. The family's forest hideout was quickly discovered by German soldiers. Awraham Rosenblatt tried to run but was cut down by German marksmen. The other forest Jews were captured and sent to the death camp of Plaszow near Krakow. In the Plaszow camp, with the exception of Chaya Rosenblatt and two other Jewish women, the forest Jews of Radomysl were all murdered.

As the Russians advanced, prisoners of Plaszow were lined up and marched at gunpoint through the ice and snow toward the Bergen Belsen concentration camp. This death march went on for 14 days. Only 40% of those who began the march reached Bergen Belsen alive. Chaya Rosenblatt was shoved into a Bergen Belsen barracks with 800 other inmates in a space meant for 50. When the British army liberated Bergen Belsen in May 1945, Chaya had a severe case of typhus and was struggling to stay alive. British doctors hospitalized her immediately. Her recovery was painfully slow. When she could finally be moved, the British sent Chaya on a ship to Sweden.

As Chaya recovered she looked back on what she'd gone through, the memory of her baby foremost in her mind. Chaya knew the child was still in Poland, living with the Balczyniak family in the area of Radomysl. Among the different organizations and people she sought out to help her retrieve the child was an influential Swedish Jew named Paul Olberg in Stockholm. He replied to Chaya's inquiries in Yiddish directing her to contact the "Bund" office in Lodz, Poland. She did but nothing happened.

She then contacted the office of the Chief Rabbi of the Polish Army, Rabbi Kahane, and told him the story. The case was handed over to Yeshayahu Drucker. Chaya also learned to her chagrin that obtaining the release of Jewish children from Christian families or institutions, especially once the child had been baptized, was both a difficult and expensive procedure.

A distant relative of Chaya Rosenblatt wrote that she had seen Edzio in Poland. Determined to retrieve her son, but still too weak to return to Poland, Chaya headed to France to her sisters who had survived the war. From France she contacted the Jewish community office in Mielec, Poland. Chaya's letter was read by most of the Mielec Jewish survivors. Coincidentally, one of the Mielec survivors owned a piece of land that he wanted to sell and he realized this was an opportunity to sell the land.

Mr. Balcyzyniak, the farmer who had taken in the Rosenblatt baby, wanted to buy the property from the Jew, but could not come up with the cash. So a plan was devised. Chaya would raise the money for Balcyzyniak in exchange for the baby, and Balcyzyniak would pay the Jewish landowner, who would use the money to get out of Poland.

Yeshayahu Drucker visited the child and brought him candies and toys at the remote Balczyniak farm. Each time Balcyzyniak and his wife refused to give up the child. Drucker estimated that he would have to pay Balcyzyniak about $2,000 to free Chaya's son. Chaya, of course, did not have $2,000, or anywhere near it. But an American journalist named Reuven Island suggested he help her write her war experiences for the New York Yiddish daily newspaper "Der Tog." Chaya agreed. The articles ran from June 16, 1946 to July 5, 1946. The last article ended with a plea in Yiddish for contributions. Chaya received the fee from the newspaper articles as well as the money raised from the fundraising campaign.

The ad read:

A FUND IS BEING CREATED IN ORDER TO RANSOM THE CHILD OF CHAYA GARN–ROSENBLATT

"A committee has been established to help Chaya Garn–Rosenblatt ransom her child from non–Jewish hands. A drive is being started to create a fund to help this holy cause. Contributions can be sent to the "Fund." All contributions must be sent to the Chaya Garn–Rosenblatt Fund, c/o The Day, 183 East Broadway, New York 2, N.Y"

At the time, Rabbi Kahane's office used a rubber stamp for official documents. The top of the stamp read, "The Polish Army, General Headquarters." Beneath this heading, in smaller letters, "Military Rabbinate." Drucker was in the habit of only applying the upper half of this rubber stamp when using it on official documents. He wrote a letter in formal Polish army terminology that the "Polish Army was interested in restoring the child located at the Balczyniak farm near Radomysl to his biological mother." Neither the child's mother nor her place of residence was mentioned. The letter was signed in the formal manner with the appropriate stamp, lacking the "military rabbinate" line. Without any prior notice, Captain Drucker presented himself at the police station in Radomysl dressed in his officer's uniform with a hat that had a rim similar to the one worn by the Polish U.B. (Urzad Bezpieczenstwa – Office of Public Security or Polish secret police). Drucker slammed the letter on the desk of the chief of police. The police chief looked up and was terrified when he saw Drucker in his quasi Polish secret police hat, carrying an official letter with the Polish army stamp. He treated the affair as official Polish business of the highest level. The police chief glanced over the letter as Drucker told him, "We know that the farmer has incurred considerable expense raising the child. And he is to be repaid in full." Drucker then laid a brown paper package on the table. "Here is a package containing more than one million zlotys" (about $2,500, a huge amount of money in those days) "that will be left with you so that the farmer can buy himself the farm a Jew is offering for sale if he releases the child." The Jewish survivor who wanted to sell the farm to Balczyniak was conveniently present at the police station.

The local police chief was so distraught by the scene that he sent two policemen to bring the farmer and the boy to the station. Balczyniak arrived carrying the two–year old boy. When the police chief tried to explain the situation, Balczyniak refused to listen. The police chief then strongly hinted that he had the means to force Balczyniak to accept the deal. Balczyniak, frightened by the threat, finally realized he had no choice but to release the boy. He received the package of money in return. At this point the Jewish owner of the farmland entered the room and Balczyniak gave him the money. Balczyniak now owned a farm, but no longer had a son, even if the boy was not really his.

Drucker scooped up the boy, left the police station, slid into his Polish army car, the motor already running, and drove away, heading toward Krakow. During the trip from Radomysl to Krakow, Drucker spoke with the boy, who already knew him from Drucker's previous visits. The youngster asked Drucker, "Uncle, do you have a rifle?" "No," Drucker answered, "but I have a gun. Why do you ask? Why do I need a rifle?" "In order to kill Jews," answered the boy. Other than that revealing conversation the trip was uneventful. The car reached Krakow safely. Drucker headed straight for the home of his younger brother Aaron, who had married after the war and settled in Krakow. Yeshayahu Drucker took the boy and bought him some clothing since the farmer had not packed clothing for the child. He then took a picture of the child and send it to Edzio's mother in Paris who had never seen her boy.

Meanwhile Drucker took Edzio Rosenblatt out of Aaron's house and drove him to the Jewish orphanage at Zabrze. Edzio was the youngest child at the orphanage and quickly became the favorite of not only the teachers but also the other children, who treated him as a beloved mascot.

Like the other children at Zabrze, Edzio waited for a way to leave Poland. Most of these children left Poland, some legally and others illegally. The "Brichah" or escape movement transported most of the older children to the displaced persons camps in Germany or Austria. Some transports of children went directly to France. The children's transports that left Poland usually combined children from different Jewish orphanages: religious, secular, Zionist or non–Zionist, including the children of Zabrze.

Zabrze orphanage

Zabrze staff and children at a Lag B'Omer celebration

As a rule, the children were assembled in the city of Lodz, which had the largest Jewish population in postwar Poland. Almost as soon as he arrived in Zabrze, preparations were begun for Edzio "Stanislaw" Rosenblatt to be reunited with his family. Being a very small child, he, of course, needed special care and attention. As the necessary preparations were made, Drucker wrote to Chaya Rosenblatt in Polish informing her that her son Edzio would be leaving Poland and hopefully would join her soon in Paris. On January 19, 1947, Edzio left Poland with a transport of Jewish children for France. Drucker sent a cable to Chaya saying that Edzio had left Poland. Mother and son would soon be united.

Drucker's cable to Edzio's mother

Orna Keret

Orna Keret was another Jewish youngster redeemed by Captain Drucker. She was born in Warsaw and was one of the survivors of the Warsaw ghetto. Her mother and brother had been rounded up and taken to a concentration camp and murdered. Her father had paid a Polish Christian family to care for her, providing her with legitimate identity papers of a Christian girl. She never saw her father again.

Orna lived with the family for nearly two years. After the war the family took her to a Christian orphanage. She became such a good Christian that when Captain Drucker came to retrieve her, having received her name from a list provided to Rabbi Kahane's association, she refused to go. "Jews," she said. "They want to murder me and take my blood to make Matza." Such was the anti–Semitic atmosphere in which she was raised. However, she went with Drucker to Zabrze.

She did not remain in Zabrze for long. The famous Herzog children's transport was in the final stages of preparation to leave Poland. Orna waited with the other children for the train to move. To pass time, she took out a Polish language version of Upton Sinclair's "Oil." The train stood idle, waiting for the arrival of Rabbi Herzog and his entourage. They waited. . And waited. According to one account, there was a problem because Rabbi Herzog had all the documents. The Polish conductor was not going to let anyone on the train until he saw the documents that allowed the children to travel. No matter what arguments were made, the train stood empty, the children forced to wait on the platform in Katowice.

According to this account, as the minutes turned to hours, the teachers' anxieties grew. The anticipation and energy the children had when they arrived dissipated. Now many were spread out on their suitcases, using their coats as blankets, sleeping. The teachers were wondering "What if Rabbi Herzog never shows up? Then what? Back to the orphanages? But how, it was already midnight. How could 500 children and their minders be transported back to the different orphanages in the middle of the night?" Panic was not far behind these thoughts. Then there was the danger of gangs of thugs, and the larger danger, being stuck in Poland. The sounds of the city had quieted. Now every trash can that was knocked over, or cat that howled, sent the teachers scurrying to protect their charges.

Another account had the children waiting on the train, not on the platform.

Major Sobol, the Polish security officer in charge of the train, had ordered all children and escorts to board the train and stay within until the train moved. Meanwhile, the train stood and waited, and waited for the arrival of Rabbi Herzog. Finally, late in the evening, Rabbi Herzog and his entourage arrived at the station and boarded the train that immediately began to move to the Czech border.

:

Esther (Goldblum) Kastenbaum

Esther was not a youngster but needed a home, a job and a sense of security in post war Poland. Zabrze needed help and lots of help with all the children, especially the youngest ones. Ester devoted herself to them.

Esther Goldblum was born on January 14, 1924, in Skarzysko Kamienna near Radom, Poland. Her father was Yehiel Yossef Goldblum and her mother was Tzikla (Rafalowicz) Goldblum. Esther had two sisters: Dora, who later altered the name to Dorotea, born in 1921, and Reuvna born in 1936. Their father was a watchmaker and had his own store. He made a nice living and provided for the family who lived upstairs while the store was downstairs. Their mother devoted herself to the family. The Goldblum's did not live in a Jewish district although the family maintained a traditional Jewish home and the father prayed daily. Holidays were observed in the traditional religious sense of a Polish Jewish family.

The children attended regular school and suffered greatly as a result of anti–Semitic behavior on the part of the Polish students and teachers in the schools. The number of Jewish children was always small in the classes, thus an easy target for the anti–Semitic bullies who received encouragement from some teachers for their behavior. Esther had one Jewish school friend but managed to have a non–Jewish school acquaintance who lived in her building and frequently provided her with the homework when she was absent from school for religious observances. As an obedient child she attended school and assisted her mother with various home chores.

The German attack on Poland had immediate consequences for the Goldblum family. A local "volksdeutch," that is, a Pole of German origin, appeared at the home of the family and demanded that the Goldblum family hand over the apartment to him. All pleas were in vain and the family finally had to move to a small one–room flat. One of the grandmothers joined them in this apartment.

Esther, like all Jewish children, was now forbidden to attend school. She assisted her father in the store and helped him bury a great deal of jewelry and precious items that would later save her life and that of her sister. The Germans vandalized the remains of the store and sent Yehiel Goldblum and his older daughter Dora to work in an armament plant. Esther remained at home with her mother, sister and grandmother. She spent her time chatting or playing with some other Jewish friends inside her home or those of her playmates. Going out in the street was dangerous, since Germans constantly appeared and grabbed people for work details.

The Germans soon created a Judenrat (Jewish council) in Skarzysko Kamienna and selected Yehiel Goldblum to be a member of it. This office executed all the wishes of the Gestapo, including providing slave labor for German needs. Still, the Judenrat also tried their best to serve the local Jewish community by providing free or subsidized meals or medications for the poor Jews in town. They helped to organize the painful transfer of the Jewish population in Skarzysko Kamienna to the ghetto of the city. The Goldblum family did not have to move since their one room flat was in the ghetto area. Conditions were crowded and hunger was prevalent in the closed ghetto. Yehiel managed to provide his family with food, according to Esther. She did not go hungry but suffered from boredom and fear. The Germans constantly raided the ghetto for one thing or another and it was unsafe to be on the street. One never knew whether one would be dragged to a work detail or sent to a labor camp, never to appear again. Yehiel Goldblum was picked up by the Germans despite his official position on the Judenrat and sent to work in Radom.

The Skarzysko Kamienna ghetto was ordered to be closed in December 1942 and the Jewish population was told to move to the ghetto of Szydlowiec, a predominantly Jewish town. The family hired a horse–drawn cart and moved their few belongings to the new ghetto that received not only the Jews of Skarzysko Kamienna but of the entire area. The town of Skarzysko Kamienna became "Judenrein" or free of Jews with the closure of the ghetto.

The Szydlowiec ghetto was bursting at the seams. Hopelessness was pervasive in the ghetto. While Esther and her family were in this ghetto, their father repaired clocks for the Germans in Radom and was busy looking for someone who could help his family. He talked to several Jewish co–workers and one of them told him that he knew of a Pole in the city of Rozwadow who could help him but it would cost a great deal of money. Goldblum paid the man for the information—a name and address—Rudolf Siec in Rozwadow. He contacted Siec and said he would pay all the expenses if Siec could save his family. Goldblum then let his family know to expect the arrival of a helper.

Rudolf Siec came to Szydlowiec and took Dora to Rozwadow where he rented a one–room flat for her. He then returned to the ghetto, provided Esther with Aryan papers and took her to live with a Christian family. She waited for the arrival of Reuvna and mother who were supposed to join her. But Siec kept making excuses, the ghetto gates were closed or the Germans were detaining Poles and sending them to work in Germany. In reality the ghetto of Szydlowiec had already been liquidated. Finally, he told Esther the truth, there were no more Jews in Szydlowiec. Siec then moved her to the apartment to live with Dora. The sisters did not know if they could believe Siec, but had no way of checking events outside.

Meanwhile a relationship developed between Dora and Rudolf Siec. Esther never found out if the relationship was spontaneous or imposed. The sisters never talked about it. Esther would have to stay in the closet when Siec visited Dora.. The situation was getting very irritating and Siec decided to look for a place in a nearby village. But such a place would cost money and they were running low on it.

Siec and Esther decided to return to Skarzysko Kamienna where the Goldblum treasure was still hidden in a cellar. The risks were great that she might be spotted or denounced but there was no choice, for without money they had no chance of survival. Esther knew the hiding place and managed to extract most of the small hidden jewels and stones and put them in a bag. The big items like candelabras were left hidden since they would attract attention. She returned to the meeting place with Siec and they left safely for Rozwadow. She gave everything to him and he paid for all their expenses by selling the treasure bit by bit. The bulk of it he buried in the village where his mother lived.

Siec refused to work for the Germans and was always involved in petty small deals of one kind or another. He decided to rent a room for Esther in the village of Malczet near Rozwadow with a Polish family. He told them that she was the child of a Christian–Jewish couple and paid them 1,500 zlotys a month. Esther remained there for about a year and a half. The only contact she had with Dora was through Siec when he came once a month to pay the couple their rent. He was also her only contact with the world. She had to hide whenever guests or neighbors arrived. Sometimes the appearances were sudden and she could not make it to the safe hideaway so had to improvise a hiding place. Life was lonely and boring but she always hoped for better things.

Then one day, Siec came and took Esther to Rozwadow where she was reunited with Dora. He had decided to move them all to Czestochowa as the front line approached Poland. Czestochowa was a very religious Catholic city in Poland. The trip went smoothly. Even though they were carrying false papers, Esther was terrified that she might be recognized when they passed Skarzysko Kamienna.

In Czestochowa there was tension in the household. Dora's family was growing and Esther felt uncomfortable, especially because of some of the things Siec said to her. She found a room where she could live on her own. Soon after she developed a rash on her legs that evolved into an infection and required medical treatment. A Polish doctor treated her and cured the infection.

The city was liberated by the Russians and Esther decided to return to Skarzysko Kamienna alone since Dora refused to leave the city. There was no organized system of transportation but she managed to reach the town and found their flat occupied by a Polish family. Somehow Esther managed to find a place with a Jewish family and began to await the arrival of her other family members. She was in the city several weeks but no one arrived. Rumors and warnings began to circulate to the effect that all Jews had to leave town if they wanted to stay alive. She saw no reason to stay and decided to return to Czestochowa.

The three of them left Czestochowa for the port city of Gdynia where Siec began to work and to drink. He became very abusive to the sisters. Esther decided to leave by herself for Lodz where there was a large Jewish community. She reached the city and met an old acquaintance of the family who invited her to stay with them.

Esther quickly discovered that no one in her family had survived the war. Her father died on one of the death marches toward the end of the war. Mrs. Goldblum had become sick with typhus in the Szydlowiec ghetto and was probably killed by the Germans who eliminated people with infectious diseases. Esther's younger sister was sent to a concentration death camp. The entire family was wiped out with the exception of Dora, Esther and a cousin named Chana Wohlhandler, the daughter of her mother's sister, Lea (Rafalowicz) Wohlhandler.

Chana was hidden by a Christian family who refused to let her go after the war despite Esther's pleas. The Polish family refused to even discuss the matter. But Esther refused to give up hope and decided to travel to Warsaw to seek help from Rabbi David Kahane, chief Jewish military chaplain of the Polish Army. She had heard of the many positive deeds that he performed on behalf of Jewish people.

Esther reached Warsaw in 1946 and managed to speak to Rabbi Kahane, who introduced her to Captain Yeshayahu Drucker, who also worked in the Chaplain's office. Drucker asked her the details of the case and took notes. He also took a great interest in Esther's life story and asked if she would help with the work of rescuing Jewish children from Christian homes. Drucker told Esther that he needed a young Jewish person who could act as a model for the Jewish children raised in Christian homes, many of whom were presently imbued with anti–Jewish feelings. He explained that a young female would have an easier time establishing a relationship with other youngsters.

Esther agreed to assist Rabbi Drucker in his work rescuing Jewish children from Christian homes and taking them to the Zabrze orphanage. At the orphanage they received the warm and individual attention necessary to overcome their traumatic experiences during and following the war. Because the children were in such need and there were so many arrangements to make, Esther ended up helping in a variety of ways. Capitan Drucker devoted a great deal of time to the youngsters at the orphanage and spent almost every weekend with the children. He even went on hikes with them when he had free time.

On occasion Esther would travel with Drucker on his missions. He even managed to rescue her cousin Chana. Chana was very upset and traumatized by the change of homes and it took some time for her to relinquish her attachments to the Christian home. Although Esther devoted a great deal of time comforting Chana and trying to restore her confidence, she continued to present special problems.

Children kept arriving and departing to various destinations, notably to Palestine and England. The very young children were often adopted by English Jewish families as soon as they arrived at the British airport. Rabbi Shonfeld of London prepared all the necessary arrangements and flew to Poland to escort the children to England. The military chaplain's office handled the Polish side for the necessary exit papers. Esther was assigned to accompany the third transport that was heading to England. She decided to visit her sister, who by now had children with Siec, to say goodbye because she would be leaving Poland. The sisters would not see each other again. Dora and Rudolph were later killed by Poles and to this day nobody knows the cause.

The transport consisted of 100 small children. Esther was assigned five children to tend to, including Chana Wohlhandler. The transport and the preparations were excellent and the trip was smooth. All small children were immediately taken by their adopted parents at the airport in accordance with the adoption papers. Esther was taken to Rabbi Shonfeld's home where she stayed for some time until further arrangements were made. She remained in England for two years and studied nursing as well as English. At first Esther visited the homes of the adopted children but as time went by she stopped the visits. She then decided to leave for Israel and arrived in 1948. She was immediately drafted and sent to the army camp of Beit Lid and then to an army hospital as a nurse.

Chana Wohlhandler did not take to her adopted English Jewish family and was placed in a youth hostel. She left for Israel the following year where she married and raised a family. Esther continued as a nurse following the war and married Zigmunt Kastenbaum in 1951, with whom she had a son and daughter.

By chance Esther met Batia (Akselrad) Eisenstein, whom she had known in Zabrze, and learned that Yeshayahu Drucker was in Israel. Esther and Drucker had not spoken or written to each other since she left Zabrze. They reestablished contact and Esther continued to maintain close relations with the Drucker family until he passed away.

Benyamin Nussbaum

**Benyamin Nussbaum on the left and Adolf Muntz on the right.
Picture taken after the boy was redeemed by Drucker.**

Benyamin Nussbaum was the son of a wealthy and influential Jewish family in Krosno, Galicia, Poland. With the liquidation of the Jewish ghetto in Krosno, the Nussbaum family managed to find a hiding place for Benyamin. This was very difficult since most non–Jews were afraid to hide Jewish children especially boys that were circumcised. Apparently, the Nussbaum's made some sort of deal with a family to take the child. The Nussbaum's were murdered in the Shoah as were most of their family.

Benyamin was hidden during the war. Once the war was over, he was baptized and sent to a Jesuit school to become a priest. Batia Akselrod had actually seen Benyamin acting as an altar boy at the church of the Capuchin Order in Krosno. Apparently, when the transports of repatriated Poles returned from the Soviet Union to Poland some Jews returned to Krosno. Among them was Adolf Muntz who had been friendly with the Nussbaum family and knew Benyamin. He started to make inquiries regarding the boy but encountered only closed doors. Muntz was not related to the family and could not take legal action so he decided to contact Rabbi Kahane. The matter soon reached the desk of Drucker who visited Krosno to make the necessary inquiries. Drucker hired a lawyer who petitioned the court and the religious institution settled the case without a legal fight. Drucker paid and took the boy to Zabrze where he remained a short period of time. Benyamin was sent to France with a transport of Jewish children and later reached Israel.

Children and staff at Zabrze . Seated in the first row on the right is Benyamin Nussbaum.

[Page 128]

Chapter V
Partial list of Jewish Children at Zabrze

Following World War II, Polish passenger trains frequently carried armed military escorts to protect the train passengers from armed ambushes.

Traveling by train in Poland following World War II was a very risky business. As mentioned before, most of the Jewish children who reached the Zabrze orphanage were there because of the efforts of Captain Yeshayahu Drucker personally or through the various religious Jewish associations that were established by Rabbi David Kahane in Poland. Some children were also brought by relatives when they were unable to support the children. The associations paid handsomely for each child who was rescued from a non-Jewish family or an institution. There was no extensive haggling over the price that had to be paid for the redemption of a Jewish child. Rabbi Kahane insisted that each party who hid a Jewish child was entitled to fair compensation for the cost of caring for the child during the war period.

Every child arriving at Zabrze needed medical attention and mental guidance to return to some form of "normalcy." The children were highly traumatized by events they had witnessed and the constant fear they felt from their environment. Because many of the children had been placed in Christian homes at early ages they had very little knowledge of Judaism and continued to attend Catholic services while at the Zabrze home. They had also often grown up in an anti-Jewish atmosphere, had been taught to hate Jews, so they had to be introduced to their real heritage slowly. These situations demanded that the staff provide very individualized attention to many of the traumatized children.

Security was a major issue. The home had to be carefully watched so that nobody attacked the place. The expenses of the home were enormous and Zabrze constantly needed money and big money. The Joint Distribution Committee in Poland was the biggest contributor to the orphanage of Zabrze. David Guzik, Joint Director in Poland, placed youth support projects at the highest level. As early as July 1945, Zabrze was receiving Joint Distribution Committee ("Joint") funding, illustrated by the budget sheet of the JDC in Poland. The JDC not only provided funding to the home but also American food products. David Danieli recalled that he had arrived at Zabrze prior to Passover 1946 and ate "Manischewitz" matzoth that were very tasty. He also saw gefilte fish, macaroons and other American Passover products, items that he had never seen in Poland. He recalled that the children were checked by doctors and some children received enriched nutritional foods to regain their strength. The Joint Distribution Committee also provided money allocations for the medical care of children.

The Joint continued to provide crucial funding for the home in the succeeding quarters. The expense sheet shows the variety of programs that the Joint funded. Drucker was constantly on the road traveling through remote areas to locate Jewish children. Some children were redeemed by the local Jewish religious associations and the bills were presented to Rabbi Kahane. Some non-Jewish families presented the Jewish children to the Jewish religious associations without asking for money while others demanded extravagant sums.

Then, on March 5, 1946, there was a terrible accident and David Guzik, the Joint's director in Poland, was killed on a return trip from Paris to Warsaw. His airplane crashed at the Prague airport and all passengers died. The Joint Distribution Committee (JDC) in Poland went into shock. As mentioned earlier, Guzik was one of the few JDC officials in Poland to survive the Shoah. Following the liberation of Poland he was immediately appointed director of the JDC in Poland. He was well connected with the Polish agencies that helped him to launch all kinds of aid programs for the surviving Jewish Shoah victims who were in great need.

American Joint Distribution Committee, Warsaw,/Poland/
Specification of expences on January 1 - 1946

	I	II	III	IV	Total V	VI
		569.900		1.376550		1946450
1.Child - Care						
a/children-house Otwock	177800		432000		609800	
" Zakopane	102600		333750		436350	
" Zabrze	35000		30000		65000	
" Zatrzebie	47000		61300		108300	
" Ecterswalden	50000		-		50000	
" Rabka	-		20000		20000	
" Oaza	-		10000		10000	
" Chorzow	-		10000		10000	
" Sielsk	-		8000		8000	

American Joint Distribution Committee, Warsaw/Poland
Specification of expenses on January 1–1946
We reproduced the budget sheet since the copy was very poor.

	I	II	III	IV	V	VI
1. Child care		569,900		1,376.558		1,945,450
Children house – Otwock	177800		432000		609800	
" – Zakopane	102600		333750		436350	
" – Zabrze	35000		30000		65000	
" – Zatrzebie	47000		61300		108300	
" – Ecterswalden	50000		–		50000	
" – Rabka	–		20000		20000	
" – Oaza	–		10000		10000	
" – Chorzow	–		10000		10000	
" – Sielsk	–		8000		8000	

This document was recently released by the JDC record division of the Polish JDC archives. The copy is barely legible. We decided to reprint the table. Zabrze is described in red. The sums are quarterly sums distributed by JDC to the various homes. This is a partial list of homes. The page goes on to indicate other expenses namely for special health homes and special care institutions.

Dr. Joseph Schwartz seated third from left, (center in trench coat) with JDC staff in Warsaw, Poland 1946

Guzik organized a staff that began to function immediately despite the terrible conditions in Poland at the time. The staff reached 130 people in 1947. Warehouses, storage depots, distribution centers had to be organized for the first JDC shipload of goods that had already arrived on October 8, 1945 at the Polish port of Gdynia. The cargo consisted of powdered milk, vegetable oil and other basic food necessities. More and more cargoes of goods would arrive with time. The merchandise was shipped to the various points of distribution and helped maintain the surviving Jewish population in Poland. The aid also included medication, clothing and tools.

The JDC also helped directly and indirectly the following Jewish organizations and associations:[1]

This vast aid organization suddenly lost its driver. The JDC director of Europe, Dr. Joseph Schwartz, rushed to Warsaw to support and maintain the Polish JDC operations. The Jewish institutions relied greatly on the help they were getting from the JDC. Schwartz wanted to make sure that the aid program continued to flow.

Schwartz called on William Bein to assume the JDC directorship in Poland. Bein had been the JDC director in Poland prior to World War II and was therefore familiar with the country. He immediately stepped in to assume the leadership of the organization. Help was needed by local surviving Jews and by repatriated Jews from the Soviet Union. Bein began to tour the various Jewish communities and Jewish orphanages throughout Poland, acquainting himself with the specific needs of the Jewish community, especially the needs of the young Jewish people.

: the Central Committee of the Jews in Poland (CKZP) and the health care organization TOZ, for example, the Central Committee received about 3.5 billion Polish zlotys in the years 1945-1949. But the Joint also supported Jewish political parties and social organizations, including the Bund labor union, the Zionist and religious organization Mizrachi-Torah v'Avodah, the Ichud Zionist Democratic political party, the Hasdomer Hatsair and Poalei Tsiyon-Left Jewish labor parties, the Jewish religious labor party Poalei Amunai Yisrael-Łódź, the Zionist and socialist labor party Poalei Tsiyon-C.S.-Hitachdut, the Union of Non-Party Zionists, and the General Jewish Union of Non-Party Jews, youth associations such as Hehaluts-Pionier [Pioneer], the Haluts socialist youth organization Dror (from 1948, the Union of Haluts Poalei-Tsiyon Dror Borochow Youth in Poland), and the Coordinating Committee for Children and Youth Affairs of Ichud and Hehaluts-Pionier, and religious organizations, mainly the Organizational Committee of Jewish Religious Congregations, the Chief Religious Council, and the Aguda religious kibbutzim. Hebrew schools were also maintained with AJDC funds.

In addition to the Joint's support of the above-mentioned institutions, it also focused its activity and interest on academic, cultural, and artistic associations. It supported the activity of the Central Jewish Historical Commission (which became the Jewish Historical Institute in 1947) a

William Bein, director of the Joint Distribution Committee in Poland, speaking with youngsters in a Jewish home for children in Srodborow, Poland

Drucker continued his activities and brought many children to the Zabrze home. When he had time, he would spend Shabbat at the Zabrze home with the children. He became their father and counselor. Drucker managed to create a photo album with pictures of some of the children at Zabrze. He brought the album with him when he moved to Israel and eventually gave it to the "Museum of Lohamei HaGeta'ot". Unfortunately some of the photos have no names and Drucker did not remember many of the names of the people in the photos. Still, there is an extensive list of names that are printed in this book. The following is a list of the names of the children at the Zabrze home that appear in the Drucker album, copied with permission.

ADLER	Hela
AGART	Shmuel
AKIERMAN	Batia
AKRABSKA	Yanka
AKSELROD	Batia
ALMOG	Shimon
ALONI	Hana
ALTMAN	Yossef
AUGMAN	Lillie
BENDER	Naomi
BERGMAN	Shoshana
BERLINSKI	Esther
BERNER	Lusia
BERNSTEIN	Simona
BLASSBERG	Ella
BLEIBERG	Dola
BORENSTEIN	Wira
BORENSTEIN	Zosia
BRANDES	Ryfka
BRENDER	Rivkah
BRENDER	Binyamin
BRENDER	Zwicka
BRESLAW	Nechema
BUKOWSKA	Stefa
CHALKES	Z
DANIELI	David
DAWIDOWICZ	Ludyta
DIAMAND	Frida
DIAMAND	Paula
DINGOTLI	David
DITMAN	Dwora

DOMB	Cesia
DRUKER	Ninka
ECKERT	Shmuel
EPSTEIN	aleksander
ETTINGER	Ewa
FALEK	Stasia
FALUCH	Irena
FELDMAN	Nehema
FENNER	Salomn
FISHBEIN	Henryk
FISZMAN	Marysia
FRAUEMGLASS	Klara
FRIEDLER	Eugenia
FRIEDMAN	David
GESUNDHEIT	Samuel
GETTENBURG	Stefania
GLOWINSAKA	Roma
GLUTZENSTEIN	Eugenius
GOLDBERGER	Lea
GOLDFREIN	Hadassa
GOLDWASSER	Krysia
GORSKA	Lydia
GRIN	Chaika
GROSS	Niunnia
GROSSBERG	Helinka
HEFER	Michal
HEIMAN	Arthur
HEIMAN	Arthur
HERTZ	Miriam
HOFER	Sonia
HOFFMAN	Hanna
HOFFMAN	Jerzy
HOTER–YISHAI	Yaakov
HUTTERER	Szymon
INBAR	Tz'ura
INDIK	Muszka
ISRAEL	Rivkah
JAKUBOWICZ	Basia
KAC	Jozef
KADER	Wita
KAFRI	Mordechai
KAGANOWIC	Liucia
KAPELI	Naumi

KAPUSZCIEWSK	Yankel
KARNI	Marila
KASTENBAUM	Esther
KEVET	Orna
KLEINER	Inka
KLEINKOPF	Abraham
KLEINMAN	Hava
KLEINMAN	Eva
KOCZY	Florian
KOCZY	Hulda
KORN	Shlomo
KORNBERG	Mania
KOZOCH	Fela
LANDAU	Marin
LANDAU	Rita
LANDAU	Marin
LANDAU	Rita
LANDWIRTH	Danka
LANGBERG	Henryk
LAOS	Tusia
LEFKOWICZ	Riszard P
LEICHETR	Sara
LENCICKI	Aaron
LERER	Mina
LESLAU	Chana
LEV ARI	Hana
LEVANON	Rachel
LEWI	Halina
LEWITEK	
LIBMAN	Hava
LICHT	Leon
LICHT	Charlotta
LICHTENTHAL	Micia
LIVNA	Noa
LUBLINER	adam
MAARAVI	Pnina
MAIER	Henryk
MAIZLISH	Hieronim
MARGEL	Hana
MARKS	Ruth
MASS	Celina
MATYL	Rivkah
MAYER	Heniek

MAYER	Sonia
MAZA	Alfred
MER	Djunia
METZGER	Joseph
MOTYL	Regina
NAJSRATER	Estera
NEBENTZAHL	Leah
NELSON	Hana
NEUBENFELD	Lipka
NEUMAN	Sabina
NIESSENTZWEI	Ewa
NORTMAN	Sara
NUSSBAUM	Beni
NUSSBAUM	Abram
NUSSIMOV	Hava
PAKTOR–PICHOTKA	Batia
PEITZNIK	Jezik
PELED	Ilana
PIECZNIK	Jezik
PIOTERKOWSKI	Ryszard
PORILES	Ryszarda
PRIFER	Zenia
RADZIECHOWSKA	
REICH	Hannah
REUVANI	Lea
REUVEN	Yehudit
ROM	Djunia
ROMEK	Romek
ROSENBERG	Marysia
ROSENBLAT	Eduard
ROSENBLAT	Stanislaw
ROSENCRAC	Aliza
ROTHOLC	Ryszaed
ROZEN	Rozia
ROZEN	Lila
RUBENSTEIN	Fania
RUBINRAT	Marysia
RUBINSTEIN	Halika
SAASIA	Miriam
SADEH	Hana
SADEH	Moshe
SCHARK	Klara
SEIDEMAN	Basia

SEIDEN	Wisia
SERBERNIK	Danka
SHADMI	Chana
SHAEFFER	Shoshana
SHAFRIR	Hana
SHARON	Sara
SHAEFER	Shoshana
SHEINFEKD	Batia
SHOR	Hanka
SHPIEGLER	Shlomo
SHPIEGLER	Zvi
SHPIEGLER	Shlomo
SHPIEGLER	Zvi
SHRAGGER	Rivkah
SHTERFELD	Arie
SHTERFELD	Arie
SILBERSHTEIN	Masha
SILBERSHTEIN	Masha
SNIADOWSKI	Abraham
SNIADOWSKIi	Chune
SNIDOWSKI	Abraham
SNIGODOWSKI	Elhanan
SOBEL	Tzvi
SOBEL	Yehuda
SOBEL	Henryk
SOBEL	Tzvi
SPATZ	Dawid
SPIEGLER	Salomon
SPIRRER	Henryka
STEN	Ephraim
STIEGLITZ	Leon
STREIT	Felusz
STRUK	Danka
SWIATOWIC	Zipporah
SZERL	Ben
TAL–SHAHAR	Shaul
TAUBENFELD	Alicja
TAUBER	Majson
TEITELBAUM	Halina
TEMPELHOFF	Pavel
TENENBAUM	Ilana
TILMAN	
TOTENGRAEBE	Eliszewa

TZAPTER	Tzvi
UBMAN	Lillie
ULKINDITZKI	Yehudith
WACHTER	Edzia
WAGNER	Madeleine
WAINMAN	Samuel
WALBERSTEIN	Moshe
WALD	Daniel
WALDHAMMER	Hanka
WALTUCH	Helena
WARSZAWIAK	Sara
WARSZAWSKA	Keysia
WASSERMAN	R
WATENBERG	Hana
WATTENBERG	
WEINLER	Andzej
WEINMAN	Wolf
WIENER	Sala
WILCZENSKI	Yehudit
WITUS	
WOHLHENDLER	Chawa
ZAIDMAN	Dawid
ZALCMAN	Alicia
ZALCMAN	Golda
ZAMTCHIK	Ella
ZAUBERMAN	Nina
ZAWARNICER	Ewa
ZILBERFEIN	Nusia
ZILBERMAN	Naomi
ZONENSHEIN	Rachel
ZONENSHEIN	Tzippa
ZONENSHEIN	Rachel
ZUCKERMAN	Abraham
ZUCKIERMAN	Salomon

:

The list contains 262 names. Some of the names are misspelled but the existing spelling that is basically Polish is maintained in order to adhere to the authenticity of the document. The list is not complete because many children were not recorded or joined transports soon after they arrived at the Zabrze home. The home and the rescue operation were Drucker's "raison d'etre." Rabbi Kahane helped Drucker with all his activities and made sure that he had the finances to carry on his projects.

Rabbi Kahane not only pressed the Joint Distribution Committee for more money but also urged the various Jewish communities in Palestine, the United States and Britain to provide financial support for his homes. The Association of Religious Communities in Poland established another home for Soviet repatriated Jewish orphans in Puszcze Gestcza in Silesia. The home operated for about a year and a half and closed with the end of the massive repatriation of Polish citizens from the Soviet Union. Both institutions received large contributions from Jewish communities throughout the free world.

As mentioned before, Rabbi Itzhak Halevi Herzog, chief rabbi of Mandate Palestine and Rabbi Kahane were awash with letters, pleas and appeals from Polish Jewish survivors to help locate their Jewish children hidden with Christian families or institutions. The letters informed the rabbis that for one reason or another these Christian saviors sometimes refused to restore the children to their families. Rabbi Kahane and Rabbi Herzog also received similar pleas for help from rabbis in Britain and the United States.

Even before the war ended, the rabbi's office in Jerusalem was being flooded with letters of relatives who implored the Chief Rabbinate for help locating children who had survived by hiding in Christian homes or institutions. According to a New York Times report from Cairo, Egypt On February, 14, 1946, Rabbi Herzog estimated that there were approximately 20,000 Jewish children in Europe, not including the Soviet Union, who had survived the Holocaust.[2]

Often the Christian families would grow attached to the children and be reluctant to part with them. There were of course all kinds of legal problems that frequently prevented the redemption of the children. Jewish orphans who had no relatives in Poland presented a particular problem. Without a Polish citizen to press their claim, no legal action could be taken to return these children to their Jewish heritage.

Rabbi Herzog and Rabbi Kahane realized that other methods needed to be applied. Both men were firmly committed to bringing these Jewish children out of their Christian environment and restoring them to their place in the Jewish community. Rabbi Herzog was reported as having said that "every Jewish orphan who had survived the Holocaust represented one thousand who had perished." Both men also realized that after a million and a half Jewish children had been murdered, along with five million Jewish adults, the continuity of the Jewish people was in jeopardy. Every Jewish child brought back into the Jewish world would help repopulate the decimated Jewish people. But these actions required money and the Jewish communities responded by sending funds directly to the Jewish religious associations in Poland or through the Joint, as the document below indicates.

Letter addressed to Rabbi Herzog to help remove a child from a Christian home to a Jewish institution. The letter mentions all the previously unsuccessful efforts to settle the matter. Some references and addresses are provided for the child. Notice the written comment in pencil made at Rabbi Herzog's office in Jerusalem: "Send letter to Drucker."

```
RL 6766                                    Warsaw, January 31st, 1949
Loan and Relief Dpt.
```

```
         To:     AJDC - New York

         From:   AJDC - Warsaw

         Re:     Donation from the United Galician Jews for a children's
                 Home in Poland

Attention Mr. . Torosansky

         We refer to your letter dated January 1st regarding the
         donation from the United Galician Jews for a religious
         children's home in Poland.

         You probably know that the Jewish Congregation subsidised by
         us maintains some children's homes which are conducted in the
         religious spirit.

         We should like to suggest that the United Galician Jews assist
         the Children's Home in Zabrze. This is a well-organised
         home and would put any donation which it may receive to good
         use.

         Looking forward to your further communication, we remain.

                                         AMERIC N JOINT DISTRIBUTION
                                         COMMITTEE
```

Contribution made by the Association of the United Galician Jews to the Zabrze home via the JDC organization in Poland.

These donations kept flowing to Poland and helped the Jewish religious associations and the Jewish religious homes to provide the needed services to the Jewish community. The fact that Rabbi Kahane was the Chief Chaplain of the Polish Army established him as the leader of Polish religious Jewry. His office became the center of information regarding Jewish religious and non-religious matters in Poland. Rabbis wrote letters to him and frequently sent contributions or gifts to his office so that he could provide the restored Jewish communities with prayer books or bibles or prayer shawls. Drucker, of course, saw to it that the Zabrze home received all the religious items that the children needed.

Footnotes

VII   Introduction to the inventory of the archives of the American Joint Distribution Committee in Poland, 1945–1948. New York Times, February 14, 1946.

[Page 148]

Chapter VI

Competition

Yeshayahu Drucker not only spoke Polish fluently but looked Polish. This would prove invaluable when Drucker presented himself at the home of a Polish farmer and talked about a Jewish child who lived with the family. The farmer would assume that the Polish government wanted the matter settled. Drucker had lists and addresses of Jewish children in non–Jewish homes. His job was to travel around Poland and locate the hidden Jewish children. Then the process of negotiations started. Sometimes he had names and addresses from letters supplied by Rabbi Kahane, Rabbi Herzog or other Jewish sources. There was also testimony by surviving Jews providing information about the location of Jewish children in non–Jewish homes. Drucker would arrive in his uniform in a military car driven by a military chauffer, supplied by Rabbi Kahane. No Polish farmer could believe that he faced a Jew.

The fact that Drucker approached the holders of the Jewish children with money incentives and praise for their action during the war placed the negotiations on a friendly basis and contributed to the high degree of his success. Often his first approach was rejected, but Drucker would stubbornly persist. He would visit frequently, bringing candy and toys for the children and gifts for the family. Slowly he would begin to negotiate with the Polish families or Christian institutions. Occasionally, if a family did not negotiate honestly or refused to negotiate at all, he resorted to guile and even force to bring the Jewish children from their Christian homes. Although he sometimes used forceful methods to get the child, he always paid for the child's upkeep during the war.

The redemption campaign of the AJRC proved to be very popular with the surviving Jews in Poland who finally found someone to actively help them in their struggle to recover missing members of their family. But, these successful efforts also created resentment at the Jewish Education Department of the Central Committee of Polish Jews. The Committee had the full backing of the Polish government in Warsaw. The Committee's Education Department, under the leadership of Dr. Shlomo Herszenhorn, ran most of the Jewish orphanages and Jewish education programs in postwar Poland. Herszenhorn was an important Bund leader and a member of the Central Committee. His first children's home was opened in Lublin in July 1944 with that city's liberation. Following the end of the war the Education Department immediately proceeded to set up homes for surviving Jewish orphans. These homes provided some Yiddish culture, language and history but were devoid of Zionism, Jewish religion or Jewish history. The homes also followed the new Polish curriculum that was heavily oriented toward Communist ideals. Rabbi Kahane was interested in the restoration of Jewish life in Poland and did not like the content of the educational programs at the homes.

The Polish government refused to involve itself in a fight between the Central Committee and the AJRC because they did not want to antagonize Jewish organizations throughout the world. The Communist controlled government wanted to gain from a show of fairness toward the Jews in its fight with the reactionary Polish government in exile in London. So the Central Committee was told to keep away from the AJRC and had to accept the decision.

The Central Committee did not concern itself with Jewish children in non-Jewish homes unless they were mistreated. The AJRC, that is, Drucker, actively searched for Jewish children hidden in Christian homes and institutions. On occasion, relatives of the children at the homes of the Central Committee induced the children to leave these homes and move to Zionist homes where they received a Zionist education. These acts irritated the Central Committee that constantly shifted to the political left. Soon another more dangerous threat appeared.

Zionist parties in Poland began to emerge and create Jewish institutions, orphanages and kibbutzim for older youngsters. Most of them were impressed by AJRC activities in Poland. Soon there was tremendous competition among the various Zionist organizations in retrieving Jewish children from Christian places. The fight became intense and acrimonious with the arrival of large numbers of repatriated Jewish orphans from Russia. Various Zionist homes began to entice youngsters to leave their current Zionist homes and join others. The competition also greatly increased the price of redemption of Jewish children. Some people even demanded cash in dollars. The homes of the Jewish Central Committee were also affected by the enticements and desertions of Jewish children but they could do little since the Polish government did not want to interfere. These homes tried to educate the Jewish youngsters in a theoretical view of Polish spirit that did not exist. Even the children saw that they were being attacked because they were Jewish. Many of these children left these homes and joined Zionist homes or kibbutzim in order to get out of Poland.

Then, Arieh Sharid, an emissary from Palestine, suggested that all the Zionist parties form a head office called "The Zionist Coordination Office" under the leadership of Leib Koriski from Kibbutz Yagur in Palestine. He coordinated the activities of redeeming Jewish children. The office established four homes where youngsters remained for some time until they left Poland. The office also began to establish and coordinate various Zionist orphanages for Jewish orphans who returned from Russia.

Most of the Zionist organizations that belonged to this office were non-religious and their orphanage homes followed a secular Zionist base of instruction. Rabbi Kahane and Rabbi Becker helped to establish religious Zionist homes under the auspices of the Mizrahi and Hapoel Hamizrahi political movements. Similar homes were established by the non-Zionist Orthodox Agudat Israel party. The religious parties were not part of the

"Koordinacija" Central Committee. The aim of the office and the Zionist homes was to prepare the children to head for Palestine. Indeed, transports of children constantly left Poland, some legally as was the case of the large Herzog children's transport described in other chapters. Some large transports of children went to Britain with Rabbi Solomon Schonfeld and other children headed to the DP camps in Germany and Austria. Many Jewish children left Poland illegally by various means. Some children were officially adopted by Jewish families abroad. The Polish government was aware of the situation but refused to stop these illegal activities for fear of tarnishing further its bad reputation regarding Jews in Poland.

The Zabrze home and the Geszcze Puste or Gluszyca home were not part of the Zionist Coordination office but programs of the AJRC in Poland. The AJRC was essentially under the auspices of the Polish Army which paid the salaries of the organization leaders, Rabbi Kahane and his assistants, Captains Drucker and Becker. Both homes prepared the children for Jewish life and intended to send them to Palestine. It is estimated that 600–700 children stayed at the Zabrze home for various periods of time until they left Poland. Drucker opened the home in Geszcze Puste or Gluszyca in Lower Silesia specifically for Jewish orphans who were repatriated to Poland from the Soviet Union following the end of the war.

Youngsters from a children's home in Gluszyca (Geszcze Puste), in the Walbrzych region of Lower Silesia. This was the Gluszyca home that also belonged to the Association of Jewish Religious Communities in Poland and was also headed by Rabbi David Kahana.

Youngsters from the children's home in Geszcze Puste (Gluszyca near Walbrzych Poland.

The Zionist homes and the AJRC homes stressed Palestine, Zionism and the Hebrew language while they distanced themselves from Polish culture and the Polish school curriculum. The homes devoted themselves to the children and to their needs, which were enormous. The children demanded constant individual attention because of their traumatic experiences. They acted out their fears, imaginary or real, and the staff had to help and offer guidance to the youngsters. The homes used a great deal of social psychology to draw the children out of their isolation by involving them in big plays that required many children. According to David Danieli, the Zabzre home staged celebrations on the birthdays of Theodor Herzl, the founder and leader of political Zionism, and Chaim Nachman Bialik, the great modern Hebrew writer.

Guests and Zabrze staff with Yeshayahu Drucker dressed in military uniform seated in the center of the picture holding a baby. The home celebrated the birth of Herzl and his picture is displayed.

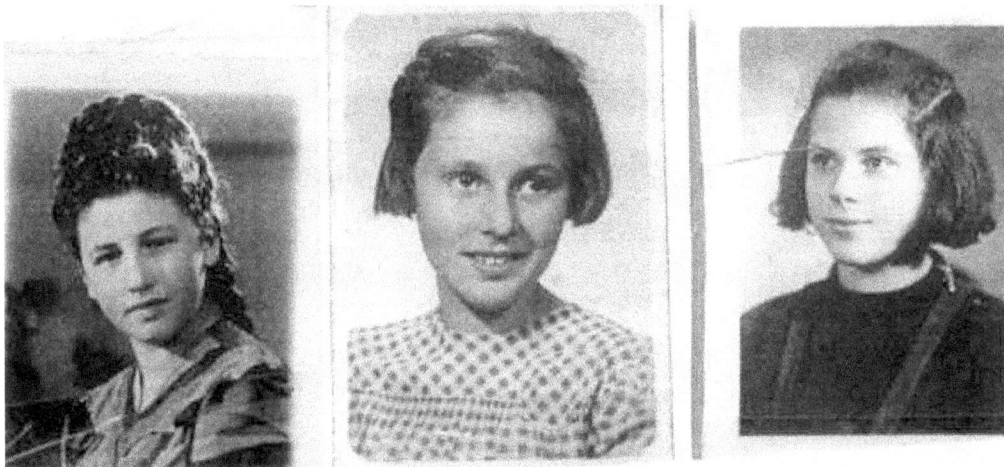

Former residents at Zabrze

Children at Zabrze stage performance

Danieli and some former residents of Zabrze helped to identify the children. Since there was no room to write all the names, they wrote numbers on the picture and then attached names to the numbers. Thus, we have names and pictures of children at Zabrze.

List of children in the picture.

1. Yanka Akarbaska
2. Charlotka
3. Fela Kozok
4. Ella Blasberg
5. David Hubel, head teacher
6. Eva, the beautiful
7. Roda Rob
8. Mr Gottlieb
9. Hanka Shor
10. Dr. Geller
11. Yehudit
12. Dr. Nehema Geller, headmistress of Zabrze
13. Batia Sheinfeld
14. Rivka Brander
15. Mrs. Gottlieb
16. Miriam Mocha
17. Rivka Gottlieb
18. Helina Hoffman
19. Berek Wattenberg. Gym teacher and security officer at Zabrze
20. Mother of Yehudit
21. Tilman
22. Shmulik
23. Sonia Mayer and her brother
24. David Fridman
25. Emil Akart
26. Yehuda and Tzvi Sobel
27. Eva and Marianka Klarsfeld
28. Benyamin Brand
29. Aryeh
30. Unknown

Attached is a partial list of children who stayed at the orphanage of Zabrze. The list was also provided by David Danieli.

Akrabska Yanka
Almog, Shimon known as Szymek
Alexandrowitch,
Anbar, Tzura known as Cessia Domb
Aloni, Hannah known as Halinka Hoffman
Augman, Lillie known as Lila Rozen
Bergman, Shoshana known as Stein
Bernstein Simona known as Simona Neufeld
Berter, Noami
Blassberg Ella
Bleiberg, Dora
Borenstein, Wira
Brander, Benyamin
Brander, Rivka
Charlotka
Danieli, David known as Danielski
Dingotli, David
Eckart, Shmuel known as Emil
Eisenstein, Batya known as Basia
Feldman, Nehema
Feldbaum, Ilana
Feinhut, Esther
Friedman, David
Goldfreund, Hadassah known as Irka Kleiner
Gottlieb, Rivka
Hefer, Michal known as Luska
Hertz, Miram known as Geula, Theresa
Hooter–Yishai, Yaakow known as Yaakov Shtekel
Hoffman, Helina
Hutterer Szymon
Israel, Rivah known as Renia Motil
Kafri, Mordechai known as Marek Fiszler–Bocian
Kapeli, Naomi known as Umka
Karat, Orna known as Fela Kozuch
Karni, Ariela
Kastenbaum, Esthen known as Edzia
Klarksfeld, Eva
Klarsfeld, Marianka
Kleinman, Hava
Korn, Shlomo

Levari, Hannah known as Hania
Levanon, Rachel
Libes, Noa
Maaravi, Pnina
Libman, Hava known as Eva
Margalit, Shulamit
Margel, Hannah known as Halinka
Marks, Ruth known as Roma
Mayer, Sonia and brother
Mazo, Alfred known as Fredek Maly
Milman
Mocha, Miriam
Nebentzahl, Lea known as Basia Zmaluchow
Nelson, Hannah known as Helinka Grossberg
Nussbaum, Beni
Nussbaum, Abek
Paktor–Pichotka, Batia known as Basia Pactor
Peled, Ilana known as Lidka Blum
Reida, Anna
Reuvani, Lea known as Lusia Goldberg
Reuven, Yehudit known as Tania Wasserman
Rob, Roda
Rosenblat, Edward–Stanislaw
Rubinraut, Maryska
Sadeh, Hannah known as Henia Reich
Sadeh, Moshe known as Marianek
Segal, Tziporah
Shafrir, Chaim
Shafrir, Hannah known as Evia Bauman
Shargar, Rivkah known as Rivtche Brander
Sheffer, Shoshana known as Ruzia Rosen
Sheinfeld,Batia
Shor, Hanka
Shterfeld, Arie known as Lowka
Snidowski, Abraham known as Abram
Snigodowski, Elhanan known as Hune
Sobol, Yehuda
Sobel, Tzvi known as Heniek
Sten, Ephraim known as Duzy Fredek
Tal–Shahar, Shaul known as Pavel Tempelhoff
Taubenfeld, Alicja
Tempelhof, Polus
Ulkinditzki, Yehudit known as Wizia Zayden

Wattenberg, Hannah
Ubman. Lillie
Zamtczik Ella
Zavia, Miriam **Staff at Zabrze**
Geller, Dr. Nehema, principal
Hubel, David, head teacher
Wittenberg, Rudolph, gym teacher
Mr. and Mrs. Gottlieb, kitchen staff
Meltzer brothers – medical staff
Strunwasser, Klara
Kastenbaum, Esther **Distant supervisors**
Rabbi David Kahane – head of the home of Zabrze
Rabbi Yeshayahu Drucker
Rabbi Aaron Becker

Dr.Nechema Geller and Rabbi David Kahana visit the home of Gluszyca

From left to right: **Michal Heffer, formerly Hinda Zorkowska; Nina and Tziporah –
former residents at Zabrze**

Children at the Zabrze home

Photos are from the Yeshayahu Drucker collection of pictures that passed through
Zabrze.
The album is presently at the Lochamei Hagettaot Museum at Kibbutz Lochamei
Hagettaot in Israel.

Photographs of life at the Zabrze home

Top middle photo shows Dr. Nechema Geller with two young boys: Witek Bernbobil and Fercig Maze.

Bottom left: historical play of Ruth, and the Lag B'omer celebration at the home.

[Page 162]

Chapter VII
The Mass Exodus of Polish Jews

The Zionist homes and the AJRC homes worked with the "Aliyat Hanoar " or youth immigration department in Palestine, a department of the Jewish Agency of Palestine. This office organized the children transports that left Poland legally and illegally. Children were assembled in small groups and sent with the "Brichah" or escape movement through Czechoslovakia to the German and Austrian D.P. camps or France where they joined Zionist homes. The Polish homes also sent children with families that were leaving Poland. The arrangements were cumbersome and time consuming while the Jewish situation in Poland was getting worse by the day. Anti–Semitism spread like wild fire across the country. Anti–Jewish acts were common as were pogroms. The height of the hysteria took place in the city of Kielce where a Polish mob attacked Jewish inhabitants on July 4, 1946 [1]. Forty–two Jewish Shoah survivors were killed and over 40 injured. Polish police units joined the pogrom. Special forces had to be sent to restore order in the city of Kielce.

The burial of the Jewish victims following the Kielce pogrom.

Fear seized the Jews of Poland. The fact that Polish security forces actively participated in the pogrom gave the Jews no hope. The Polish government already had a reputation among non–Jews of being dominated by Jewish interests and did not want to encourage this idea by interfering on behalf of the Jewish community. The government was also fighting for survival as the country approached a state of anarchy.

Even before the Kielce pogrom, Jews started to leave the war ravaged country. This trickle became a flood following the Kielce pogrom where Jews were accused of making matzoth with Christian blood. Jewish institutions in Poland introduced strict security measures. According to David Danieli, security was tightened at the Zabrze orphanage. The boys that usually slept on the upper floor were moved downstairs near the entrance and the girls were moved upstairs. Danieli went to his old neighborhood, dug up several guns that he brought back to the home and gave to Rudolf Wittenberg. The latter gave the guns to members of the "Ichud" kibbutz who were living at the Jewish compound while preparing themselves for Aliyah to Palestine. The older youngsters assumed defensive positions around the compound. Danieli was given two of his guns back to help defend the orphanage. Apparently, other weapons were also found for self–defense. It was a particularly difficult time for people who had already been through so much.

Jews throughout Poland and other areas of Eastern Europe became terrified at the situation. Since the Polish government was powerless to act, it decided to let the Jews leave, regardless of the consequences. Of paramount importance was the stability of the Polish government. The Polish Assistant Minister of Defense, Marshal Marian Spychalski, was ordered to conduct secret negotiations with Yitzhak (Antek) Zuckerman, one of the leaders of the 1943 Warsaw Ghetto uprising and a member of the Central Committee of Polish Jews. An agreement was reached whereby Jews could leave Poland, no transit papers would be necessary, but they could take no gold or foreign currency. All transportation arrangements were the responsibility of the Polish Brichah as were all medical issues and special problems. The Polish government and institutions were not officially involved in the Jewish exodus. The agreement was secret and not announced publically by the parties involved. It was to commence on July 27, 1946, and end about February 1947.

Yitzhak (Antek) Zuckerman

Marshal Marian Spychalski (center)

Children transport arrives at Nachod camp.

The Village of Nachod on the Czech side of the Czech–Polish border.

The Brichah, with the financial assistance of the Polish JDC, agreed to funnel the massive exodus across different points along the long Polish–Czech borders. In 1945, 5,000 Polish Jews crossed the Polish–Czech border illegally. Following the Kielce pogrom, a mass movement of Polish Jews began to head to the Czech border. In May of 1946, 3052 Polish Jews crossed illegally to Czechoslovakia, in June of 1946, 8,000, in July of 1946, 19,000. August 1946, 35,346, in September 1946, 12,379 Jews crossed the border illegally [2]. During 5 months 77,777 Polish Jews crossed the Polish–Czech border at a single place called Nachod. Of course, there were other crossing points along the border namely at the village of Broumov. The number of Polish Jews leaving Poland were staggering in relationship to the total numbers of Jews following World War II. Of course, Polish Jews kept returning to Poland from Russia and soon joined the Brichah transports.

All of these Jews poured into Czechoslovakia illegally through various Polish border points namely Krosno, Dukla, Nowy Sacz, Kattowice, Walbrzych. Some Polish Jews actually left Poland legally to various Western countries and the USA. The total Jewish population in post–war Poland was 42,662 Jews in May 1945 [3]. By July 1946, with the massive arrival of repatriated Polish Jews from the Soviet Union, the number swelled to 240,489. But this number constantly declined with the mass departure of Jews as indicated above. The number of Jews in Poland at any given time following the war could not be ascertained due to the fluctuations.

Polish Jews crossing the Polish–Czech border in broad day light.

Polish Brichah transporting Jews across the Czech–Polish border

Israel Gaynor Jacobson, JDC director in Czechoslovakia

Zdenek 'Zoltan' Toman (Asher Zelig Goldberger), Czech Deputy Minister of the Interior

Transport of Polish Jews leaving Nachod camp on their way to the Austrian or German D.P. camps

The temporary refugee camp of Nachod had to be expanded rapidly to cope with the large number of arrivals. The camp would handle about 1,000 refugees for a day or two and then ship them on to Austria or Germany. The JDC in Paris sent huge stockpiles of food, clothing, and medicines to these reception camps to provide the refugees with the basic necessities before their departure from Czechoslovakia. In spite of the haste of organization the reception camps performed extremely well under the leadership of the JDC director of Czechoslovakia, Jacobson. The Czech government, particularly the assistant minister of the interior, Zdenek Toman or Asher Zelig Goldberg, helped the situation by granting the necessary permits for all theseoperations within Czechoslovakia. They gave the JDC and the Brichah a free hand in the country. Both Jewish organizations used it to the full extent. They enabled the Czech Brichah to work very closely with the Polish Brichah. The Brichah organization was run along national lines namely Polish Bricha or Italian Bricha. Each Brichah unit was familiar with the language, territory and customs of the country. The Polish Brichah was not of great use in Germany, but did develop excellent relations with the Polish border guards as the picture below shows.

Polish Jewish children leaving Poland following the Kielce pogrom

Polish border guard officers with Polish Brichah officials

Translator's Footnotes

VIII   Bauer, Yehuda, Out of the Ashes. pp.81–82 Pergamon Press
IX   Bauer, Yehuda, Brichah, New York, Random House, 1970, p.204
Dobroszycki, Lucjan, "Survivors of the Holocaust in Poland– A Portrait based on Jewish
Committee Records 1944–1947", Armonk, New York, M.E. Sharpe, 1994, p.10

[Page 182]

Chapter VIII
The Herzog Children's Transport

Jewish children continued to arrive at the association and Zionist homes. Most Jews wanted to leave Poland as quickly as they could. Some were single parents and did not want to drag their children through the borders so they brought them to the various Zionist homes with the understanding that the children would leave Poland for Palestine where the families would be reunited. The Jewish community of Zabrze continued to absorb many Jewish newcomers from Poland and from the repatriated Jewish masses from the Soviet Union. A synagogue was established in Zabrze with the help of the AJRC and some Jews chose to settle in Zabrze. Batia Akselrod recalls enjoyable moments shared with the Geller's at their apartment. There was a constant stream of Jews to Zabrze but most did not stay.

Jewish children from Teheran, Iran arrive in Palestine

Rabbi Herzog watched with trepidation as events unfolded in Eastern Europe, especially Poland. But there was little he could do except write letters and send money to the Association homes in Poland. The English government kept him in Palestine and would not permit him to leave the country. Herzog took a great interest in Jewish children. He helped absorb the Jewish children that arrived in Palestine during World War II with the Polish Army headed by General Anders.

He now wanted to help the Jewish orphans in Europe. Finally the British relented and permitted him to leave Palestine on January 20 1946. His first stop was Cairo, Egypt and then he continued to Italy where he met Jewish Shoah survivors, Jewish community leaders, soldiers of the Jewish Brigade and rescued Jewish children. Everywhere he urged the Jewish leaders to do everything in their power to help redeem the Jewish children still held in non-Jewish homes or institutions.

הועד היהודי האמריקאי המאוחד לסיוע (ג'וינט)
AMERICAN JEWISH JOINT DISTRIBUTION COMMITTEE
OFFICE FOR THE MIDDLE EAST AND BALKANS   המשרד למזרח התיכון ובלקנים
CHARLES PASSMAN, DIRECTOR   צ' פסמן, המנהל הכללי

Jerusalem,   כ"ד כסלו תש"ו   ירושלים
P. O. B. 645 PHONE 3745   29.11.45

לכבוד
הרב יצחק אייזיק הלוי הרצוג,
רב ראשי לארץ-ישראל,
י ר ו ש ל י ם.

רב ראשי נכבד מאד,

הנני מתכבד למסור לנ"ל לידיעה
כב"ת את נוסח המברק שקבלנו היום ומסרנו
בפריז:

"Guzik Warsaw requests you advise Chief Rabbi
Herzog Jerusalem   quote

Many thanks in my and Rabbi Steinberg's
name for consolation words Polish Jewry
stop
Entrance visa Poland arranged   stop
Please contact Polish Government rep-
resentative Jerusalem for visa   stop
All religious communities Poland look
forward to your visit   stop
Please advise date departure representative
Jewish religious communities Poland Rabbi
Dr. Kahane Aleja Schucha 16/43

                                        unquote "

בכל הכבוד,

(פ) כותר
צ' פסמן.

This cable awaited Rabbi Herzog on his arrival in Jerusalem

The visa was issued by the Polish government in Warsaw following pressure by David Guzik, director of JDC in Poland and Rabbi Steinberg. This document would enable Herzog to travel to Eastern Europe without British permission.

Rabbi Herzog then flew back to Jerusalem to testify before the Anglo–American Commission for Palestine. On his arrival in Jerusalem, a surprise awaited him, namely a visa to enter Poland. He testified at the hearings and then returned to Europe and traveled to England, France, Belgium, Holland, Switzerland and the American zone of occupation in Germany where he met Jewish Shoah survivors in the D.P. camps. The rabbi was shocked by the conditions, especially the orphanage homes in the camps.

Rabbi Itzhak Eisik Halevi Herzog and his son Yaakov Herzog
arrive at the D.P. camp in Fohrenwald, Bavaria, Germany.
To the left of Rabbi Herzog dressed in military uniform is Rabbi Wohlgelernter, Vaad Hatzala representative in Europe.

In London Rabbi Herzog urged Jews to contribute money to save Jewish children from non–Jewish homes. He also discussed plans of mass transportation with Rabbi Wohlgelernter, Vaad Hatzala representative of the American Orthodox rabbis in Europe and liaison officer with the United Nations Relief and Rehabilitation Administration (UNRRA). Both rabbis wanted to speed up the rescue of Polish Jewish orphans. They decided to ask UNRRA to help transport the children to France without the need to smuggle them over unfriendly borders. The rabbis used all their connections to influence UNRRA to prepare a plan of action. UNRRA cooperated and began making the arrangements. Meanwhile Rabbi Herzog obtained visas to enter France and Belgium for the children.

Rabbi Herzog and his son Yaakov left Paris and headed to Prague. Transportation in Europe was still limited to military personnel and only UNRRA could provide extensive means of transportation. So the Rabbi traveled under UNRRA auspices. He arrived in the Czech capital on July 25, 1946 and met Elfim Rees, UNRRA representative in Czechoslovakia. They discussed arrangements for a transport to be led by the Rabbi of 1,250 passengers – 500 adults, and 750 children. The transport would arrive from Poland and have to remain in Czechoslovakia for about six weeks until accommodations in France were ready. Rabbi Herzog, UNRRA and the Czech government conducted discussions on the length of the stay. The Czechs wanted the transport to leave the country as soon as possible. Then Rabbi Herzog took ill and was sent to the hot springs of Karlovy Vary where he stayed for one week. He returned to Prague and finalized the stay of the transport, then flew to Warsaw, with Yaacov, Rabbi Zeev Gold, the Rabbi's secretary and Rabbi Solomon P. Wohlgelernter.

The Polish government did not want to take risks with the safety of the Rabbi even though he was not an official guest of the government. For security purposes, the Herzog entourage was installed at the "Warszawa" [1] hotel by Rabbi Kahane. Several army officers were assigned to guard him reinforced by a few more Polish Jewish officers enlisted by Kahane.

Rabbi Kahane acted as the host and was pleased to finally see the man with whom he had often corresponded. They exchanged ideas and plans. Rabbi Kahane told Herzog in detail of the Jewish situation in Poland, and that there was a mass exodus of Jews from Poland. Rabbi Herzog decided to insist that his visas be used. It was true that Jews could leave Poland illegally or semi–legally by heading to the Czech border and then to Germany and Italy. But this lengthy trip involved so much suffering, pain and exhaustion, while his plan envisioned transports of Jewish children and youngsters from Poland to France by rail – easy and simple.

Rabbi Kahane began to prepare a list of children that would be leaving Poland with Rabbi Herzog. The Zabrze home received a sizable number of seats aboard the train as did the home of Gluszyca. Other religious homes like the Mizrahi and Agudat homes were given a number of seats and all the homes were told to prepare lists of children and the adults who would escort the transport.

In Warsaw, Rabbi Kahane introduced Herzog to various Polish Jewish leaders and Polish government officials including Poland's Prime Minister Eduard Osobka–Morawski. During this cordial meeting Rabbi Herzog asked the Polish leader to pass legislation to the effect that all Jewish children still in Poland be listed as Jews even if they were no longer living in Jewish homes or with Jewish families. He also asked the Polish prime minister to permit 750 Jewish orphans and 500 yeshiva students to leave for Palestine. The Polish government decided to allow the children to leave Poland.

Soon Rabbi Kahane was told that a Polish Red Cross train would be heading to Paris to bring home disabled Poles from France. The train could be used to transport the Jewish orphans to France. The entire operation was under the auspices of UNRRA which would pay for the transportation. [2] The Polish government side stepped the entire issue by handing the transportation matter to the Polish Red Cross and UNRRA.

In Warsaw, preparations began to organize the children's journey to France. Rabbi Kahane met with the AJRC leaders and representatives of Agudat Israel, Poalei Agudat Israel, the religious Zionist Mizrachi and Hapoel Hamizrachi movements in Poland, and apprised them of the plans and the need to prepare for the imminent departure of the children. Due to limited time and the difficulty of assembling such a large group, the original plan for 1250 travelers was drastically reduced.

Meanwhile, Rabbi Herzog visited the city of Lodz and on his way back to Warsaw, he decided to stop off at the Jewish cemetery in the city of Suchaczew where Rabbi Awraham, the author of 'Avnei Nezer', was buried. The tombstone was gone but he did find the tomb of Rabbi Awraham's wife, daughter of the Rabbi of Kotzk. He spent some moments in prayer and contemplation when Poles began to assemble and the security forces ordered the Rabbi to leave immediately for the train station. [3]

The AJRC organized a dinner honoring Rabbi Herzog where he encouraged them to have faith. He also addressed English and American correspondents in Warsaw on the Jewish situation in Poland. Following the news conference, he was urged to leave Poland immediately. He left Warsaw for Prague at 10:30 p.m. on August 13, 1946. The Polish guards remained with the Rabbi until the Czech border [4].

On August 19, 1946, the final transport plan entitled "Transport 750" was ready and presented to Rabbi Solomon P. Wohlgelernter, liaison officer for Rabbi Herzog and UNRRA. He called Rabbi Herzog and Rabbi Kahane and transmitted the plan to them. It was very detailed and covered almost all possible eventualities. According to the plan, the train, consisting of 44 passenger cars, would leave Lodz on Wednesday, August 21, 1946, stopping in Katowice where most of the children would board, and arrive in Prague on Friday, August 23, 1946. The document listed the entire leadership of the transport and their positions. The Polish government was represented by Wanda Siwek, an official of the Polish repatriation office. Security was represented by Major Sokol and medical facilities were the responsibility of Dr. Alfred Kalmanowicz. The Vaad Hatzala was represented by Rabbi Simcha Wasserman , Recha Sternbuch and Rabbi Solomon P. Wohlgelernter.

MINUTES OF CONFERENCE — 19TH AUGUST, 1946

15.00 Hours. UNRRA 15 Ross Street.

SUBJECT:- TRANSPORT FROM LODZ TO PRAGUE OF 750
JEWISH ORPHAN CHILDREN.

PRESENT:- Mr. M. Berger — Chief, Welfare and Repatriation
Division, UNRRA.

Rabbi S. Wasserman
Mrs. Biwek Wanda T.O.R.
Mrs. Palmowska Janina Polish Red Cross
Mrs. Sternbuch Recha
Rabbi Solomon M. Wohlgelernter
Mr. O.V. Horn — Voluntary Liaison Office, UNRRA.
Miss J. Hof — Interpreter - UNRRA.

After some discussion the following was agreed:-

Routine of journey

Wednesday, 21st August. 22.22 hours train leaves Lodz with 100 to
200 children. The Polish Red Cross will provide the train with
food and with all supplies, including facilities for children under
three.

Thursday, 22nd August. 08.00 arrive Katowice. Children to be taken
to Children's Home Zabrze for meals, washing etc., Ten buses are
being arranged by Rabbi Wohlgelernter, who will check arrangements
on Tuesday and Wednesday.
16.00 hours Children will return to train, together with other
children from Zabrze, Bytom, Katowice and Krakow areas.
18.00 hours train to leave Katowice.
19.00 hours (approx) Supper on train. Polish Red Cross will
provide this food.

Friday, 23rd August. Breakfast on train before arrival at Prague.
Train may be instructed to stop 30 km. before Prague to unload, but
breakfast will be served sufficiently early.

Additional Data.

1.   The train will be composed of 44 coaches of all kinds,
including Red Cross sleeping cars. There will be 380 beds and
approximately 30 beds in each sleeping coach. Children if
necessary to sleep two in each bed. The separation of boys from
girls by ages and sex will be the responsibility of the leaders.

2.   Lists of children by groups of 25 (or less) have been
prepared. Each group will have a leader who is also an instructor.
These leaders are to have passports for themselves.

3.   Visas for the children will be for each group as listed.
The children will not have individual visas. This is in accordance
with the wish of the Czechoslovak Government. Rabbi Wohlgelernter
will be responsible for informing UNRRA Poland of the official
identity numbers of each group visa.

4.   The leaders will travel with their respective groups and
will be responsible for ensuring:-

        (a) the safety of the children

        /(b) checking.........

**The UNRRA plan for transporting the Polish Jewish youngsters out of Poland
part 1**

- 2 -

(b) checking by numbers and names
(c) feeding of children
(d) supervision of children's hand baggage.
(e) obtaining sanitary and medical attention when necessary.

5.   The train will be staffed as follows:-

(a) Major Sokol - in charge of technical and operational matters.

(b) Dr. Alfred Kolznnowicz - in charge of medical matters.

He will have assistants:-

(i)   3 other doctors   } provided by Polish Red Cross.
(ii)   12 nurses   }
(iii) 2 doctors   } provided by Jewish organisation.
(iv)   30 leaders   }

6.   The Polish Red Cross will provide food, water, and all medical supplies, and will prepare and serve all meals on the train.

7.   Rabbi Wohlgelernter will make all arrangements for baggage - hand baggage through group leaders. He will arrange marking, collection and loading of baggage. Marking will be either singly or by groups as convenient. He will arrange special transport at Katowice and Prague for conveyance of baggage as well as of children. No sorting of baggage will be done at the stations or train.

8.   Rabbi Wohlgelernter will arrange for the leaders to meet Major Sokol in Katowice to receive his instructions.

9.   Rabbi Wohlgelernter will make special transport arrangements for children under three at Lodz and Zabrze (Katowice). The Polish Red Cross will provide all facilities and supervision for under threes from Lodz, and will ensure adequate sanitary arrangements for all on the train.

10.   Rabbi Wohlgelernter will be responsible for checking lists with special reference to the ages of the children. UNRRA H.Q., will extract from the list the under-threes in order that they may have special attention. He will refer names of any children apparently over 16 to Rabbi Wohlgelernter.

11.   Rabbi Wohlgelernter will telephone to UNRRA Prague from Katowice stating the actual numbers of children and of adults on the train.

In order to make a double check a message will be sent by the Czech Repatriation Mission in Katowice to Prague, No.61849 UNRRA. UNRRA Prague will send a representative to the frontier until the departure of the train from Lodz.

12.   All messages to Prague in connection with this operation will be sent through UNRRA Warsaw only.

13.   For purposes of contact between Warsaw and Katowice the following address in Katowice will be used:- Dr. Schebesta, ulica Koscielna 8, Katowice.

14.   UNRRA Warsaw will arrange for a photographer to be at the train for the purposes of UNRRA records and for future publication when considered advisable by UNRRA. Until then no publicity will be given to this operation.

The UNRRA plan for transporting the Polish Jewish youngsters out of Poland
Part 2

The plan had two major drawbacks, there was no continuation provision following the arrival in Prague and no one specific leader named. Rabbi Kahane instructed Drucker to supervise the loading of the train [5] in Lodz on Wednesday, August 21, 1946. The Rabbi's office in Warsaw directed all homes to proceed to Lodz or Katowice. Transportation was a problem in Poland especially for groups that wanted immediate tickets. Furthermore, there was a problem of safety for the Jewish children on Polish trains. But these decisions had to be made quickly. Even the UNRRA plan called "Plan 750 "only listed 750 youngsters plus escorts. This number would be further reduced the day of departure

Recha Sternbuch, was one of the first to board the train in Lodz with a group of yeshiva boys who brought a Torah scroll they had saved during the war and carried with them all across Russia. Rabbis Wohlgelernter, Drucker and Becker were on the train to greet the children. The loading proceeded according to plan, with half the cars assigned to the Mizrahi party and the other half to the Agudat party.

The youngest member of the Herzog transport

Group leaders, namely Moshe Einhorn, Yeshayahu Spiner, the late Meir
Weissblum, and Recha Sternbuch soon assumed their posts. When the train
arrived at Katowice, it was shunted to a side line where the various groups
proceeded to board including the Zabrze contingent that was part of the
Mizrahi group. David Danieli described in a previous chapter how the Zabrze
group of children received the news of departure and proceeded to the train
station.

**The Herzog children's train reached the main Prague railway station
where Rabbi Herzog, seen standing on a small platform, thanked the
Czech government and Czech officials for their hospitality.**

The train stood in Katowice for a long time until Rabbi Herzog who was
detained in Warsaw finally arrived late in the evening and the train started to
roll to the Czech border. Prior to the border crossing, some stowaways were
discovered aboard the train. The Polish guards counted and recounted the
passengers and discovered that there were 10 extra passengers. The
stowaways were removed and the journey continued. But the train was still far
away from Prague as the Sabbath approached. Rabbi Herzog and the children
left the train in Ostrava–Moravska where they spent the Sabbath and resumed
the journey the next day. They arrived in Prague to a tumultuous reception.
This was one of the largest Jewish children transports to transit
Czechoslovakia and contained a sizable number of Zabrze and Gluszyca
children. The transport consisted of 500 children, 101 teachers and
supervisors and Rabbi Herzog and his entourage. The children were moved to
the big reception center of Dablice where they would spend six weeks until
accommodations in France were ready. Only then did the Herzog Children's
Transport leave Czechoslovakia for France.

The children left Poland but relatives continued to search for them there. Below is a letter sent from England inquiring about two orphans who survived the war. The letter was sent to the JDC office in Poland who traced the children and replied to the distressed family.

```
10785/56/D/Secr.                          March 12th,  7
File No. 242

          Jewish Refugees Committee
          Bloomsbury House
          Bloomsbury Street
          L o n d o n  W C 1.


          Gentlemen,

                    Immediately upon receipt of your cable regarding
          Ryfka and Berl Brander we contacted the Children's Home in
          Zabrze and now received the information that the children
          left Poland in August 1946 for France. The children are full
          orphans and they have no relatives in Poland.-

                    Their present address is. Colonie de Vacances,
          Shirmeck, Bas Rhin, France.-

                    We are giving you for your information the children's
          identifying data.
                    Brander Ryfka, born January 12,1935 in Brzozow near
                    Sanok.
                    Brander Berl, born in December 1937.

          Father's name Pinkas, mother's Esther M.N. Roth. Sara Bart,
          the children's aunt was their guardian and was residing in
          Bytom but she also left recently for abroad.-

                              Very truly yours,

                              American Joint Distribution
                                   Committee


                              William Bein
                              Director for Poland
```

Letter searching for Jewish children after the war. The children were located. They had left the Zabrze home with the Herzog children transport and reached the home of Schirmack near the city of Strasburg in France. Notice the signature on the letter.

Rabbi Herzog, chief rabbi of Palestine, pleading with UNRRA official in Prague to let his transport of children enter Czechoslovakia

Children outside Zabrze Orphanage

Transports of children continued to leave Poland but on a much smaller scale and more frequently. The children transports went directly to France. Batia Akselrad–Eisenstein, one of the Jewish children hidden during the war and then brought to the Zabrze orphanage by the efforts of Drucker, was constantly hoping that she would be returned to her Polish adoptive family in Krosno as they had promised her. While Batia waited in vain for her foster family to rescue her from the orphanage, other events soon took control of her destiny. "The news quickly spread," she said, "that the children from Zabrze would soon leave for Palestine. A second children transport was being organized. Like everyone else, I began to pack. I was ready for the trip. I still thought my 'mother' would come and get me once we reached the train station. A small number of us Zabrze children were driven to Katowice where we boarded a train to Lodz. I looked for my 'mother' at the Katowice railway station but couldn't find her. We only spent a short time in Lodz. Living conditions there were unpleasant. The second train was finally organized. I remember waiting again for my 'mother' to come and get me before the train left. I was crying. But the train left without me ever seeing her. We rode in cattle cars but the trip was pleasant. The train rolled through Poland and after a delay at the Polish–Czech border, it then continued to travel through Czechoslovakia, then Germany, stopping in Paris. We received a tumultuous welcome at the Paris train station. I remember that Rabbi Herzog's son Yaacov was there to greet us on behalf of his father, who was recuperating in Palestine from his last long journey." According to Batia, the Zabrze children were then sent to the southern French city of Perigueux where they would remain for the next two years. They would all arrive in Israel with the creation of the new State.

The second Herzog transport to France

The Rothschild estate near Perigueux where Jewish children spent two years preparing to settle in Palestine

The Zabrze home had a number of small toddlers who presented particular problems. Obviously, they could not be sent illegally across the borders. Most of them were flown to England by Rabbi Salomon Schonfeld, son in law of the Chief Rabbi of England Joseph H. Hertz. Rabbi Hertz raised substantial sums of money in England to support the Jewish orphanages in Europe. Rabbi Schonfeld was heavily involved in rescuing Jewish children from Europe before World War II, regularly bringing children from Germany and Austria and placing them with religious Jewish families. With the end of the war he immersed himself in rescuing Jewish children from non–Jewish homes. He worked very closely with Rabbi Kahane and helped financially and materially the Jewish homes. He made all the arrangements in England to transport the young children and place them with Jewish families. Rabbi Schonfeld took several transports of small Jewish children directly from Poland to England. Rabbi Kahane did not like to send Jewish children to England but the necessity of the situation forced him to consent. Poland was in turmoil, the small children needed special care that could not be assured in Polish homes. So he consented to send them to England where they would be provided with good homes. Most of the children were adopted and raised to maturity.

Rabbi Salomon Schonfeld dressed in military uniform

Translator's Footnotes

X Kahane, David Rabbi. After the Deluge, Jerusalem, p89.
XI   Kahane, Deluge, p.88
XII   Sharagai, Zalman. Mission to Europe, Jerusalem, p.66
XIII   Ibid. pp 72–74
Testimony of Yeshayahu Drucker at Yad Vashem in Jerusalem

[Page 192]

Chapter IX
Normalcy Returns to Poland

On February 27, 1947, the Polish borders were closed in accordance with the Spychalski–Tzuckerman agreement. The number of Jews crossing the border illegally into Czechoslovakia steadily declined as the Jewish population in Poland shrank. Repatriation of Polish Jews from the Soviet Union was reduced to a trickle since the mass of Polish Jews had already returned to Poland. The Polish Brichah still organized some illegal crossings but these were small operations. The Polish government slowly gained control of the country following national elections won by the Communist Party. The various security forces and the army slowly restored order. Jews also began to feel a bit safer. The Jewish community in Zabrze steadily grew in numbers. Children continued to arrive at the Zabrze home and Captain Drucker was very busy locating and redeeming Jewish children from non–Jewish homes and institutions. The Geszcze Puste home closed since few repatriated Jews now arrived in Poland and even fewer Jewish orphans. Most of the residents and staff of Geszcze Puste were sent abroad while the borders were still open. The home had existed for about 18 months.

The Zabrze old age home was located on the top floor

The remodeled old age home of Zabrze

RL 6367   November 12th, 1948.

          TO: AJDC, New York

          FROM: AJDC, Warsaw

          RE: Landsmannschaft BYDGOSZCZ

Gentlemen,

This is in reference to your letter dated October 22, 1948.

We wish to inform you that we have communicated with the Bydgoszcz
Landsmannschaft and asked them for a more detailed statement regarding
the payment, and for a complete and thorough report of their activities.

We specifically stressed the urgency of their pointing up in the report
the amounts spent for housing and house furnishings.

To date we have already paid out the amounts earmarked for the three
Homes for Aged:

                    in Zabrze   -   Zł1000.-
                    in Krakow   -   Zł1000.-
                    in Lodz   -   Zł1435.-

These homes will put at the disposal of the Bydgoszcz Landsmannschaft
special rooms. There will be plaques placed on the doors and the main
walls of these rooms dedicated to the memory of the donors, Lena and
Zelig Cohen.

We will promptly send on to you receipts of the above payments, as well
as letters of appreciation and photographs of the plaques.

Cooperative in the name of "Lena Cohen"

We enclose herein copies of letters received from the Bydgoszcz
Landsmannschaft as well as the newly-established Workers' Cooperative,
in the name of "Lena Cohen", concerning the payment Zł10,000 earmarked for
them.

**The Polish Joint Distribution Committee allocated money to the old age home of
Zabrze**

The old age home which had been created by the Central Committee of Polish Jews after the war and funded by the Polish JDC, received mostly Jewish Shoah survivors who had no place to go and were unable to move about. The home would continue to function until 1953 when it was closed and remodeled as a state home for chronically and terminally ill patients. Currently, the building houses a nursing home.

Below is a registration card of a new Jewish arrival in Zabrze. The Zabrze community received many Jewish residents, especially repatriated Jews. Regina Viertel had come from the area of Lwow that was now part of the Soviet Union. Her registration card indicates the number 1,905, implying that the Jewish community of Zabrze had already received close to 1,905 Jews by June 1946 and Jews were still coming. Of course, many of those Jews did not stay long. Regina Laur Viertel was born on September 17, 1876, to Chaskiel Laur and Rajzla Schauer, in Kolomyja, Eastern Galicia. She registered in Zabrze on the 25th of June, 1946. The Jewish community office in Zabrze was located at 3 Brysza Street in the building of the so–called Small Synagogue. Before the war, the building was called Small Synagogue. It was built in 1898. During the expanding work on the large synagogue in Zabrze, the building served as a house of prayer, while at the same time it held the archives of the Jewish community and housing for employees of the municipality. In August 1902, its interior was rebuilt. A mikveh (ritual bath) was built in the basement. During the World War II, in October 1939, the Germans converted the building into a music school. Later, the Hitler Jugend school was located there.

Registration card of Regina Viertel, maiden name Laur, on arrival in Zabrze on

June 25, 1946

Following the war, a local branch of the Committee of Polish Jews opened an office to assist Jewish refugees who wanted to settle in the city, such as Regina Viertel.

As mentioned above, the Polish government was slowly gaining control of the country. More and more police forces were created to cope with the lawlessness. The U.B. or Urzad Bezpieczenstwa or Polish secret police force was greatly expanded and given large powers. The Polish Communist Party demanded action. Even the Central Jewish Committee of Polish Jews that was by now Communist dominated demanded immediate steps to prevent Jews from legally leaving Poland. It also demanded that the educational programs of the Jewish orphanages be realigned with the regular Polish school program. Pressure was also applied on Rabbi Kahane to merge his Zabrze home with those of the Central Committee homes. He used all his influence to delay the demands. But now Zionist orphanages and institutions were being watched. The Polish government tightened control of Jewish legal emigration but permitted Jews to move to Palestine. The U.B. or Polish secret police began to follow Zionist activists. A significant change was taking place regarding Jews and Jewish organizations, especially those involved in Zionist activities. The president of the Central Committee of Polish Jews, Emil Sommerstein, was still recovering from a heart attack he had suffered abroad. His place was soon assumed by a strong Communist and the shift of the committee's political orientation became obvious. The Communist members of the committee became vociferous in their demands that all Zionist activities throughout Poland cease. The Polish government took matters in hand.

The Zionist kibbutzim and homes increased the tempo of their transports out of Poland. Then, out of the blue, the Polish government decided to honor the Zabrze home and invited a contingent from the home to participate in the official celebrations in memory of the Jewish revolt in Warsaw. Drucker and some children from the Zabrze home took part in the 1948 parade marking the fifth anniversary of the Jewish revolt in the Warsaw ghetto. The Zabrze contingent also attached a plaque in memory of the revolt. The home made extensive preparations for its participation in the parade and wore their best clothes for the occasion.

Zabrze official delegation headed by Dr. Nechema Geller
Behind her stands Rudolf Wittenberg, gym teacher of the Zabrze home, and to his left
is Captain Drucker dressed in military uniform

**Zabrze children waiting their turn to enter the parade in memory of the Jewish
revolt in Warsaw**

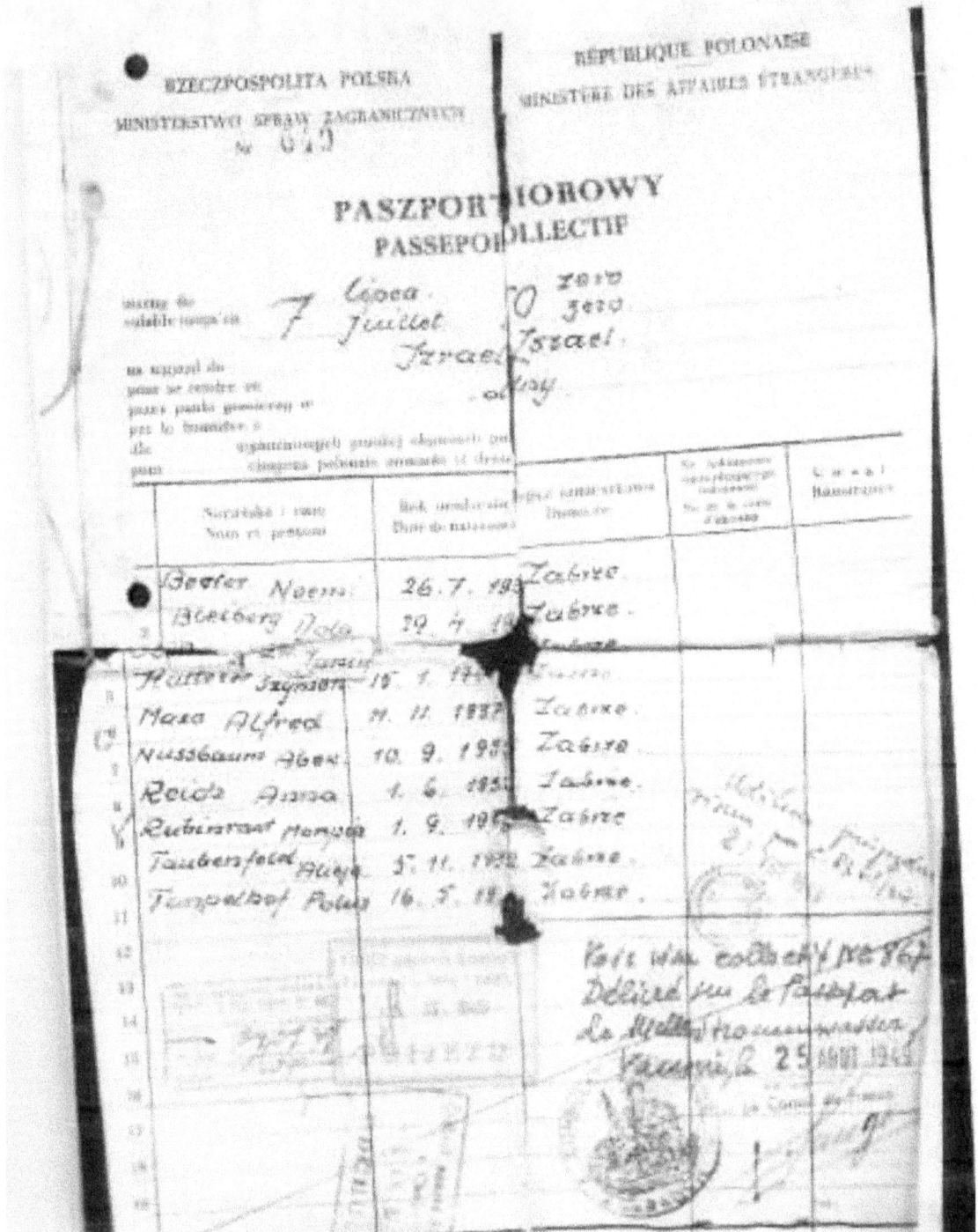

Group passport for Polish children traveling to Israel.
All children listed were from the Zabrze home
They traveled via Czechoslovakia to Germany and France and then sailed to Israel

The U.B. began to intimidate the Palestinian Zionist representatives in Poland. They were urged to leave the country. Leib Koriski, head of the Koordinacja office, was placed under special surveillance. The Zionist homes tried to send all their children abroad. Zabrze was no exception as the document above indicates.

In 1949, Rabbi Kahane decided to leave Poland for Israel and managed to take with some of the children with him. Upon his arrival he was appointed Chief Rabbi of the Israeli Air Force. Drucker was appointed to replace Kahane as Chief Chaplain of the Polish Army.

The office of the Chief Rabbi was diminished in importance since the number of Polish Jewish soldiers constantly declined. Drucker continued his activities in redeeming Jewish children but it became more difficult by the day. Poland was becoming a Communist dictatorship where movements were strictly controlled. Many checkpoints and roadblocks were set up and traveling across the country became very difficult. The cold war atmosphere swept Poland.

[Page 205]

Chapter X
The End of the Jewish Community of Zabrze

**The great Yiddish actor Solomon
Mikhailovich Mikhoels, murdered in 1948
by the Soviet secret police in Minsk, Soviet
Union**

In Eastern Europe new winds began to blow. The Soviet Union was having problems with Yugoslavia, which refused to follow Stalin's political line. Marshal Tito of Yugoslavia and Stalin in the Soviet Union were constantly at odds but Stalin could do little since there were no Soviet troops in Yugoslavia. The pro–Soviet elements in Yugoslavia were rounded up and disarmed. Tito was ready to fight and had the support of the West, particularly the United States. Stalin had to accept defeat but ordered the Soviet secret services to tighten control over his empire to make sure that no more Tito–type situations arose. The various communist parties in Eastern Europe were ordered to seize power or tighten the reins of power. The cold war climate escalated between the Soviet Empire and the West. Organizations and institutions were advised to desist from dealing with Western entities. Fear and panic swept the Communist world as the cold war grew.

Stalin's paranoia with Jews began to emerge into the open. Soviet papers began to write anti–Jewish articles. The Yiddish theater in the Soviet Union was being dismantled and in 1948 Stalin had the great Yiddish actor Solomon Mikhoels bludgeoned to death and his body run over by a truck as a thinly veiled hit–and–run accident in the city of Minsk. Mikhoels received a state funeral, but most of the Yiddish actors and writers were arrested or exiled. The Moscow Yiddish Theater was dissolved. Jewish culture was ended in the Soviet Union.

The Soviet secret services received orders to begin to replace the Jewish Communist leaders in the various East European countries, including Zdenek Toman, one of the first casualties of the new policies. He was a Jew, well connected with Zionist and Jewish American organizations, had lived for many years in Britain, and was very independent and sure of himself in relation to the Soviet secret service. He was also very close to the Czech establishment, particularly Jan Masaryk. The decision to destroy Toman was made in typical Stalinist fashion: he was promoted to the Czech Ministry of Interior but lost the position of head of state security. He lost control over the security forces to one of his subordinates in the fall of 1947. Toman was neutralized by the change and lost his power in Czechoslovakia. Other important Jewish Communist leaders, including Rudolf Slansky, general secretary of the Czechoslovak Communist Party, would soon suffer the same fate. Ana Pauker, leader of the Romanian Communist Party and Foreign Minister of that country would also be arrested and charged with anti–party activities.

Ana Pauker, Romanian foreign minister

Similar events involving Jewish officials would begin to occur in other Soviet satellite countries including Poland where the hard liners or pro–Stalin faction gained control of the party and the government. Wladyslaw Gomulka was removed from power and later jailed.

Harsh police measures soon followed in Poland. Leib Koriski, Palestinian emissary and head of the "Koordinacja" office, was arrested and released on condition that he stop his activities in Poland. He continued his "Koordinacja" activities and was arrested again and interrogated. The police insisted that he provide evidence that all children who had left Poland had done so legally. While Koriski was in jail, Pinhas Kribus, another Palestinian emissary, was appointed to replace him. But the police hampered all activities of the "Koordinacja" office. Koriski was released and forced to leave Poland. All Palestinian officials including Sarah Dushnicka–Shener and Menachem Kondo, were also forced to leave the country. No new entry visas were granted to Zionist emissaries. Rachel Sternbuch, who was a Swiss citizen, represented the "Vaad Hatzala" organization in Europe, especially in Poland. This organization was created by American orthodox rabbis to help orthodox rabbis and yeshiva students in Europe. She was also very active on behalf of redeeming Jewish children from non–Jewish homes and institutions. She was arrested, kept in jail for a short period of time and then escorted to the border.

Active Jews were called to the police and questioned. All were told that they were being watched. Even the members of the Bund or Jewish Socialist movement were being followed. The Bund was the best organized movement in postwar Poland. It had a wide variety of institutions and branch offices in many cities in Poland. The organization frequently cooperated with the Communist Party in Poland. The Polish government decided to attack the Bund on two fronts. One way was to order the police to check and control the party activities. The Polish government also urged the Bund members to join the Polish Communist Party. The simultaneous pressure was too difficult to fight and the Bund decided to close its doors in Poland. Most Bund members left Poland and headed to Australia, Europe, Argentina and even Israel, which they had so fervently opposed.

The Zabrze home was not a Zionist institution so it continued to function and even received some of the children from Zionist homes. But Drucker knew they had limited time to get the remaining children out of Poland. Some children were given to Polish families for adoption as the case illustrated below indicates. Drucker was under constant pressure to unite the Zabrze home with the homes of the Central Committee. He delayed and used the time to remove the children and staff from the home. This was challenging since the secret police watched and recorded their movements. It became particularly difficult to obtain legal documents.

l-szy wypis aktu notarialnego. - Numer repertorium : 3144/49.-
AKT NOTARIALNY. - Dnia ósmego września tysiąc dziewięćset cter -
dziestego dziewiątego roku (8.9.1949), przede mną Mgr.Mieczysła -
wem Galeńskim, Notariuszem w Gliwicach, jawią się w kancelarii
notariatu przy ulicy Powstańców pod numerem 23 - nieznani mi
osobiście :   1.- Dr Emilia S a l i t - A l e k s a n d r o -
w i c z, lekarz, zamieszkała w Gliwicach przy ulicy Chodoby nu -
mer 6 - wykazująca tożsamość swej osoby dla braku rekognoscentów
legitymacją numer 11361 wydaną przez Państwowy Instytut Przeciw -
rakowy w Gliwicach dnia 25 czerwca 1949 -   2.- Major Wojak Pol -
skich Jezajasz D r u c k i e r, zamieszkały w Warszawie Aleje
Szucha numer 16 - wykazujący tożsamość swej osoby legitymacją
oficerską numer 0783 wydaną przez Ministerstwo Obrony Narodowej
dnia 10 maja 1947. ---- Stawający zawierają wobec mnie następu -
jącej treści : - A K T P R Z Y S P O S O B I E N I A. -----
I.- Wedłg złożonego w aktach Sądu Grodzkiego w Gliwicach IV Ns.
738/49 wierzytelnego odpisu passportu Dr Emilia Salit-Aleksan -
drowicz, urodziła się dnia dwudziestego czwartego kwietnia tysiąc
dziewięćset trzeciego roku (24.4.1903), a według złożonego w
wierzytelnym odpisie w tych samych aktach poświadczenia obywa -
telstwa wydanego przez Zarząd Miejski w Zabrzu Pol.III-31-0/306
z dnia 31 maja 1948 - Sulamit (Stefania) G o t t e n b e r g

**This Polish document states that on"September 8, 1949 appeared before me
Doctor Emilia Siliat Aleksandrowicz from the city of Gliwice. She officially
adopted Sulamit Stefania Gottenberg from the nearby orphanage of Zabzre. The
release from the orphanage was signed by Major in the Polish Army named
Jezajasz Druckier (Yeshayahu Drucker) service number 0783, residing at 16
Szucha Alee, Warsaw. 12 Copy of adoption paper of Sulamit Gottenberg in
Gliwice, Poland."**

Many Zionist officials began to leave Poland for Israel. Slowly but
effectively, the Zionist political parties and their cultural institutions were
forced to close their doors. The Jewish communities including Zabrze lost a
good part of their Jewish population. Many Jewish activities stopped in Zabrze
as the number of Jews steadily declined. Then on December 31, 1949, the
Polish government informed the Joint Distribution Committee in Poland that it
had to stop all activities on Polish soil. William Bein, head of the Polish Joint
Distribution Committee tried to intervene but in vain. The decision shocked
the entire Jewish community for the Joint Distribution Committee had
extensively supported the Jewish communities and all Jewish institutions.
Institution after institution closed. Yeshayahu Drucker closed the Zabrze
home and returned the key to the AJRC, which in turn gave the key to the
Central Committee of the Polish Jews.

The end of Jewish communal and cultural institutions came with the
closure of the organization known as the Central Committee of Polish Jews
then headed by Hersz Smolar. Even this official organization representing the
Jews of Poland was closed down despite the fact that it had become a mere

mouthpiece of the government. All branch offices of the Central Committee were closed including the office in Zabrze. The most prominent official Jewish institution in Poland following the Shoah, the Central Committee of Jews in Poland (Centralny Komitet Żydów w Polsce; CKŻP) attended to the needs of Jews from the fall of 1944 until 1950. Originally chaired by Emil Sommerstein, it had sponsored a variety of programs, providing food, shelter, education, medical assistance, cultural activities, and employment services and vocational training. The CKŻP also supervised the repatriation of Jews from the Soviet Union and assisted with legal emigration.

Emil Sommerstein, Head of the Central Committee of Polish Jews

The dissolution act in effect left Polish Jews without any Jewish organization. The Polish government would eventually establish a mere cultural association of Jews in Poland. The Jewish community remained isolated shadows within the country. The Polish government also closed the exit gates of Poland to Jews. All visa applications to Israel were denied. State–sponsored anti–Semitism swept Poland.

The Zabrze home was converted to a general public old age home that would continue to operate until 1953. The Jewish community of Zabrze withered as most of the Jews left the city. The town has no Jews at present.

[Page 229]

Chapter XI

Pan Kapitan

The children at the Zabrze home referred to Yeshayahu Drucker as "Pan Kapitan" or sir captain. He was their father, counselor, adviser and spiritual master. He devoted most of his free time to the home and the children. They became attached to him and saw in his devotion to them a sort of paternal love. The children at Zabrze demanded a great deal of individual attention which they had been deprived of for years and he provided it. He hated to see them leave Poland but realized that they must go since the situation in Poland was intolerable.

Some say Yeshayahu Drucker was driven by an inner force to save as many Jewish children as possible. He was familiar with prewar Polish Jewry. He had witnessed the results of the war as a simple infantryman in the Polish liberating Army. Drucker was determined to save the few remnants of once great Polish Jewry, not for personal gain or fame but for the Jewish nation. To Drucker, Jewish history was a long chain of life that had to be continued regardless of the destructive events. In order to continue this unbroken chain, living Jews were needed, yet so few Jews survived that there was a real and present danger that Jewish life might end. It was this fear of extinction of the Jewish people that drove Drucker to save one soul after another in order to continue the chain of Jewish life. He personally led many of the hidden children to the orphanages and foster homes in Poland and took an interest in their problems. He maintained contact with the children until they left Poland and even later continued the communications when they were all in Israel. To him these children were part of the surviving nation that had to be nurtured and restored to life.

Drucker's job was not pleasant and required great tact. Some of these hidden children had become accustomed to their new Christian homes where they had been placed by their Jewish parents to hide them from the Nazis. The children felt comfortable in their Christian surroundings, safe from the turmoil of war whirling around them. Some of the Christian families behaved like excited new parents, especially childless couples. Over the years, many of the families became attached to the children and thought of them as their own. No doubt this was a dilemma even for Drucker. Should he let things stay as they were or restore the children to their Jewish roots? So many Jewish families had been decimated during the war, with not a sole living relative on earth. He could not stand by and permit the disappearance of even more Jews from the Jewish community. It became obvious to Drucker that he could not leave the matter as it was, that he had a moral and religious obligation to act on behalf of the lost Jewish families so these hidden children could assume their natural role as a part of the Jewish people

In 1948 Captain Drucker was promoted to the rank of Major in the Polish Army. He married a survivor of the war named Miriam Wolfeiler whom he met while she was working at the Zabrze home. Their daughter Rachel, named in honor of Drucker's mother, was born in Warsaw. Because of the dire situation for Jews in Poland and the promise of the new state of Israel, Drucker decided to take his wife and daughter and follow his rescued children. He retired from the Polish army and in 1950 the family left Poland and settled in the coastal town of Bat Yam, near Tel Aviv. Miriam soon gave birth to a son, Yoel.

Word quickly spread among the graduates of the Zabrze home throughout Israel that Captain Drucker had arrived in Israel. They began to write him letters and call him. He was busy adapting to life in a new country like so many other immigrants. Still, he met his adopted children. They came to him with their problems and their questions. He became a one–man welfare agency for they had nowhere else to turn. Eventually, Drucker found a job with the Jewish Agency, a position he held until his retirement.

A gathering of former residents of the Zabrze orphanage in Israel

The rescued children appreciated his efforts and expressed their thanks by throwing a surprise birthday party for him in the city of Holon.

Yeshayahu Drucker at a reunion with former Zabrze Jewish orphans on the 26th of May 1999 in Israel

Reunion of former Zabrze residents with Yeshayahu Drucker
Standing from right to left: **Tziporah Domb, Fela Koshok, Hawa Klarsfeld and Shoshana Stein**
Sitting from right to left: **David Danieli, Yeshayahu Drucker, and his wife Marioska or Miriam**
Man standing in the back unknown

Yeshayahu Drucker in a pensive mood in Israel

Later, Drucker was somewhat disappointed to see what happened to these children. The ill prepared new country was not always able to provide the guidance and nurturing the children needed. At that time, the State of Israel was already engaged in the fight for its survival, the War of Independence. Thousands of Jewish refugees were arriving daily. The pressure to absorb new immigrants and deal with their problems took a back seat to the threat to the new Jewish state's existence. The government and institutions were overwhelmed by the great tasks they faced and the children of Zabrze and other foster homes were mostly left to fend for themselves. Despite his own absorption and adaptation problems, Drucker again stepped in and offered his assistance and help to all those who turned to him. Once in Israel he again became fixated on the "hidden children" who he had rescued.

Yeshayahu Drucker died on September 15, 2004. The news spread among the surviving Zabrze graduates in Israel. They flocked to the unveiling of the tombstone from all over Israel to pay their final respects to the man who devoted himself to them.

**The unveiling of a tombstone for Yeshayahu Drucker.
Mrs. Drucker and her daughter were present at the ceremony**

Yeshayahu Drucker's tombstone in Israel

Michal Hefer, a former resident of Zabrze eulogized Yeshayahu Drucker

"קפטן דרוקר" היה איש אציל נפש, בעל שאר רוח, שמפעל הצלת הילדים היהודים מידי
הנוצרים היה מפעל חייו.

לקפיטן דרוקר היתה עבורנו כל הסבלנות והאהבה להם נזקקנו ג'אשות אחרי השואה האיומה.
הוא היה המשפחה שלנו. אנחנו, ששרדנו יחידים בודדים ממשפחות שלמות, ראינו בו אח
גדול. גם כשהיינו בצרפת, ממתינים לעלייה, לשם שלח אותנו על מנת להרחיקנו מפולין
המסוכנת, כתבנו אליו, וכל מכתב התחיל ב "אחי היקר". ואכן היה איש יקר, שהסתכן בלי
גבול וללא כל חשבון עבור "ילדיו".

כשהלך להוציא ילד שלא תמיד רצה לחזור לחיק היהדות, או שמצליליו נקשרו לאותו ילד ולא
אפשרו לו לעזוב, היה עליו לעיתים לחטוף את הילד או לפנות לבית המשפט ובלבד להצילו!
כשבא הרב דרוקר ביחד עם בן דודי, הסופר הארדי יהודה אלברג, ז"ל, להוציא אותי מכפר
פילצ'יצה, ליד העיר קלצה, מעט אחרי הפוגרום שהפולנים ערבו ב-1946 ביהודים ששבו
ממחנות ההשמדה, כמעט הרגו אותנו ביער, בדרך אל החופש. רק תושייתו של הרב דרוקר
הצילה אותנו.

עם זאת, לא פעם סיפר לי על הלבטים הקשים שהיו לו לקחת ילד קטן מתוך משפחה חמה:
אשר גידלה אותו מספר שנים כבנו/ביתה, מבלי שהיה מודע כי אינם הוריו האמיתיים, ולהעבירו
לבית יתומים. או להוציא ילדה גדולה יותר ממשפחה מצליליה ולקרוע אותה שנית ממסגרת
חייה על מנת להחזירה לחיק עמה.

היום אני יודעת את התשובה. עשית נכון "קפטן דרוקר!". פעלת מתוך אהריות לאומיה
וגדלות נפש. אתה היית הקורצ'אק הפרטי שלנו, סמל ומופת!

כעת, כשהגעת לבית הדין של מעלה, שם בודאי הודו לך בשמנו, ילדי ז'בז'ה, ובשם שאר
הילדים שהצלת, מפני שעם ישראל הוא כאותו "עוף החול" המוזכר בבראשית רבה, י"ט. שם
כתוב: "עוף אחד ושמו חול... אלף שנה הוא חי, ובסוף אלף שנה אש יוצאה מקנו ושורפתו,
ומותיר בו כביצה, וחוזר ומגדל איברים וחי".
אתה עזרת לנו לחזור, לגדל איברים ולחיות!

תודה לך קפיטן דרוקר.
תנחומינו לרעייתך מרים ולמשפחתך.
יצענו לך רבבי צפרה של ישראל הקטנה, אליה שלחת אותנו לקיים חיים חדשים.
יהי זכרך ברוך.

מיכל הפר
כפר ויתקין, 15.10.04

Translation of the Hebrew eulogy to English
Translated from Hebrew by William Leibner

Captain Drucker was a noble person endowed with a sensitive soul who immersed himself in the task of saving Jewish children from Christian homes. This endeavor became his raison d'etre. He had all the patience and love for us and we needed heaps of it following the Shoah. He was our family. We saw in him our big brother for we had no one to turn to, yet we all had large families that vanished during the war. Even when we left Poland where we were in terrible danger and arrived in France, we continued to correspond with him. Our letters usually began with "Dear Brother." Indeed he was a dear man who risked his life for the sake of his "children."

He frequently went on missions to extract Jewish children from Christian homes knowing well that some of the children no longer wanted to return to the Jewish fold or the adopted parents refused to part with the child. Then Yeshayahu Drucker attempted to negotiate the release of the child. If negotiations failed he then resorted to the courts or even to strong–arm tactics in order to save the child. When Yeshayahu Drucker came with my uncle Yehuda Elberg, a Yiddish writer, to take me away from the village of Pilczica near Kielce shortly after the terrible Kielce pogrom of 1946 aimed at the surviving Jews, we were almost killed in the forest on our way to freedom. But thanks to the quick thinking of Yeshayahu Drucker we were saved.

Yeshayahu Drucker frequently had moral doubts as to his activities, for he realized that some of children had finally found a home where they were accepted. They had lived with the family for a number of years and frequently did not even know that these parents were not their biological parents. Then to come and break up the relationship was very painful. Furthermore, some of the children were older and even more sensitive to being traumatized again. But Yeshayahu was determined to save these children for the Jewish nation. I now understand your motive, Captain Drucker, you did it on behalf of the Jewish nation and sacrificed personal feelings. You were our Janusz Korczak, our standard bearer.

And now you will appear before divine judgment and you will be graciously thanked in all likelihood on behalf of all the children of Zabrze and all the other children who you saved. For the nation of Israel can be compared to that famous legendary bird of the sand that is mentioned in Genesis Raba, 19, where it is written "The bird lived for a thousand years, then it was consumed by fire but the remains provided the necessary elements for the rebirth of the bird." We are in the same situation, Captain Drucker, you have provided us with the necessary elements to grow again.

Thank you Captain Drucker,
Our condolences to your wife Miriam and to your family.

May the gentle soil of this small country accept you who has sent us to it to resume a new life.

May your memory be blessed forever.

Signed,
Michal Hefer. Dated 15/10/2004.

Miriam Drucker passed away a year later.

May their memory be blessed forever.

Invitation letter to the former residents of the Zabrze home to come and participate in a reunion that would discuss their past experiences and interactions

The meeting was scheduled to take place on December 17, 2010 at Yad Vashem in Jerusalem. The program of the day consisted of four parts; light refreshments, group discussion, lunch, group discussion, and a memorial service at the "Memorial Hall" of Yad Vashem. The picture on the invitation is that of the Zabrze home with Dr. Nechema Geller, David Hubel and the children.

Drucker devoted himself to rescuing Jewish children and placing them at the Zabrze home.

Most of them reached Israel where they established families and integrated into society. Yad Vashem decided to honor the man and his deeds by assembling the surviving former children of Zabrze to a reunion at Yad Vashem in Jerusalem. Invitations were sent and those that were able participated in the event including Drucker's daughter and son. The participants described their experiences during the war and their relationships with Drucker. The entire session was recorded on video. The participants also laid a wreath at the "Memorial Hall" of Yad Vashem and memorial services were held.

Some of the participants at the reunion of Zabrze graduates as they discussed their experiences

Group picture of Zabrze participants at the reunion

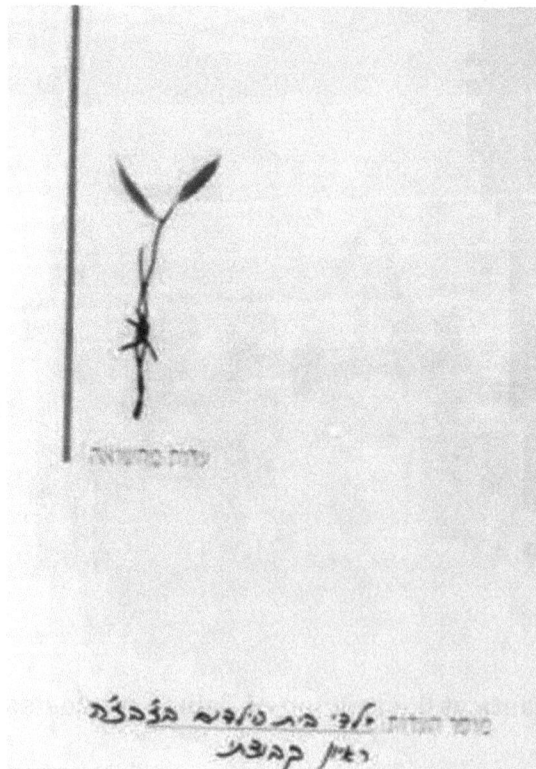

Yad Vashem video dedicated to the children of the Zabrze home and to the memory of Yeshayahu Drucker

Nechema Geller must be remembered as the head Mistress of the Zabrze Home, she devoted herself to the children and gave them the necessary forces to continue life. She was an educated woman that that survived the Shoa and devoted herself to the Jewish children. She remained with the institution until it was closed.

David Hubel, master teacher at Zabrze set the tone of the school. An old Zionist, he implanted the ideas of Zionism amongst the youngsters and gave them courage to face the uncertain future. He left Poland with a transport of children to France where he married. He reached Israel and became a teacher.

[Page 237]

Chapter XII

Pictorial Chapter of Zabrze

Survivors of the Zabrze children's home in at Yad Vashem in Jerusalem

The Jewish compound in Zabrze survived the war relatively intact. The compound consisted of an old age home, school house and offices.

The old age home in Zabrze

The Polish Jewish Association of religious communities headed by Rabbi Kahane received the building that was converted to an orphanage. The upper floor became the old age home.

Children and staff at the entrance of the Zabrze orphanage

Zabrze home for the kibbutzim that remained for short periods of time and then left Poland for Palestine. The building also had a synagogue for the Jews of Zabrze

Zabrze elementary Polish school that older children from the home had to attend in accordance with the Polish educational laws. The Zabrze home accepted Jewish toddlers as well as adolescent youngsters.

Zabrze children visiting the city with their teacher

Dr. Nechema Geller, head mistress of the Zabrze orphanage seated with small children at the Zabrze home

From left to right: **Michal Heffer, formerly Hinda Zorkowska; Nina and Tziporah – former residents at Zabrze.**

Yeshayahu Drucker spent a great deal of time in Zabrze and took many pictures of the children and the home. He assembled them into an album when he came to Israel. The album of pictures was donated to the Museum of the Lochamei Hagataot.

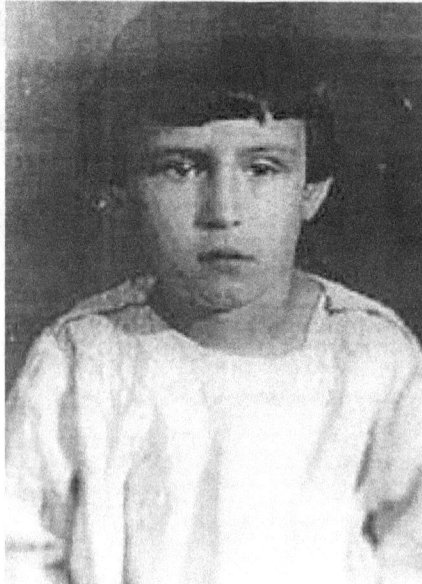

Klara Frauenglass at Zabrze

Page from the Drucker album at Zabrze

A page of Drucker's album showing children and their activities

Celebrations of Jewish holidays and festivals at Zabrze

Students and staff attend celebration of Hertzl Day at Zabzre

Zabrze staff

Zabrze home receives special honors from the Polish government. The home was invited to send a delegation to the memorial parade of the Jewish revolt in the ghetto of Warsaw in 1943.

The Zabrze contingent ready to enter the memorial procession in Warsaw

Zabrze delegation reviews the procession of the children

Zabrze children leaving Poland for France

Swimming instruction at Zabrze

Exercises at Zabrze

Hiking at the Zabrze home

Zabrze children memorialize the Warsaw Ghetto revolt

Gymnastic activities at Zabrze

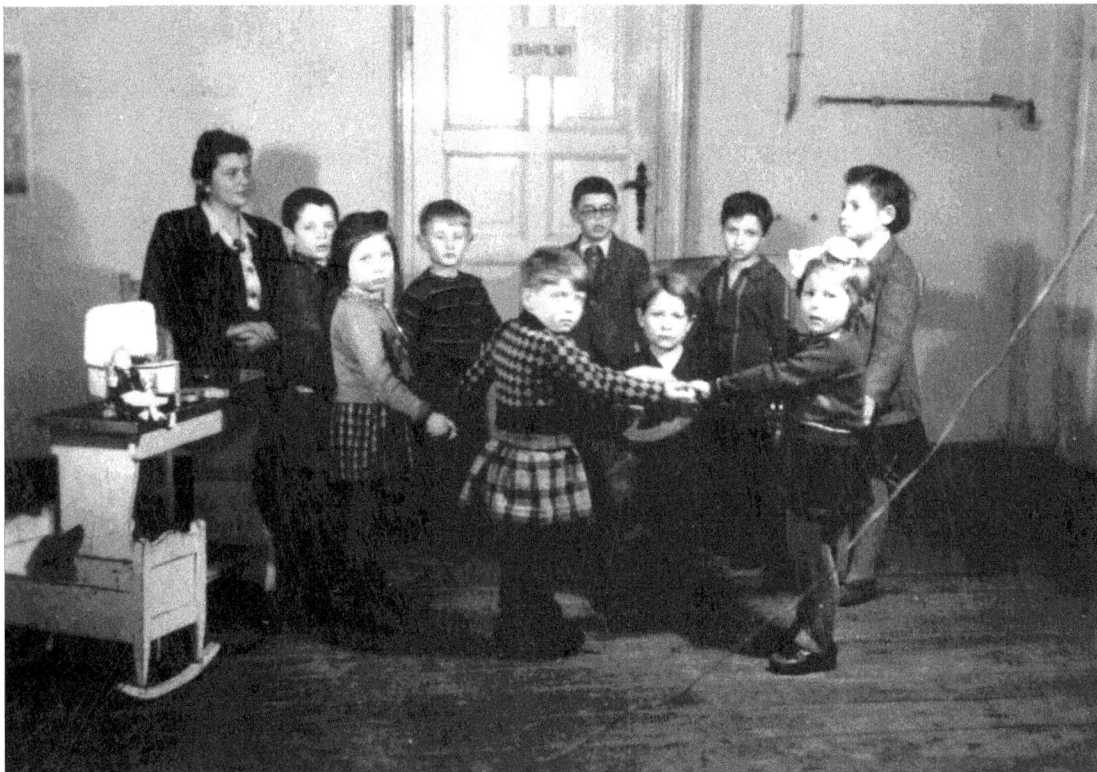

Young Children at Zabrze learn to dance

Friday evening meal by the Shabbath candle lights

[Page 257]

Chapter XIII

Bibliography

XIV   Pamphlet published by the Zabrze museum in Polish. The material was assembled by the museum staff and published in 1990 in Zabrze, Poland

XV   Schroder, Hermann Von, Dr., Hindenburg, Essen, Stadtischer Archvdirector , 1985

XVI   Dobroszycki, Lucjan, "Survival of the Holocaust in Poland– A Portrait based on Jewish Committee Records 1944–1947", Armonk, New York, M.E. Sharpe, , p.10

XVII   Szulc, Tad, The Secret Alliance, New York, Farrar, Straus and Gitroux, 1991, p.129

XVIII   Polish JDC documents pertaining to Zabrze recently released.

XIX   Interviews with David Danieli, Batia Eisenstein, Shlomo Korn, Michal Hefer, Orna Keret, Edzio Rosenblat, Esther Kastenbaum.

XX   The New York Yiddish daily newspaper "Der Tog."

XXI   Introduction to the inventory of the archives of the American Joint Distribution Committee in Poland, 1945–1948.

XXII   New York Times, February 14, 1946.

XXIII   Bauer, Yehuda, Bricha, New York, Random House, 1970, p.204

XXIV   Yad Vashem video recording of the reunion of former Zabrze residents

XXV   Yeshayahu Drucker's Testimony at Yad Vashem

XXVI   Yeshayahu Drucker's Album of pictures at Kibbutz Lochamei, Hagetaot Museum

[Page 259]

Chapter XIV
Partial list of the Jews of Zabrze
Names collected by William Leibner

Legend

SH	Shoah
KILL	Killed in World War I
YV	Yad Vashem
P	Private research
ZB	Book on Zabrze

Surname	First name(s)	Gender	Remarks
ABRAHAM	Alfred	M	YV, SH
ABRAHAM	Hans	M	YV, SH
ABRAMSOHN	Annmarie	F	YV, SH
ARONSOHN	Margret E	F	YV, SH
AUFRECHT	Otto	M	YV, SH
AUFRECHT	Nathan	M	YV, SH
AUFRECHT	Ema	F	YV, SH
BADER	Berish	M	YV, SH
BADRIAN	Ilse	F	YV, SH
BANDMAN	Rosa	F	YV, SH
BANDMAN	Salo	M	YV, SH
BAUMGART	Ernest H	M	YV, SH
BAUMGART	Margot	F	YV, SH
BAUMGART	Grete	F	YV, SH
BAUMGART	Fritz	M	YV, SH
BENGER	Erich	M	ZB, KIL
BENGER	Martin	M	ZB, KIL
BERG	Arnold	M	YV, SH
BERGER	Irma	F	YV, SH
BLANDOWSKI	Max	M	ZB, KIL
BLANDOWSKI	Moritz	M	ZB, KIL
BOEHM	Ilse	F	YV, SH
BOEHM	Charlotta	F	YV, SH
BOEHM	Simon	M	YV, SH
BOHM	Max	M	ZB, KIL
BORINNSKIS		M	ZB
BORINSKI	Mariana	F	YV, SH
BRAUER	Berta	F	YV, SH
BRAUER	Alfred	M	ZB, KIL
BRAUER	Max	M	ZB, KIL
BRAUER	Artur	M	ZB, KIL

BRAUER	Salo	M	ZB, KIL
BRAUN	Lydia	F	YV, SH
BRAUN	Betty	F	YV, SH
BRAUN	Fela	F	YV, SH
CHOJENSK	Genia	F	YV, SH
CHOJENSK	Miriam	F	YV, SH
CHOJENSK	Max	M	YV, SH
COHEN	Ruth	F	YV, SH
COHEN	Louis	F	YV, SH
COHEN	Werner	M	YV, SH
COHEN	Siegbert	M	YV, SH
COHEN	Heinz	M	YV, SH
COHN	Robert	M	YV, SH
COHN	Kurt	M	YV, SH
COHN	Ernestine	F	YV, SH
COHN	Karl	M	ZB, KIL
COHN	Herbert	M	ZB, KIL
COHN	Siegfried	M	ZB, KIL
CULMAN	Gertrude	F	YV, SH
CULMAN	Hilda	F	YV, SH
DANIEL	Max	M	ZB, KIL
DANTZIGER		M	ZB, Community officer
DLAZER	Friweda	F	YV, SH
DOCKOS		M	ZB
EHRLICH	Sara	F	YV, SH
EHRLICH	Metha	F	YV, SH
EHRLICH	Feodor	M	YV, SH
EHRLICH	Michal	M	YV, SH
EHRLICH	Feodor	M	YV, SH
EHRLICH	Mata	F	YV, SH
EHRMANN	Else	F	YV, SH
EISNER	Kaethe	F	YV, SH
EISNER	Luis	M	YV, SH
EISNER	Wilhelm	M	ZB
EUGEN		M	ZB
FABISCH	Henrich	M	ZB, KIL
FABISCH	Max	M	ZB, KIL
FARTIG	Tia	F	YV, SH
FARTIG	Awraham	M	YV, SH
FARTIG	Chana	F	YV, SH
FARTIG	Israele	F	YV, SH
FINKELSTEIN	Flora	F	YV, SH
FINKELSTEIN	Rosa	F	YV, SH
FINKELSTEIN	Gunter	M	YV, SH
FRANKEL		M	YV, SH
FRANKEL	Erwin	M	YV, SH

FREI	Franz	M	YV, SH
FREI	Orzola	F	YV, SH
FREI	Roza	F	YV, SH
FREI	Irema	F	YV, SH
FRIEDLANDER	Hugo	M	ZB, KIL
FROEHLICH	Kurt	M	YV, SH
FROEHLICH	Berta	F	YV, SH
FROEHLICH	Max	M	YV, SH
FROELICH	Dora	F	YV, SH
FROHLICH	Max	M	YV, SH
GERSTEL	Eva	F	YV, SH
GERSTEL	Alfred	M	ZB, KIL
GERSTEL	Leo	M	ZB, KIL
GERSTEL	Wilhelm	M	ZB, KIL
GLASER	Ewald	M	ŻB, KIL
GLASER	Leopold	M	ZB, KIL
GLASER	Max	M	ZB, KIL
GLASER	Rheinhold	M	ZB, KIL
GLASER	Noa	M	ZB
GLAZER	Frieda	F	YV, SH
GLICKSTEIN	Esther	F	YV, SH
GOLDMAN	Ernest	M	YV, SH
GOLDMAN	Arthur	M	YV, SH
GOLDMAN	Tina	F	YV, SH
GOLDMAN	Eugenia	F	YV, SH
GOLDMAN	Arthur	M	YV, SH
GOLDMAN	Jeanny	F	YV, SH
GOLDMAN		M	ZB
GOLDMAN	Channan	M	YV, SH
GOLDMANN	Elma	F	YV, SH
GRUNBERG	Salo	M	ZB, KIL
GRUNBERG	Siegfried	M	ZB, KIL
GRUNBERGER	Kurt	M	YV, SH
GRUNWALD		M	ZB
GUNTHER		M	ZB, Dr.
GUTHAMER		M	ZB, Lawyer
GUTMAN	Friedenke	F	YV, SH
GUTTENHEIMER	Ernest	M	YV, SH
HAMBURGER	Simon	M	ZB
HANDLER		M	ZB
HANDLER	Heinrich	M	ZB
HANDLER	Lobel	M	ZB
HANDMAN	Salomon	M	YV, SH
HANSDORFF	Walter	M	ZB, KIL
HERTZBERG		M	ZB
HERZBERG	Frank	M	YV, SH
HERZBERG	Oskar	M	YV, SH

HERZBERGER	Margarete	F		YV, SH
HERZKO	Max	M		ZB, KIL
HIRSCH	Else	F		YV, SH
HOFFMAN	Samuela	F		ZB
HOLTZMAN	Pinhas	M		YV, SH
HUJANSKI	chaja	F		YV, SH
HYMAN	Hilde	F		YV, SH
JACOBI	Berthold	M		ZB, KIL
JOTKOWITZ	Leopold	M		YV, SH
KAATZ	Else	F		ZB, social worker
KAATZ	Saul	M		ZB, SH, Rabbi
KAISER		M		ZB
KALLMAN	Alphonse	M		YV, SH
KALLMAN	Lotte	F		YV, SH
KALLMAN	Charlotta	F		YV, SH
KAMM	Harry	M		YV, SH
KANZIERS	Paula	F		YV, SH
KATZ	Paula	F		YV, SH
KATZ	Shaul	M		YV, SH
KILSTEIN	Fridel	F		YV, SH
KILSTEIN	Tziporah	F		YV, SH
KILSTEIN	Jakow	M		YV, SH
KILSTEIN	Osna	F		YV, SH
KIWI	Arena	F		YV, SH
KLAPHOLTZ	Awraham	M		YV, SH
KLUGER	Franziska	F		YV, SH
KLUGER	Fanny	F		YV, SH
KOCHMAN	FrEidrich	M		YV, SH
KOCHMAN	Erich	M		YV, SH
KOCHMAN	Julius	M		YV, SH
KOCHMAN	Friedrich	M		YV, SH
KOCHMAN	Julius	M		YV, SH
KOCHMAN		M		ZB
KOHN	Yehuda	M		YV, SH
KOHN	Dora	F		ZB, teacher
KOLTON	Max	M		YV, SH
KOPLPWITZ	Minna	F		YV, SH
KOSCHITSK	Miriam	F		YV, SH
KOSCHITZKY	Shlomo	M		YV, SH
KOSCHITZKY	Kalman	M		YV, SH
KOSCHITZKY	Mania	F		YV, SH
KOSCHITZKY	Yechezkel	M		YV, SH
KOSCHITZKY	Awraham	M		YV, SH
KOSCHITZKY	Chaim Y	M		YV, SH
KOSCHITZKY	Kalman	M		YV, SH
KUTTNER	Alfred	M		YV, SH
LABAND	Manfred	M		ZB, KIL

LAMM	Kurt	M	ZB, social worker
LANG		M	ZB
LESCHNITZER		M	ZB
LIEBERMANN	Ernestina	F	YV, SH
LANDESAR	A	M	ZB
LECHCZINER	Ferdinand	M	ZB, KIL
LOBINGER	Hartwig	M	ZB, KIL
LOBMAN	Max	M	ZB, KIL
LUNDGARD	Martha	F	YV, SH
MACHOWSKi	Alfred	M	ZB, KIL
MANDOWSKI	Kurt	M	YV, SH
MANDOWSKI	lLina	F	YV, SH
MANDOWSKI	Helga	F	YV, SH
MANDOWSKY		M	ZB, community head
MARKUS		M	ZB
MARKUS	Raphael	M	ZB, head of the social services
MAY	Alwine	M	YV, SH
MAY	Leopold	M	YV, SH
MAY	Georg	M	YV, SH
MICHAELIS	Juliusz	M	YV, SH
MICHAELIS	Margareta	F	YV, SH
MICHAELIS		M	ZB, treasurer
MICHAELIS	J.	M	ZB, teacher
MORGEBNSTERN	Emanuel	M	YV, SH
MORGEBNSTERN	Ernest	M	YV, SH
MORGEBNSTERN	Holda	M	YV, SH
MUENZER	Else	F	YV, SH
MUSMAN	Herta	F	YV, SH
NATHANSOHN	Paula	F	YV, SH
NEBEL	Louiza	F	YV, SH
NEBEL	David	M	YV, SH
NEBEL	Rosa	F	YV, SH
NEBEL	Else	F	YV, SH
NEBEL	Simon	M	YV, SH
NOTLAMANN	A	M	ZB, KIL
PERL	Alfred	M	ZB, KIL
PINKUS	Salma	F	YV, SH
PINKUS	Alfred	M	YV, SH
POLLACK	Polly	F	YV, SH
POLLACK	Huda	F	YV, SH
POLLACK	Eugen	M	ZB, KIL
POLLACK	Ludwig	M	ZB, KIL
POLLACK	Samuel	M	ZB, KIL
POLLACK		M	ZB
PRAGUER	Ruth	F	YV, SH

PRAGUER	Rudi	M	YV, SH
PRAGUER	Ernest	M	YV, SH
PRAGUER	Julie	F	YV, SH
PRAGUER	Oskar	M	YV, SH
PRAGUER	Ernest	M	YV, SH
PREISS	Werner	M	YV, SH
PREUSS	Frieda	F	YV, SH
PREUSS	Oskar	M	YV, SH
PROSKRO	Daniel	M	YV, SH
PROSKRO	Joana	F	YV, SH
RASMUSSEN	Else	F	YV, SH
RINKEL	Alfred	M	ZB, KIL
SACHS	Julius	M	ZB, KIL
SACHS		M	ZB
SAMTER	Eliasz	M	YV, SH
SANDBERG	Josef	M	YV, SH
SANDBERG	Lina	F	YV, SH
SCHALLANACH		M	ZB
SCHIFTAN	Herman	M	YV, SH
SCHIFTAN	Hnnah	F	YV, SH
SCHIFTAN	Nathan	M	YV, SH
SCHIFTAN	Rachel	F	YV, SH
SCHIFTAN	Berta	F	YV, SH
SCHINDLER		M	ZB, Lawyer
SCHIROKAUER	Rosa	F	YV, SH
SCHIROKAUER	Siegfrid	M	YV, SH
SCHNEEMAN	Hulda	F	YV, SH
SCHNEJMAN	Friedrich	M	YV, SH
SCHRIKAUER	Rosa	F	YV, SH
SCHULER	Salomon	M	ZB
SCHUTZ	Heinrich	M	ZB, KIL
SCHUTZ	Wilhelm	M	ZB, KIL
SCHWEITZER	Victor	M	YV, SH
SCHWEITZER	Johanna	F	YV, SH
SCHWEITZER	Willy	M	YV, SH
SEIDLER	Felix	M	ZB, KIL
SHIFTAN	Rachel	F	YV, SH
SHIFTAN	Ruth	F	YV, SH
SHIFTAN	Hanah	F	YV, SH
SIEGRIST	Alice	F	YV, SH
SILBERMANN	Arnold	M	ZB, KIL
SILBERSTEIN	Max	M	YV, SH
SILBERSTEIN	Ruhama	F	YV, SH
SILBERSTEIN	Sarah	F	YV, SH
SILBERSTEIN	Moshe	M	YV, SH
SIMON	Herman	M	YV, SH
SINGERMANN	H		

STEINITZ	Fritz	M	ZB, KIL
STEINITZ	Ernest	M	ZB, KIL
STIEBEL	Erich	M	ZB, KIL
STRAUSS	Marie	F	YV, SH
STRAUSS	Meier	M	YV, SH
SUESMAN	Paula	F	YV, SH
SXHLESINGER	Fritz	M	ZB, KIL
SXHLESINGER	Ludwig	M	ZB, KIL
TANDESAR	Max	M	ZB, KIL
TICHAUER	Ella	F	YV, SH
TICHAUER	Salo	M	ZB, KIL
TICHAUER	Fritz	M	ZB, KIL
TOTSCHEK	Heinrich	M	ZB, KIL
TROUGOTT			YV, SH
UCKO	Gertrude	F	YV, SH
UCKO	Lotte	F	YV, SH
UCKO	Sally	F	YV, SH
UCKO	Gertrude	F	YV, SH
VICTOR	Artur	M	ZB, rabbi, died
WACHSMAN	Ella	F	YV, SH
WACHSMAN	Edgar	M	YV, SH
WACHSMAN	Eliyahahu	M	YV, SH
WACHSMANN	Ella	F	YV, SH
WARTENBURG	Hans	M	YV, SH
WASSERTEIL	Marcus	M	YV, SH
WASSERTEIL	Marta	F	YV, SH
WASSERTEIL	Esther	F	YV, SH
WEICHMANN	Max	M	YV, SH
WEICHMANN	Johanna	F	YV, SH
WEICHMANN	Hans	M	YV, SH
WEICHMANN	Victor	M	YV, SH
WEINSTEIN	Frieda	F	YV, SH
WEISS	Daniel	M	YV, SH
WEISSBERGER	Ilona	F	YV, SH
WEISSBERGER	Ernest	M	YV, SH
WEISSBERGER	Eva	F	YV, SH
WEISSENBERG	Hulda	F	YV, SH
WEISSLER	Kurt	M	YV, SH
WEISSLER	Kurt	M	YV, SH
WIELAND	Mathilde	F	YV, SH
WIESENKOWIZ		M	ZB
WOLFF	Roseman	F	YV, SH
WOLFF	Lucie	F	YV, SH
WOLFF	Gerhardt	M	YV, SH
WYGAS	Edith	F	YV, SH
YASCHIKOWITZ	Fridl	F	YV, SH
YASCHIKOWITZ	Josef	M	YV, SH

YASCHIKOWITZ	Heintz	M		YV, SH
YASCHIKOWITZ	Walter	M		YV, SH
ZALMANOWITZ	Yeshayahu	M		YV, SH
ZILBERSTEIN	Leibisch	M		YV, SH
ZILBERSTEIN	Dawid	M		YV, SH
ZVIKLITZER	Anita	F		YV, SH
ZWEIG	Helga	M		YV, SH
ZWEIG	Margarethe	F		YV, SH

[Page 267]

Chapter XV
Census of Jews in Zabrze Following World War II

The census below was conducted at the request of the Central Committee of Polish Jews in liberated Poland, headquartered in Warsaw. The Central Committee received funds from the Polish government to distribute to the localities. The organization frequently requested information from the branch offices such as the number of Jewish residents, orphanages, children etc. to aid in distributing the funds. In March of 1946, the Zabrze Jewish committe received a request to list the Jewish population as well as the various Jewish institutions in the city. The information was also given to the Polish Joint Distribution Committee who provided assistance based on a per capita basis. The reply sheets also made the Central Committee aware of special local needs or problems.

A copy of the Zabrze Jewish Committee reply appears earlier in the book. The reply also contained a list of all Jewish residents in Zabrze in March 1946. A copy of this list managed to reach the United States Holocaust Memorial Museum in Washington D.C. Michlean Lowy Amir graciously sent us a copy of the document.

Below is the list of Jewish residents of Zabrze in 1946.

Surname	First name	Year of birth	Place of birth	Trade	Parents
ACHT	Anna	1914	Zbaraz		
ACHT	Maria	1922			
ARATEN	Markus	1903	Sandomierz		
ASZKENAZI	Nusen	1922			
AZEIF	Ester	1921	Kovno		Marfel & Chaja
AUERBUCH	Rubin	1869	Skalat	agent	Markus & Ruchla
AUERBUCH	Fryderyka	1873			Leib & Jenta
AFTERGUT	Pepi	1926			Gustav & Roza
ASZKENAZE	Nunia	1922	Budzianow	tailor	
BAJUK	Zelig	1917	Dzialdowo		Markus & Celina
BARANOWICZ	Lea	1921	Lomza	seamstress	Iser & Szajna
BARANSKA	Maria	1915	Warsaw	clerk	
BARDYGA	Wolf	1902	Rowna	merchant	Jakub & Rywka
BARDYGA	Zisla	1915	Rowna		Chaim & Lea
BATALION	Adolf	1901	Stryj		Lake & Regina
BATALION	Bronislawa	1914	Stryj		Eliasz & Helena
BAUM	Fela	1916	Czernowce		Boruch & Anna
BAUM	Sala	1929			
BAUM	Selman	1924	Skalat	barber	

BAUMGOLD	Chaim	1916	Warsaw		Szmul & Sala
BELICKI	Chaim	1884	Rowno	merchant	Iiasz & Ida
BERLINSKI	Aba	1912	Jastzubie		Izrael & Rajzlo
BIBRING	Abram	1900	Stanilawow	baker	Mojsz & Chana
BIREN	Berek	1920	Bedzin	electrician	
BIRENBAUM	Ignac	1912	Radom	driver	Abraham & Jeti
BIRENBAUM	Jeremiasz	1906	Baden		Abraham & Etta
BLINDER	Pesia	1935	Sokoliki		
BODNER	Ichak	1920	Piotrkow		Pinkas & Brandla
BORTEN	Ajzik	1905	Kolomjja	druggist	
BORTEN	Roza	1912	Rowno		
BORTEN	Salomon	1936			Ajzik & Roza
BORTEN	Mozes	1845			Ajzik & Roza
BRAJTBERG	Chaskel	1817		butcher	Icek & Sala
BRAKSMAJER	Leon	1910	Czrtkow	clerk	Chaim & Helena
BREUER	Pepe	1930	Mikulice		Hersz & Roza
BRODER	Jozef	1930	Czerniowce		Adolf & Berta
BRODER	Izak	1920	Czeniowce		Adolf & Berta
BROMBERGER	Hanna	1922	Chrzanow		
BURSZTYN	Jozef	1920	Stanilawow	mechanic	Shaja & Lea
CORNFORF	Szmul	1912	Molo		Chaim & Chaja
CORNFORF	Genie	1906	Molo		Shlome & Cipe
CORNFORF	Chaim	1936	Molo		Szmul & Genia
CUKIER	Jechiel	1905	Warszawa		Mojacz & Lucila
CUKIRMAN	Henryk	1927	Bedzin	locksmith	Mozes & Fela
DIAMANT	Wolf	1907	Krosnobrod		Benjamin & Bronia
DIAMANT	Regina	1906	Krosnobrod		Luzer & Henia
DIAMANT	Benjamin	1932	Krosnobrod		Wolf & Regina
DIAMANT	Icek	1935	Krosnobrod		Wolf & Regina
DYTMAN	Bela	1922	Warszawa	legal clerk	Henryk & Gustawa
EPPEL	Benjamin	1916		farmer	Jankel
EBERT	Adolf	1893	Bursztyn	merchant	Litman & Sala
FEIGENBAUM	Sara	1919	Tranystow		Feivel & Dwoira
FEILER	Jacheta	1924	Chorzow		Dawid & Mindla
FEILER	Rachela	1925	Chorzow		Dawid & Mindla
FEILER	Leopold	1912	Chrzanow	merchant	Mozes & Rachela
FELDMAN	Jalina	1927	Krakow		Herszel & Jadwiga
FELSENHARD	Ludwika	1913	Warszawa		
FELSENHARD	Krystina	1943	Warszawa		
FENINGER	Maks	1905	Jaworow	locksmith	Izak & Adela
FESTING	Otto	1902	Krakow	druggist	Salomon & Fanny
FESTING	Bela	1913	Krakow	doctor	Leib & Elzabieta
FESTING	Ina	1940	Krakow		Otto & Bela
FINDER	Rudolf	1915	Czortkow		Salomon & Fanny
FINDER	Malwina	1887	Libuszyn		August & Anna
FINKELSZTEIN	Szaja	1922	Rowno		Naftali & Jenta
FLASZNER	Abraham	1925	Trembowla	electrician	Chaskel & Tauba

FRANKEL	Juda	1919	Glabina	locksmith	Froim & Maria
FRANKEL	Tena	1922	Krosnobrod		Markus & Jenta
FRANKEL	Feiga	1944	Dzambul		Juda & Tena
FRECHTMAN	NTON	1930	Brody	shoemaker	Aleko & Klara
FRIEDLANDER	Markus	1909	Stryj		Jakub & Regina
FRIEDLANDER	Sabina	1915	Stryj		Mendel & Chana
FRIEDLANDER	Regina	1887	Stryj		Wolf & Chana
FRYDMAN	Bela	1913	Krakow		Szmul & Gitla
FRYDLER	Janusz	1899	Stryj	miller	Samuel & Gitla
FRYDLER	Sara	1912	Stryj		
FRYDLER	Genia	1941	Stryj		
FRYDLER	Gitla	1887	Stryj		
FISHLER	Jenny	1924	Chemnitz		Lezer & Wizzi
FISHLER	Abram	1898		clerk	Chaim
FUNKEL	Samuel	1887	Klewon		Jakub & Cipa
FUNKEL	Zelig	1887	Bekawicka		Gershon & Chana
FUNKEL	Pavel	1922	Lwow		Rubin & Amalia
FUNKEL	Mieczyslaw	1931	Golub		Aleksander & Roza
FUSSMAN					
GARFUNKEL	Mieczyslaw	1915	Warszawa		Leon & Dwora
GELINA	Zofia	1912	Bialoczerkew		Shulim & Jenta
GELINA	Bronislawa	1936	Bialoczerkew		Auros & Oile
GELINA	Mojsze	1907			
GELLER	Maksimiljan	1901	Horodenka	lawyer	Jozef & Miriam
GELLER	Necha	1899	Horodenka		Victor & Zanna
GELLER	Abram	1901	Makowze	shoemaker	Shulim & Jenta
GERSTEL	Julian	1885	Zniatyn	hairdresser	
GERSTEL	Klara	1909	Zniatyn		Jakub & Gusta
GERSTEL	Szaja	1899	Budzanow	shoemaker	
GERTLER	Mojsze	1885	Krosnobrod	slaughterer	Hersz & Malka
GERTLER	Jenta	1888	Krosnobrod		Cedalia & Tema
GERTLER	Abraham	1928	Krosnobrod		Mojsze & Jenta
GERTLER	Josef	1934	Krosnobrod		Mojsze & Jenta
GERTLER					
GLASER	Jetti	1896	Budzanow	seamstress	
GLASER	Szaja	1930	Briansk		Szmul & Szprynca
GLASER	Jette	1899	Budzanow		
GLASER	Natan	1921	Rowno		Netel & Rozia
GLATTSTEIN	Itzhak	1915	Warszawa		Leon & Dwoira
GLEICH	Itzhak	1913	Pytaica		Mozes & Gitla
GOLDBERG	Paula	1908			Mordechai & Estera
GOLDFUSS	Natan	1908	Tarnopol	merchant	
GOLDMAN	Mojsze	1907			
GOLDSTEIN	Nina	1903	Tarnowiec		Dawid & Johanna
GOLDSTEIN	Leon	1910	Turka	merchant	
GOLDREICH	Rubin	1895	Turka	merchant	Feivwel & Zofia
GOLDREICH	Szeindel	1912	Sokoliki		Basia

GOLDREICH	Zofia	1937	Sokoliki		Rubin & Szeindel
GOLDREICH	Pesia	1944	Sokoliki		ubin & Szeindel
GOLDREICH	Samson	1911	Zysaczow	lawyer	Gershon & Lea
GOTTLIEB	Gizela	1912	Zysaczow		Markus & Amalia
GOTTLIEB	Cipa	1902	Jezierzany		Lipe & Frymeta
GRABER	Frania	1916			
GRABER	Alexander	1916		farmer	Wolf & Ida
GRIEGER	Klara	1914			
GRIEGER	Mojzes	1896	Lwow	merchant	Hersz & Hindla
GROSSMAN	Lea	1905	Lwow		Chaim & Malka
GROSSMAN	Carol	1921	Lwow		Mojzes & Lea
GROSSMAN	Lea	1920			Kalman & Hendel
GRUNZELLER	Berek	1930	Piotkow		
GRYNBAUM	Mojsze	1885	Krosnobrod	clerk	Hersz & Malka
HEBERBERG	Ruchle	1926		seamstress	Shalom & Mitia
HEFLER		1915	Zojnilow		Pridel & Ida
HEIMAN	Willi	1906	Zabrze	merchant	Siegfried & Zilli
HELMAN	Arthur	1887	Zabrze	clerk	Wilhelm & Emma
HIMMELFARB	Fela	1926	Sosnowiec		Itzhak & Sara
HIRSCH	Mozes	1904	Sandomierz		
HIRSHBERG	Joachim	1893	Tarnopol	druggist	Dawid & Fryderika
HIRSHBERG	Rergina	1898	Zloczow		Juda & Henia
HIRSHBERG	Julian	1830	Tarnopol		Joachim & Regina
HOCHENBERG	Rachela	1920	Radom		Pinkas & Chaja
HOLLANDER	Rachela	1919	Krakow	embroider	Abraham & Deborah
HOROWITZ	Marek	1908		accountant	Abe & Regina
HOROWITZ	Zofia	1913			Mozes & Frida
HOROWITZ	Zachariasz	1936			Zofia
HUBEL	Leon	1905	Stryj	druggist	Eisig & Mytia
HUBEL	Dawid	1910	Stryj		Eisig & Etia
HUTTEL	Rosalia	1907	Stanislawow		Henryk & Pepa
HUTTEL	Halin	1932	Stanislawow		Jakub & Rozalia
HUTTEL	Szymon	1902	Lwow		Samuel & Remila
IMMERGLUCK	Frymeta	1925	Chrzanow		Izrael & Regina
JABLONKA	Pelike	1910	Warszawa	clerk	Abram & Szeindla
JAJES	Szymon	1919	Wilno		Jozef & Feja
KAC	Chaja	1911	Bialocrkiew		
KAC	Josef	1913	Katylekia		Aron & Sara
KAGAN	Kalman	1900	Rimpeling	druggist	Leon & Paulina
KAGAN	Janina	1911	Czerniowce	druggist	Nemzion & Augusta
KESTNER	Eliza	1908	Kopczyca		Dawid & Leonora
KESTNER	Daniel	1948			Jakub & Eliza
KIRSZENBERG	Icek	1898	Warszawa		Lemel & Perla
KIRSZENBERG	Gelina	1904	Warszawa		Josel & Roza
KLAR	Aron	1918	Mosciska		Jakub & Roza
KLER	Janka	1922			Jecjiel & Rozalia

KOBREC	Ruchel	1910	Skalat	merchant	Bernard & Rosalia
KOBREC	Majer	1919	Rowno	carpenter	Mozes & Lea
KRAFT	Regina	1922	Lodz		Majer & Chana
KRAMER	Juda	1886	Polonia		Mozes & Ruchla
KRAUTHAMER	Leon	1910	Zutowno		Josef & Anna
KUBILENSKI	Boruch	1930	Kulesze		Icek & Erena
KUNICH	Leon	1926	Rowne		Marek & Tywka
KACOWA	Zofia	1905	Rohat	druggist	
KACOWA	Zilla	1925	Tarnopol		
KACOWA	Roza	1921	Tarnopol	accountant	
KAGAN	Ciwia	1912			Jankel & Maria
KARAFIN	Lea	1892	Dubno		Abraham & Sonia
KARAFIN	Bime	1932			Lea
KAUFER	Hirsz	1913	Sochnia	merchant	
KAUFMAN	Liza	1922	Plauen		
KCZENOWSKI	Leon	1916			Jakub & Manina
KELLER	Eliasz	1899	Zurowno		Mendel & Bela
KENIUK	Czeslaw	1905			Czeslaw & Zofia
KLEMPNER	Ichhak	1927	Dubno		Abraham & Sara
KLINGER	Jerzy	1918	Przemysl	dentist	Itzhak & Klara
KRIEGG	Szmul	1897	Tarkowice		Lea
KLEJTNER	Michal	1929	Dubno		
KOCZY	Hilda	1888	Zabrze		Julian & Charlotta
KOPEC	Michal	1917	Laszow		
KOPEC	Jan	1925			
KORCH	Hirsz	1909	Rowno		Luzer & Chana
KORCH	Ruchla	1909	Rowno		Luzer & Mariam
KOSSOWER	Jozef	1915	Tarnopol	druggist	
KOSSOWER	Taube	1919	Tarnopol		
KOSSOWER	Michal	1942	Tarnopol		
KASZMAN	Mendel	1896			Dawid & Berta
KASZMAN	Regina	1896			Jakub & Berta
KRYMER	Szulim	1908			
KUDZINSKI	Leon	1915	Radom	tailor	Hersz & Mala
KUFHER	Lyda	1908	Turka		Szymon & Paula
LAMMEL	Lola	1923	Sosnowiec		Salomon & Perla
LANGENBERG	Hersz	1935	Skalat		Ruchel
LANGENBERG	Blanka	1936	Skalat		Ruchel
LANGENBERG	Estera	1925	Zawierce		Chaim & Chana
LASSAK		1902	Szczyno	clerk	Salo & Augusta
LASTER	Dawid	1919	Weodenka		Jakub & Berta
LEIMANN	Aron	1876	Zytolerz		Marek & Ita
LIBMAN	Juda	1928	Tiankowce		Izrael & Chana
LIEBLEIN	Carol	1918	Stanislawow		Henryk & Zina
LINEK	Helena	1916	Lodz		Izrael & Vera
LINHARD	Abraham	1899	Sambor	baker	Salomon & Chawa
LINTOWSKA	Clau	1825	Chozow		Mozes & Hedwiga

LIPSZYC	Tonia	1919		seamstress	Moszek & Chaja
LONEK	Jozef	1916	Czenstochowa	clerk	Salomon & Clara
LOWENTAL	Marcel	1919	Przytik	accountant	Jozef & Chaja
LOWENTAL	Paula	1989	Radom		
LOWENTAL	Majer	1912	Przytik		Itzhak & Sara
LUFT	Izak	1911	Lwow	musician	Jakub & Ruchla
MAJEROWITZ	Krystina	1941			Adolf & Ruchla
MANDELBAUMl	Aron	1916	Zamosc		Mordke & Mariam
MANDELBAUMl	Laja	1914	Zamosc		Mordke & Mariam
MANTEL	Zofia	1910	Zloczow		Adolf & Rachela
MARGULIES					Adolf & Amalia
MATZNER	Chaja	1930			Jakub & Chaja
MAUZENGISSER					
MAUZENGISSER	Barbara	1925	Ujhest		Leon & Anna
MEJACH	Laizer	1945	Dzambul		Aron & Leja
MEISNER	Etel	1909	Kolomaja		Jocel
MEISNER	Dawid	1941			
MEISNER	Jozef	1910	Sadowa	doctor	Joachim & Bela
MEISNER	Janina	1921	Lodz		Cafa
METZGER	Joel	1914	Osiecja		
METZGER	Dawid	1889	Rowno	doctor	Leib Hirsz
MICHTENBRUSER	Rywka	1943	Dzambul		Aron & Leja
MORGENSTERN	Roza	1916	Luxemburg		Mozes & Charlotta
MORGENSTERN	Chaja	1940			
MOTYL	Gatzip	1899			
NEBEL	Maxumilia	1899	Katowice		Jakub & Elizabeta
NELSEN	Bronia	1920	Warszawa		Motel & Rywka
NELSEN	Butera	1916	Dziedzice	nurse	Ignacy & Frymeta
NELSEN	Sara	1908	Tomaszow		
NELSEN	Bernard	1907	Sosnowiec	merchant	Chaim & Ruchla
NELSEN	Icek	1906	Warszawa	electrician	Leizer & Lea
NELSEN	Tauba	1907	Warszawa		Dawid & Malka
NELSEN	Nora	1933	Warszawa		Icek & Paula
NELSEN	Dawid	1944	Tashkent		
NEPERSZTEK	Leib	1915	Warszawa		Eisig & Sara
NESSELROTH	Adolf	1906	Sadowica		Salmon & Anna
NEZENKOWSKA	Mozes	1907			
NIZINSKA	Sarita	1925	Zabrze		Jakub & Anna
NUSSENBLAT	Herman	1920	Stanislawow		Majer & Eliza
NUSSMAN	Feivel	1915	Warszawa		Boruh & Cipe
OFNER	Willi	1906	Zabrze	merchant	Siegfried & Zilli
ORENSTEIN	Arthur	1887	Zabrze	clerk	Wilhelm & Emma
OFFENBERGER	Hilda	1888	Zabrze		Julian & Charlotta

PARDES	Sonia	1914	Lwow	office worker	Izrael & Emalia
PARDES	Izabela	1938	Lwow		Julian & Genia
PEARLMUTTER	Artur	1930	Skalat		Jakub
PEARLMUTTER	Jakub Szual	1903	Skalat	merchant	Markus & Pesla
PELUCH	Michal	1921	Polaskie		Mordke & Genia
PELUCH	Antonina	1927	Saratow		
PELUCH	Bela	1944	Saratow		
PERLMUTTER	Dawid	1915	Sosnowiec		Neuman & Lea
PESSLER	Adam	1904	Dubno		Herman & Sara
PESSLER	Wanda	1914	Dubno		Richar & Rebeca
PESSLER	Friedrich	1944	Dubno		Adam & Wanda
PINKOWSKI	Emil	1906		merchant	
POLISZCZUK	Abram	1930			Jakub & Elizabeta
POMANKIEWICZ	Julian	1910	Zoszow		
RASKIN	Icek	1909	Dortmund	barber	Izrael & Frida
RAZICKI	Jerzy	1920	Radom	merchant	Wolf & Teofila
RETTER	Leon	1922		student	Jakub & Miriam
RETTER	Jakub	1890		doctor	Natan & Sima
RETTER	Miriam	1889			Michal & Berta
ROSEN	Chaim	1910	Dubno	merchant	Jakub & Liza
ROSEN	Sara				
ROSEN	Szulim	1928	Matkowice		Mendel & Feige
ROSENBERG	Debora	1923	Warszawa		Itzik & Gitla
ROSENSTEIN	Chaim	1925	Piotrikow	locksmith	Pinkus & Shaidela
ROSENTZWEIG	Itcek	1907		merchant	Dawid & Lea
ROTH	Icek	1900	Krakow		
ROTSZYLD	Tuman	1888	Tczerniowce		Pinkus & Golda
ROTSZYLD	Icek-Jude	1909	Tczerniowce		Pinkus & Golda
ROTSZYLD	Malka	1916	Tczerniowce		Pinkus & Golda
ROTSZYLD	Rosen	1922	Tczerniowce		Pinkus & Golda
ROTSZYLD	Chana	1922	Tczerniowce		Pinkus & Golda
ROTTENBERG	Hirsz	1921	Dubno	merchant	Yechiel & Yetka
RABNER	Bune	1944	Kodlin		Hesziek & Nana
RABNER	Anna	1922	Rowno	nurse	Nahum & Meria
REDOK	Alexander	1899	Biaslystok	tailor	Chune & Sara
REGENBOGEN	Ezriel	1892	Sanok	painter	Lezer & Leonora
REGENBOGEN	Brajna	1897	Krakow		Ojszez & Roza
REGENBOGEN	Roza	123	Krakow		Ezriel & Brajne
REGENBOGEN	Sura	1928	Krakow		Ezriel & Brajne
REIHARZ	Natan	1904	Skolw	shemaker	Motel & Rachela
REITER	Leon	1898	Zurawna	merchant	Eisig & Etia
REITER	Rozalia	1899	Zurawna		Chaim & Lucua
REITER	Fryderik	1922	Zurawna		Leon & Rozalia
REITER	Edmund	1931	Zurawna		Leon & Rozalia
REITER	Markus	1903	Stanislawow		Majer & Blima
RIEGER	Mjzes	1912	Nowy Sacz	lawyer	Izrael & Sara

RIEGER	Rozalia	1914	Tarnow		Izrael & Sara
RIEGER	Anna	1941	Dzambul		Mojzes & Rozalia
ROLNICKI	Rachmil	1915	Warszawa	painter	Bernard & Rika
ROLNICKI	Genia		Warszawa	doctor	Nuchim & Rachela
ROLNICKI	Zofia	1944	Warszawa		Rachmil & Genia
ROSAENSTEIN	Abraham	1916	Zamosc		Mordke & Meriam
ROSENBLUM	Jakub	1907	Bedzin	clerk	Shimon & Jeannette
ROSENTAL	Philip	1928	Tluste		Mendel & Golda
ROZEN	Paulina	1914	Warszawa	seamstress	Michal & Sima
ROZENZWEIG	Menachem	1913	Zaklikow	student	Jakub & Chana
ROZENZWEIG	Rachela	1921	Sarny		Szmul & Malka
ROZWEN	Julian		Luck	engineer	Szulim & Pepi
ROZWEN	Charlotta	1917	Mosty		Meraz & Pepi
ROZWEN	Pepi	1945	Krakow		Julian & Charlotta
RUFF	Amalia	1890	Otynia		Adolf & Anna
RUFF	Gusta	1889			Zygmunt & Amalia
RUSINEK	Estera	1918	Pilica		Aba & Rywka
RUSSEK	Jakub	1897	Jeruszow		Natan & Stylia
RUSSEK	Regina	1901	Lututow		Wolf & Chana
RUSSEK	Malina	1925	Grabow		Jakub & Regina
RUSSEK	Nina	1932	Grabow		Jakub & Regina
REITER	Gusta	1903	Stanilawow		Izak & Rachla
REITER	Herman	1929	Stanilawow		Markus & Gusta
REITER	Mania	1932	Stanilawow		Markus & Gusta
REITER	Mira	1934	Stanilawow		Markus & Gusta
REITER	Izio	1941	Stanilawow		Markus & Gusta
SAFIERSTEIN	Berta	1920	Warszawa	office work	Aron & Jenta
SCHAPIRA	Aron	1906	Zuarz	electrician	
SCHLECHTER	Rubin	1921	Sosnowiec		Hirsz & Brana
SCHLOMOWICZ	Lemech	1928	Radom		Dzja & Dabina
SCHUMER	Adolf	1899	Rohatyn	lawyer	Bernard & Emalia
SCHUMER	Dorota	1903	Sanok		Leizer & Leonora
SCHUMER	Albert	1934	Sanok		Adolf & Dorota
SCHWARTZ	Berek	1917	Krasnik	shoemaker	
SCHWARTZ	Rfal	1897	Pubienko	shoemaker	Leibusz & Cila
SCHWARTZ	Chuan	1904	Fojowiec		Ber & Jeta
SCHWARTZ	Leib	1923	Chelm		Rafael & Cunan
SCHWARTZ	Borys	1930	Chelm		Rafael & Cunan
SCHWARTZ	Sonia	1933	Chelm		Rafael & Cunan
SCHWARTZ	Henryk	1901			Maximilian & Maris
SEWICKI	Alexander	1925	Amsterdam		Izak & Anna
SLORNA	Pola	1923	Bedzin	official	Chaim & Genale
SOBERMAN	Szymon	1909	Sandomierz	tailor	
STAL	Mordke	1919		footwear	Moszek & Estera
STANGER	Jakub	1920	Sandz		
STASSLER	Ruolf	1922	Pieden		Otto & Greta
STEINGOLTZ	Naftali	1893	Milusza	druggist	Feivel & Betty

STEINGOLTZ	Iwona	1905	Krakow		Franz & Flora
STERNSCHUSZ	Anna	1904	Zloczow		Franz & Tama
STERNSCHUSZ	Fryderik	1928			Adolf & Anna
STUB	Izak	1910	Kolbuszow	glass worker	Mozes & Rachela
SUSSMAN	Bela	1927	Sosnowiec	merchant	Srul & Estera
SZKILNIK	Mjer	1917	Dubno		Abram
SZORC	Sara	1897			
SZORC	Ita	1927	Kloden		
SZORC	Rozalia	1928	Kloden		
SZORC	Chaja	1934	Kloden		
SZYMANOWSKA	Zlata	1935	Skarzysta	seamstress	Leon & Razia
SCHIMMEL	Sabina	1925	Pistekowa		Mozes & Daria
SCHIMMEL	Tadeusz	1945	Sanok		
SCHNEUR	Benzion	1872	Przemysl	lawyer	Salomon & Chaja
SCHNEUR	Augusta	2895	Krakpw		Bernard & Emma
SCHNUR	Teodor	1926	Warszawa		Wolf & Ida
SCHOCHTER	Henryk	1921	Zurawno	student	Szymon & Pena
SEKINGER	Mieczyslaw	1927	Sosnowiec	electrician	Berek & Zofia
SIGAL	Sylvia	1914	Stanislawow		Froim & Izabela
SILBIGER	Helena	1916	Szieszanow	nurse	Chaim & Chana
SILBIGER	Rene	1911	Szieszanow		Chaim & Chana
SISAK	Jozef	1907	Turka	farmer	Chana
SISGAL	Berta	1906	Buczacz		Abraham & Roza
SKOLER	Aron	1893	Czortkow		Mojszez & Roza
SOLURF	Maria	1872	Rzeszow		Szymon & Pesla
STERNHAL	Daria	1904	Ottynce		Julius & Roza
SZONTAL		1888	Luck		Salmon & Chaja
TAUS	Ojszas	1914	Bedzin		Aron & Taube
TECEL	Pinkas	1892	rowno	merchant	Isak & Sara
TEICH	Emanuel	1920	Dzidziece		
TENNENBAUM	Rozalia	1901	Tarnopol	druggist	Mendel & Anna
UNFUSE	Hersz	1894	Tomaszow	butcher	Chaim & Sara
UNFUSE	Chuma	1900	Tomaszow		Hersz & Lea
UNFUSE	Raja	1927	Tomaszow		Hersz & Chuma
UNFUSE	Szmul	1929	Tomaszow		Hersz & Chuma
UNFUSE	Hindale	1933	Tomaszow		Hersz & Chuma
UNFUSE	Ryfke	1936	Tomaszow		Hersz & Chuma
UNGER	Szyfra	1914	Uszeszow	doctor	Markus & Nina
VIERTEL	Adolf	1884			
VOGEL	Juda	1913	Poniatyn		Feiwel & Sara
WIESMAN	Mozes	1898	Dubno		
WIESMAN	Rywa	1926	Dubno		Lea
WOWK	Szlome	1900	Dubno		Benjamin
WOWK	Estera	1918	Dubno	seamstress	Simon & Golda
WOWK	Michal	1932	Dubno		
WAJNBERG	Jakub	1912	Warszawa	merchant	Mordek & Estera

WAJNBERG	Sonia	1923	Projac		Izrael & Szajntle
WEISSELBERG	Jakub	1895	Stanislawow	clerk	Henryk & Nina
WEISSELBERG	Natalia	1902		druggist	Bernard & Lola
WEISSELBERG	Ludwiga	1926			Jakub & Natalia
WILK	Jakub	1910	Piasek	doctor	Dawid & Berta
WILK	Yasalina	1918	Brzezany	dentist	Izak & Roza
WILNER	Moniek	1930	Rymanow		Naftali & Fryda
WILSON	Lora	1923	Sosnowiec		Mzks & Mania
WITUCH	Mendel	1897	Sczawnica		Baruch & Blima
WITUCH	Helena	1931	Lwow		Zissel & Rachela
WITZLING	Franz	1900	Lwow		Juda & Zosia
WITZLING	Erna	1906			Juda & Feige
WITZLING	Justaw	1940			Franz & Erna
WIUKI	Iak	1919	Warszawa	watchmaker	Majer & Felicia
WIUKI	Bela	1919	Slawa		Abraham & Felicia
WOSZK	Antonina	1925	Leningrad		Michal
WOWK	Chaiim	1935	Dubno		Salomon
WOWK	Itzhak	1920			Szmul & Feige
WOWK	Szaja	1906		farmer	Gerszon & Zosia
WRECZEWSKI	Wladyslaw	1920	Warszawa	driver	Mendel & Anna
WROCZEWSKI	Szmul	1903	Lututow		Wolf & Chana
ZERZENOWICZ	Zofia	1897	Warszawa	dentist	Wolf & Estera
ZERZENOWICZ	Lila	1923	Warszawa		
ZERZENOWICZ	Debora	1929	Warszawa		
ZIMMERMAN	Mozes	1921	Boryslaw		Jozef & Regina
ZIMMERMAN	Juda	1925	Jeslow		Leib & Bela

[Page 279]

Chapter XVI

Total Register of the Population in Hindenburg/Zabrze at the End of World War II

The document below was provided by the United States Holocaust Memorial Museum in Washington, D.C. It is rare and important information to provide and is published here without changes or alterations. We would like to particularly thank Michlean Lowy Amir for her efforts in obtaining this document for us.

List of residents of Hindenburg/Zabrze

Presented by the Holocaust Memorial Museum in Washington D.C

* OS=Stand for Upper Silesia

Last name	First name	Gender	Birth date	Birth place
ACKERMAN	Marilyn	F		Radom, Poland
ADAMICK	Martha	F	23 Mar 1905	Hindenburg
ADLER	Friedrich	M	21 Aug 1889	Hindenburg
ADLER	Kurt	M	9 Jul 1884	Hindenburg
ADLER	Bruno	M	15 Jan 1884	Hindenburg
ADLER	Irma	F	28 Apr 1931	Hindenburg
ADLER	Alexander	M	15 Jun 1899	Dramatal, Beuthen
ADLER	Heinrich	M	17 Jan 1884	Krier, Pleay
ADLER	Hildegard	M	10 Mar 1905	Hindenburg, Germany
ADLER	Irma	F	28 Jun 1891	Hindenburg O.S.
ADLER	Friedericke	F	15 May 1877	Katowice (Kattowitz)
ADLER	Georg	M	4 Feb 1882	Hindenburg O.S.
ADLER	Jeanette	F	25 Aug 1925	Radom Poland
ADLER–RUBIN	Diana	F	16 Apr 1922	Tomaszow
AITCHISON	Henia	F		Warsaw, Poland
AKERMAN	Batia	F	17 Apr 1917	Radom Poland
ALEXANDER	Ida	F	19 Dec 1872	Hindenburg Ost
ALTMANN	Hans	M	06 Mar 1923	Hindenburg O.S.
ALTMANN	Margarete	F	1 Mar 1883	Hindenburg O.S.
ANGREAY	Lieselotte	F	31 Jan 1924	Hindenburg
ANGREAY	Erwin	M	16 May 1921	Kanigshatte
ANGREAY	Max	M	22 Jan 1891	Kanigshatte
ANGREAY	Olga	F	14 Nov 1886	Jedlin, Pleay
ANGREAY	Gertrud	F	2 Jan 1880	Hindenburg O.S.

ANGRES	Else	F	06 Feb 1901	Zaborze, Hindenburg
ANGRES	Margarete	F	25 Dec 1904	Hindenburg O.S.
ANGRES	Pawel	M	20 Oct 1895	Paulsdorf, Hindenburg
ANGRES	Walter	M	2 Sep 1897	Zaborze, Hindenburg
ANGRESS	Rosa	F	29 Jun 1879	Hindenburg O.S.
ANGRESS	Gertrud	F	2 Jan 1880	Hindenburg
ANGRESS	Heinz	M	22 Dec 1927	Hindenburg
ANKOWSKI	Anne Marie	F		Danzig, Germany
APT	Elfriede	F	17 May 1884	Zabrze, Schlesien
APT	Erna	F	25 Sep 1885	Zabrze, Schlesien
APT	Elfriede	F	17 May 1884	Hindenburg O.S.
APT	Erna	F	25 Sep 1888	Hindenburg O.S.
ARNADE	Elisabeth	F	7 Sep 1892	Hindenburg O.S.
ARNOLD	Bertha	F	15 Jun 1916	Hindenburg
ARONHEIM	Erwin	M		
ARONSOHN	Margot	F	21 Oct 1916	Hindenburg O.S.
ASCHER	Heinz	M	14 Jul 1911	Hindenburg
ASCHNER	Betty	F	18 Apr 1912	Hindenburg O.S.
BIGELMAN	Anna	F	26 Mar 1905	
BAHM	Bertha	F	26 Apr 1865	Zabrze
BAHM	Friedrich	M	14 Apr 19–20	Paulsdorf, Hindenburg
BAHM	Heinrich	M	05 May 1907	Paulsdorf, Hindenburg
BAHM	Charlotte	F	10 Dec 1892	Chropaczow, Beuthen
BAHM	Charlotte	F	17 Sep 1879	Antonienhatte
BAHM	Elisabeth	F	10 Nov 1892	Meiningen
BAHM	Karl	M	15 Aug 1904	Paulsdorf
BAHM	Kate	F	05 Nov 1912	Ratibor
BAHM	Kate	F	7 Jul 1888	Kanigshatte
BAHM	Markus	M	22 May 1884	Liemianowitz, Kattowitz
BAHM	Max	M	12 May 1873	Slupna, Myslowitz
BAHM	Max	M	30 Nov 1871	Hindenburg O.S.
BAHM	Rosa	F	11 Aug 1892	Kanigshatte
BAHM	Salo	M	17 Mar 1915	Paulsdorf
BAHM	Simon	M	28 Mar 1888	Tost O.S.
BAHM	Valentin	M	26 Sep 1883	Slupna, Myslowitz
BAHM	Georg	M	22 Nov 1870	Hindenburg O.S.
BAHM	Lieselotte	F	01 May 1918	Hindenburg O.S.
BAHM	Elfriede	F	24 Nov 1918	Katowice (Kattowitz)
BAHM	Werner–Otto	M	23 Jan 1923	Katowice (Kattowitz)
BAHM	Paula	F	10 May 1881	Zaborze, Hindenburg
BAHM	Willy	M	22 Oct 1886	Hindenburg O.S.
BARGER	Pelagia	F	02 Jul 1901	Hindenburg
BADRIAN	Gerhard	M	13 Jun 1921	Hindenburg
BADRIAN	Gerda	F	10 Dec 1925	Hindenburg O.S.
BADRIAN	Gunter	M	23 Oct 1926	Hindenburg
BADRIAN	Heinz	M	28 Jul 1931	Hindenburg O.S.
BADRIAN	Ruth	F	10 May 1923	Hindenburg O.S.

BADRIAN	David	M	25 Mar 1891	Pawlowitz, Pleay
BADRIAN	Eva	F	15 Dec 1931	Groay Strelitz
BADRIAN	Leo	M	24 Jun 1896	Gleiwitz
BADRIAN	Marie	F	30 Apr 1899	Raitza, Beuthen
BADRIAN	Paula	F	31 Jan 1897	Kamin, Beuthen
BADURA	Gertrud	F	16 Mar 1920	Klausberg, Beuthen
BAENDEL	Max	M	14 Aug 1866	Ruda, Hindenburg
BAER	Selma	F	5 Dec 1865	Zabrze, Schlesien
BAER	Alfred	M	29 Jun 1898	Zabrze, Schlesien
BAER	Selma	F	5 Dec 1865	Hindenburg O.S.
BAHM	Harry	M	04 Mar 1912	Nauslau
BAIER	Theodor	M	24 Aug 1931	Hindenburg
BAIER	Joseph	M		Hindenburg, Germany
BAJER	Emil	M	21 Jul 1891	Hindenburg
BAJTLER	Natan	M	08 Mar 1905	
BALBIEN	Dina	F		Radom, Poland
BALLEIER	Hubertus	M	26 Jul 1927	Hindenburg
BALLON	Lothar	M	14 Oct 1897	Hindenburg O.S.
BANKIER	Szyka	M	31 Mar 1905	
BARANOWICZ	Lea	F	04 Apr 1905	
BARON	Ruffi	F	3 Aug 1899	Hindenburg
BARON	Aug	M	27 Aug 1886	Hindenburg
BARON	Wiktor	M	21 Sep 1905	Laband
BARTECYKO	Katharina	F	22 Mar 1892	Hindenburg Ost
BARTENSTEIN	Else	F	23 Nov 1904	Hindenburg
BARTZIK	Franz	M	03 May 1907	Hindenburg
BASS	Regina	F	1 May 1877	Zabrze, Schlesien
BAUDY	Johann	M	27 Aug 1888	Schackendorf, Oppeln
BAUM	Frida	F	01 Apr 1925	Staszow
BAUMAHLOVA	Klara	F	03 Sep 1922	Kezmarok Czechoslovakia
BAUMGART	Elfriede	F	04 Dec 1908	Hindenburg
BAUMGART	Margot	F	10 Mar 1922	Hindenburg, Schlesien
BAUMGART	Fritz	M	15 Jun 1927	Hindenburg
BAUMGART	Bianca	F	9 Feb 1883	Mogilno
BAUMGART	Friedericke	F	20 Jul 1864	Eichenau
BAUMGART	Margarete	F	16 Dec 1892	Lipine
BAUMGART	Heinz	M	01 Apr 1907	Hindenburg
BAUMGART	Kurt	M	19 Dec 1923	Hindenburg O.S.
BAUMGART	Ernst	M	29 Sep 1885	Myslowice , Kattowitz
BAYER	Emil	M	21 Jul 1891	Zabrze
BECHERT	Gertrud	F	26 Nov 1899	Zaborze, Hindenburg
BEDNAREK	Paul	M	11 Jan 1902	Hindenburg
BEDNORZ	Johann	M	5 Dec 1884	Hindenburg
BEDNORZ	Lothar	M	11 Jun 1919	Hindenburg
BEDNORZ	Marie	F	11 May 1892	Hindenburg
BEER	Benjamin	M	04 Sep 1930	Hindenburg
BEHNSCH	Rosa	F	21 Jun 1885	Hindenburg

BEIN	Elisabeth	F	13 Nov 1871	Zabrze, Schlesien
BENGER	Anna	F	13 Mar 1871	Jastrzemb, Rybnik
BENGER	Else	F	28 Jul 1876	Hindenburg
BENJAMIN	Elisabeth	F	19 Nov 1901	Hindenburg O.S.
BERGER	Wolfgang	M	21 Feb 1916	Hindenburg
BERGER	Max	M	16 May 1899	Zabrze, Schlesien
BERGER	Max Markus	M	16 Nov 1856	Zabrze, Schlesien
BERGER	Irma	F	12 May 1892	Zabrze, Schlesien
BERGER	Max	U	16 Nov 1856	Hindenburg
BERGER	Arthur	M	24 Jan 1905	Lipine
BERGER	Heinrich	M	14 Jul 1872	Gleiwitz
BERGER	Irma	F	12 May 1892	Hindenburg O. S.
BERGER	Kurt	M	20 Feb 1893	Hindenburg
BERGER	Max	M	16 May 1899	Hindenburg O. S.
BERGER	Max	F	16 Nov 1856	Hindenburg O. S.
BERGER	Else	F	27 Sep 1900	Hindenburg
BERGER	Henriette	F	27 Oct 1885	Dorotheendorfj, Hindenburg
BERGER	Hilde	F	22 Nov 1895	Hindenburg O. S.
BERGHEIM	Hedwig	F	8 Jul 1870	Hindenburg O.S. (Biskupitz)
BERGMANN	Ruth	F	06 Feb 1924	Hindenburg O. S.
BERGMANN	Ursula	F	20 May 1927 7	Hindenburg O. S.
BERKELHAMER	Paulins	F	11 Apr 1905	
BERKI	Else	F	26 Jun 1896	Borsigwerk, Hindenburg
BERLINER	Erich	M	31 Oct 1907	Hindenburg O. S.
BERNATZKY	Georg	M	29 Sep 1889	Hindenburg O.S.
BERNATZKY	Rosa	F	11 May 1882	Neustadt O.S.
BERNEMAN	Guta	F	04 Apr 1922	Pionki, Poland
BERNHARD	Salome	F	17 Nov 1899	Hindenburg O.S.
BERSER	Abraham	U	15 Apr 1905	
BESWER	Abraham	M	15 Apr 1905	
BEYERMANN	Luzie	F	04 Dec 1908	Hindenburg
BIALKOWICZ	Bella	F		Garbatka, Poland
BIENIEK	Josef	M	17 Mar 1913	Hindenburg
BIMBERG	Klara	M	03 Apr 1905	
BINIAS	Martha	F	17 Dec 1883	Hindenburg O.S.
BINIOSSEK	Elfriede	F	2 Oct 1889	Schanbrunn
BINIOSSEK	Gustav	M	13 Jan 1891	Breslau
BINIOSSEK	Manfred	M	03 Jul 1921	Nassau, Neustadt O.S.
BINIOSSEK	Ulrich	M	10 Aug 1918	Nassau, Neustadt O.S.
BINIOSSEK	Ursula	F	03 Jun 1920	Nassau, Neustadt O.S.
BINKS	Danka	F	02 Mar 1920	Ciechanow, Poland
BINZYK	Hedwig	F	14 Oct 1886	Biskupitz, Hindenburg
BIRENBERG	Klara	U		
BIRNBAUM	Tedy	M		
BIRNBAUM	Ignac	M	26 Mar 1905	
BIRNBAUM	Jeremiasz	M	22 Mar 1905	

BIRNBERG	Ida	F		
BISKUP	Luzie	F	14 Dec 1910	Hindenburg O.S.
BLAAY	Lina	F	8 Nov 1859	Lindenburg, Hindenburg
BLAI	Cacilie	F		Zaborze, Hindenburg
BLANDOWSKI	Hans	M	10 Jul 1926	Hindenburg O.S.
BLANDOWSKI	Ilse	F	30 Nov 1934	Hindenburg O.S.
BLANDOWSKI	Hertha	F	14 May 1901	Greifswald
BLANDOWSKI	Salo	M	7 Jul 1895	Schwientochlowitz
BLASCHKE	Max	M	21 Oct 1873	Hindenburg
BLASCHKE	Klara	F	23 Oct 1875	Karstadt, Kreuzburg O.S.
BLASCHKE	Walter	M	2 Sep 1899	Hindenburg O.S.
BLATMAN	Tola	F	12 Feb 1924	Radom
BLAUT	Horst	M	06 May 1933	Hindenburg O.S.
BLAUT	Marie	F	10 Apr 1904	Hindenburg O.S.
BLAUT	Adolf	M	07 Aug 1929	Hindenburg O.S.
BLAUT	Artur	M	13 Feb 1928	Hindenburg O.S.
BLAUT	Eugen	M	17 Aug 1925	Hindenburg O.S.
BLAUT	Heinrich	M	10 Mar 1936	Hindenburg O.S.
BLECHER	Egon	M	15 Apr 1927	Karlovy Vary
BLECHER	Malka	F	18 Jan 1923	Radom , Poland
BLOCH	Richard	M	21 Sep 1895	Hindenburg
BLOCH	Gertrud	F	12 Mar 1897	Hindenburg O.S.
BLOCH	Herbert	M	30 Jul 1921	Hindenburg
BLOCH	Ilse	F	22 Aug 1921	Hindenburg O.S.
BLOCH	Marie	F	5 Sep 1898	Hindenburg
BLOCH	Werner	M	30 Jul 1923	Hindenburg O.S.
BLOCH	Karl	M	26 Oct 1890	Ober Glogau, Neustadt
BLOCH	Hermann	M	4 Jul 1894	Schweslerwitz, Neustadt.
BLOCH	Ellinor	M	04 Jun 1904	Hindenburg O.S.
BLOCH	Freud	F	12 Apr 1904	Hindenburg O.S.
BLOCH	Klaus–Reiner	M	18 Jul 1925	Hindenburg O.S.
BLUEH	Rosa	F	10 Nov 1874	Zabrze, Schlesien
BLUFARB–WAKSMAN	Sabina Jaffa	F	05 May 1925	Warszawa
BLUM	Kurt	M	08 May 1912	Hindenburg
BLUMENFELD	Gertrude	F	10 Nov 1881	Hindenburg O.S.
BLUMENFELD	Valeska	F	29 Mar 1876	Hindenburg O.S.
BLUMENFELD	Waldemar	M	11 Oct 1878	Hindenburg O.S.
BLUMENTHAL	Paula	F	12 May 1876	Pinne, Samter
BLUSZEZ	Martha	F	19 Jul 1905	Lazisk, Pleay
BLUTH	Max	M	10 Feb 1886	Hindenburg O.S.
BLUTSTEIN	Rosa	F	23 Aug 1923	Dortmund
BNRGER	Berta	F	03 Apr 1905	
BOCHNER	Elieser	M	10 Apr 1905	
BOCHNER	Amalia	F	19 Mar 1905	
BOCHNER	Michal	M	15 Apr 1905	
BODNER	Michel	M	28 Mar 1905	
BOEHM	Georg	M	22 Nov 1870	Zabrze, Schlesien

BOGUTH	Elisabeth	F	08 Jan 1917	Hindenburg
BOIN	Joachim	M		Berlin, Germany
BONK	Ewald	M	02 Oct 1912	Hindenburg
BOOZKA	Lorche	F	20 Mar 1905	
BOREN	Bella	F	10 Jun 1919	Kielce, Poland
BORINSKI	Marianne	F	18 Feb 1887	Wollstein, Bomst
BORINSKI	Moritz	M	11 Dec 1877	Hindenburg O.S.
BORINSKI	Eugen	M		Zaborze, Hindenburg
BORINSKI	Max	M	28 Jun 1874	Zaborze O.S.
BORNSTEIN	Emmy	F	16 Jun 1883	Zaborze O.S.
BORSCHZ	Edith	F	15 Dev 1920	Hindenburg O.S.
BORTLIK	Margarete	F	07 Feb 1911	Hindenburg O.S.
BORTLIK	Ruth	F	11 May 192 0	Hindenburg O.S.
BORTLIK	Maria	F	9 Apr 1883	Zabelkau, Ratibor
BORTLIK	Paul	M	5 Feb 1881	Roschkau, Ratibor
BORTS	Ferdinand	M	11 Dec 1880	Hindenburg
BORYCZKA	Viktor	M	6 Dec 1891	Hindenburg
BOTTENBREITER	Lieselotte	F	07 Aug 1925	Hindenburg Ost O.S.
BOTTENBREITER	Handel	F	11 Apr 1884	Neuberun
BOTTENBREITER	Samuel	M	19 Jan 1875	Eichenau
BOY	Gustav	M	20 Jul 1890	Hindenburg, Templin
BRAY	Auge	F	25 Dec 1880	Hindenburg O.S.
BRAHN	Georg	M	21 Oct 1877	Hindenburg O.S.,
BRAND	Sally	F	19 Feb 1923	Tarnow
BRAND	Anna	F		
BRANDES	Hedwig	F	30 Mar 1885	Zabrze, Schlesien
BRANDT	Margarete	F	15 Aug 1889	Biskupitz, Hindenburg
BRASCH	Ella	F	19 Sep 1887	Hindenburg O.S. (Zabrze)
BRASS	Auge	F	25 Dec 1880	Zabrze, Schlesien
BRAUER	Jakob	M	15 Jan 1872	Hindenburg O.S. (Zabrze)
BRAUER	Elzbieta	F		
BRAUER	Gertrud	F	11 Feb 1896	Hindenburg O.S.
BRAUER	Adolf	M	27 Nov 1870	Hindenburg
BRAUER	Artur	M	16 Jul 1890	Pilzendorf O.S.
BRAUER	Benno	M	3 Oct 1885	Pilzendorf, Beuthen
BRAUER	Berta	F	24 Sep 1909	Bobrek, Beuthen
BRAUER	Bertha	F	15 Oct 1859	Schildberg
BRAUER	Ernestine	F	14 Jan 1870	Zaborze
BRAUER	Jacob	M	24 Sep 1867	Ornontowitz, Pleay
BRAUER	Linka	F	13 Aug 1887	Kroschnitz, Groay Strelitz
BRAUER	Martin	M	11 Aug 1905	Klausberg, Beuthen
BRAUER	Paula	F	13 Mar 1893	Pilzendorf O.S.
BRAUER	Rosa	F	23 Sep 1903	Pilzendorf O.S.
BRAUER	Walter	M	19 Mar 1920 0	Klausberg, Beuthen
BRAUER	Jakob	M	15 Jan 1872	Hindenburg O.S.
BRAUER	Hugo	M	15 Sep 1863	Biskupitz, Hindenburg
BRAUER	Johanna	F	12 Apr 1890	Hindenburg O.S.

BRAUN	Gertrud	F	13 Jul 1890	Beuthen O.S.
BRAUNER	Wilhelm	M	10 Mar 1905	
BREGULLA	Emil	M	26 May 1893	Kanigshatte
BREGULLA	Sophie	F	3 May 1899	Kanigshatte
BREIT	Else	F	06 Jan 1909	Zabrze, Schlesien
BREITBARTH	Henny	F	9 Jan 1893	Lublinitz
BREITBARTH	Oskar	M	3 Nov 1885	Orzech, Tarnowitz
BREITKOPF	Sophie	F	07 Mar 1905	Hindenburg
BRENER	Pepi	F	13 Apr 1905	
BRESCHEL	Georg	M	18 Sep 1901	Hindenburg O. S.
BRESLAW	Mechana	F	21 Apr 1905	
BRODER	Izak	M	02 Apr 1905	
BRODER	Jozef	M	09 Apr 1905	
BROLL	Ludwika	F		
BROLL	Heinrich	M	25 May 1893	Hindenburg O.S.
BROLL	Heinz–	M	24 Jul 1928	Beuthen
BROLL	Luise	F	6 Mar 1897	Charlottenburg
BRONIATOWSKI	Michael	M	02 Jul 1935	Hindenburg
BRONNER	Hans	M	14 May 1919	Hindenburg
BROSZIASKI	Hulda	F	23 Mar 1920	Hindenburg
BRUKIER	Paula	F		Radom, Poland
BRZEZINA	Adelheid	F	12 Sep 1931 1	Hindenburg N.O.
BRZEZINA	Auge	F	24 May 1907	Hindenburg N.O.
BRZEZINA	Eva	F	28 Mar 1903	Hindenburg N.O.
BRZEZINA	Hedwig	F	25 Mar 1931	Hindenburg N.O.
BRZEZINA	Luzie	F	23 Dec 1927	Hindenburg N.O.
BRZEZINA	Hermann	M	4 Oct 1898	Tryngow
BRZOZA	Roman	M	28 Feb 1903	Hindenburg
BUCHCZYK	Josef	M	13 Mar 1899	Hindenburg
BUCHTA	Alois	F	09 May 1906	Hindenburg
BUCHWALD	Hedwig	F	22 Feb 1919	Hindenburg O.S.
BUCKOW	Martin	M	9 Jun 1884	Hindenburg
BUJAK	Paul	M	05 Jan 1910	Hindenburg
BULLA	Robert	U	04 Jun 1900	Hindenburg
BUNTZEL	Alfred	M	20 Aug 1861	Ruda, Hindenburg
BUNTZEL	Martha	F	29 Apr 1868	Ruda, Hindenburg
BURCZYK	Ernst	M	21 Aug 1898	Hindenburg O.S.
BURDA	Johann	U	23 May 1903	Hindenburg
BURKOWSKI	Otto	M	25 Mar 1905	Hindenburg
BURMANN	Linda	F	1 Jan 1893	Zarborze, Zabrze
BURSKA	Emil	M	28 Feb 1900 0	Hindenburg
BYCK	Fanny	F	26 Oct 1869	Hindenburg, Labiau
BYTOMSKI	Aug	M	29 Aug 1916	Hindenburg
CEBULLA	Max	M	11 Dec 1897	Hindenburg
CEGLAREK	Franz	M	30 Nov 1918	Hindenburg O/S
CELBRODT	Vinzent	M	30 Dec 1910	Hindenburg OS.
CENTAVER	Jette	F	22 Oct 1867	Zabrze (Westgalizien)

CENTAWER	Henriette	F	19 Oct 1868	Hindenburg O.S.
CHAVALLEK	Raimund	M	03 Aug 1909	Hindenburg
CHERNYSHOV	Aleksei	M		Krovno
CHIDECKEL	Edith	F	12 May 1922	Hindenburg O.S.
CHIDECKEL	Bernhard	M	14 Aug 1884	Gleboky, Wilna
CHIDECKEL	Margarethe	F	04 Jul 1901	Kaningshatte
CHMEL	Cilly	F	26 May 1890	Beuthen O.S.
CHMEL	Max	M	19 Jan 1892	Baurowitz, Leobschatz
CHOTZEN	Rosa	F	22 Feb 1879	Zabrze, Schlesien
CHOYKA	Johanna	F	15 Apr 1873	Hindenburg O.S.
CHROSNIK	Josef	M	22 Sep 1885	Hindenburg
CHUDERLAND	Helah	F	06 Jun 1923	Lodz, Poland
CIESLACK	Joseph	M	12 Aug 1905	Hindenburg.
CISLIK	Walter	M	15 Jun 1914	Hindenburg
CISLIK	Rosa	F	01 Jan 1910	Hindenburg
CIUPEK	Paul	M	22 Dec 1912	Hindenburg
CLIPPER	Regina	F		Radom, Poland
CLIPPER	Regina	F	01 Feb 1924	Radom, Poland
COHN	Olga	F	23 Jan 1869	Zabrze O.S.
COHN	Werner	M	11 Dec 1927	Hindenburg
COHN	Hildegardt	F	04 Jun 1914	Hindenburg
COHN	Olga	F	28 Apr 1877	Hindenburg
COHN	Olga	F	23 Jan 1869	
COHN	Auge	F	5 Jun 1872	Tichau, Pleay
COHN	Charlotte	F	16 Feb 1892	Groay Weichsel
COHN	Curt	M	14 Dec 190	Hobg.
COHN	Ernestine	F	12 Dec 1881	Woischnik, Lublinitz
COHN	Georg	M	17 Sep 1920	Nikolai
COHN	Heinz	M	07 Nov 1923	Beuthen O.S.
COHN	Hildegard	F	04 Nov 1905	Nikolai, Pleay
COHN	Loebel	M	6 Oct 1875	Langendorf, Gleiwitz
COHN	Margarete	F	27 Oct 1897	Namslau
COHN	Siegbert	M	15 Nov 1887	Nikolai
COHN	Dorothea	F	21 Jun 1912	Hindenburg O.S.
COHN	Emilie	F	13 May 1884	Hindenburg
COHN	Marta	F	22 Jun 1868	Hindenburg
COHN	Bruno	M	14 May 1901	Hindenburg O.
COHN	Martha	F	21 Jun 1868	Hindenburg O.S.
CURTIS	Rosa	F	13 Oct 1923	Mosonmagyar, Hungary
CURZYDLO	Gerhard	U	07 Aug 1912	Hindenburg
CWOLEK	Stanislaus	M	15 Apr 1913	Hindenburg
CYRON	Hans	M	10 Oct 1909	Hindenburg O. S.
CZAJA	Wilhelm	M	07 May 1908	Hindenburg
CZAJA	Theodor		23 Sep 1915	Hindenburg OS
CZAJA	Helene	F	22 Sep 1905	Biskupitz, Hindenburg
CZAJA	Robert	M	10 Jun 1894	Zaborze, Hindenburg
CZAJA	Georg	M	13 Nov 1903	Ruda, Zabrze O.S.

CZAJA	Wilhelm	U	17 May 1908	Hindenburg
CZAJA	Theodor	U	23 Sep 1915	Hindenburg
CZAPLOCK	Elfriede	F	04 Feb 1922	Hindenburg O.S.
CZARNOWIETSKI	Heinz	M	31 Jul 1923	Hindenburg
CZARNOWIETSKI	Emanuel	M	4 Aug 1886	Tost, Gleiwitz
CZARNOWIETSKI	Ida	F	22 Dec 1889	Bismarckhatte, Beuthen
CZARNOWIETSKI	Siegfr.	M	09 Aug 1920	Schlesieng
CZECH	Franz	U	23 Jan 1905	Hindenburg
CZEKALLA	Paul	M	29 Jun 1898	Hindenburg
CZEKALLA	Emil	M	23 Aug 1894	Hindenburg
CZEKALLA	Sophie	F	27 Apr 1895	Hindenburg
CZEMPIEL	Johann	M	17 Mar 1905	Hindenburg
CZERNY	Ursula	F	02 Mar 1924 4	Wyry, Pleay
CZOCK	Hildegard	F	15 Jul 1910	Hindenburg O.S.
CZOGLIA	Josef	M	30 Jul 1904	Hindenburg O.S.
CZOMBARA	Georg	M	01 Sep 1900	Hindenburg
CZOMBERA	Adelheid	F	29 Dec 1898	Hindenburg, Oppeln
CZOMBERA	Gunter	M	10 Jun 1923	Hindenburg, Oppeln
CZOMBERA	Karl	M	3 Nov 1897	Hindenburg, Oppeln
CZOSALIA	Josef	M	30 Jul 1904	Hindenburg
DAEUBNER	Johanna	F	20 Nov 1912	Hindenburg O. S.
DALLMANN	Gunter	M	21 May 1923	Hindenburg O.S.
DALLMANN	Hannelore	F	04 Sep 1928	Hindenburg O.S.
DALLMANN	Wolfgang	M	28 Jan 1931	Hindenburg O.S.
DANIEL	Bernhard	M	14 Jul 1913	Hindenburg
DANIEL	Georg	M	15 Sep 1897	Hindenburg O.S.
DANIEL	Gunter	M	28 Apr 1923	Hindenburg O.S.
DANIEL	Margarete	F	31 Oct 1895	Ossepow, Beuthen
DANIEL	Franz	M	29 Sep 1903	Biskupitz, Hindenburg
DANZIGER	Siegfried	M	13 Dec 1858	Hindenburg O.S. Zabrze
DANZIGER	Karl	M	31 Aug 1884	Hindenburg
DATTNER	Eugenie	F	22 Sep 1879	Hindenburg O.S.
DAVID	Bertha	F	21 Apr 1876	Hindenburg O. S.
DE STEIN	Eva	F		Hindenburg O.S.
DE WOLF	Frieda	F	16 Feb 1912	Zabrze
DECKRO	Frieda	F	14 Mar 1894	Hindenburg O.S.
DECKSLER	Wilhelm	M	04 Apr 1901 1	Hindenburg
DEN	Halina	F		Radom, Poland
DESTELIER	Betty	F	31 Aug 1892	Hindenburg O.S.
DESTELIER	Heinrich	M	5 Oct 1888	Kanigshatte
DEUTSCHER	Arthur	M	1 Nov 1886	Hindenburg O.S.
DIAMANTOVA	Gertruda	F	06 Oct 1924	Bratislava
DIAMENT	Henrietta	F		Lodz, Poland
DINES	HÃŒaiah	F	12 Dec 1928	Pionki, Poland
DITTERLA	Fritz	M	29 Apr 1925	Oppeln
DLUBASZ	Karl	M	26 Sep 1912	Hindenburg
DLUGI	Friedrich	M	06 Mar 1924	Hindenburg

DLUGI	Gertrud	F	22 Sep 1898	Hindenburg
DLUGI	Hannelore	F	27 May 1928	Hindenburg
DLUGI	Johannes	M	24 Oct 1937	Hindenburg
DLUGI	Karl	M	27 Oct 1899	Hindenburg
DLUGI	Renate	F	31 Dec 1934	Hindenburg
DLUGOSCH	Ernst	M	13 Jul 1931	Hindenburg O.S.
DOCTOR	Marie	F	7 Jan 1872	Hindenburg O.S.
DOLEZYCH	Agnes	F	17 Jan 1909	Hindenburg O.S.
DOLEZYCH	Eleonore	F	02 Jan 1915	Hindenburg
DOLEZYCH	Gertrud	F	18 Mar 1912	Hindenburg
DOLEZYCH	Gunter	M	22 Jun 1927	Oppeln
DOLEZYCH	Marie	F	3 Aug 1879	Groay Rauden, Ratibor
DOLLNIK	Max	M	11 Jan 1900	Hindenburg
DOMBROWSKY	Hans	M	11 Jul 1910	Neisse
DOMIN	Elisabeth	F	26 Nov 1909	Hindenburg O.S.
DOMIN	Maria	F	18 Jul 1905	Hindenburg O.S.
DOMMEYER	Margarethe	F	15 Aug 1910	Hindenburg O.S.
DOMMEYER	Karl–Heinz	M	30 Aug 1928	Ratibor O.S.
DOPPMANN	Erich	M	11 Feb 1912	Rybnik, Poland
DOPPMANN	Magdalene	F	09 Jan 1916	Makoschau
DOPPMANN	Marta	F	18 Jan 1893	Rybnik, Poland
DOPPMANN	Max	M	15 Nov 1882	Kanigsbruch
DORMAN	Ellen	F	28 Dec 1926	Tarnow , Poland
DRAGON	Ernst	M	27 Mar 1905	Hindenburg
DREAYLER	Reinhold	M	10 Mar 1901	Hindenburg
DREYER	Ilse	F	19 Mar 1915	Hindenburg
DRONIA	Marie	F	3 Dec 1876	Hindenburg O.S.
DROST	Anastasia	F	25 Feb 1893	Ruda Slaska, Hindenburg
DRYSKA	Angela	F	21 Mar 1905	Hindenburg
DUBIEL	Josef	M	23 Sep 1914	Hindenburg
DUCHNIK	Felix	M	23 May 1895	Hindenburg
DUDA	Franz	M	14 Nov 1910	Hindenburg
DUDA	Alois	F	14 Jun 1904	Hindenburg
DUDA	Maria	F	8 Apr 1892	Hindenburg
DUDA	Alois	F	14 Jun 1904	Hindenburg
DUDEK	Alfred	M	18 Mar 1905	Hindenburg
DUDIKA	Karl	M	21 Apr 1905	Hindenburg
DUNKEL	Otto	M	9 Apr 1889	Hindenburg/Templin
DUSCHA	Richard	M	14 Jan 1908	Hindenburg
DUSCHA	Konrad	M	23 Apr 1901	Hindenburg
DUYETASH	Richard	M	14 Jan 1908	Hindenburg
DUZINSKI	HÃŒavah	F	05 May 1926	Miskolc, Hungary
DUZINSKI	Rudolf	M	16 Nov 1902	Hindenburg
DYMANT	Rudolf	M	16 Nov 1902	Hindenburg
DZIADZIA	Pola	F	25 Oct 1924	Kozienice, Poland
DZINRA	Michael	M	17 Feb 1905	Hindenburg
DZINRA	Ursula	F	31 Jan 1932	Hindenburg Nord Ost

DZINRA	Adolf	M	08 Sep 1908	Ruda, Schwientochlowitz
DZIWISCH	Else	F	21 Jun 1911	Oppeln
EBSTEIN	Sophie	F	19 Mar 1905	Hindenburg
EHRENREICH	Rosa	F	2 Jun 1896	Zaborze, Hindenburg
EHRLICH	Lola	F		
EHRLICH	Georg Josef	M	22 Feb 1890	Hindenburg
EHRLICH	Erna	F	31 Mar 1892	Hindenburg
EHRLICH	Fedor	M	5 Jun 1879	Alt–Berun, Pleay
EHRLICH	Gunther	M	04 May 1923	Neisse
EHRLICH	Katharina	F	10 Feb 1882	Groay Neundorf, Kosel
EHRLICH	Katharina	F	07 Dec 1920	Strabel, Breslau
EHRLICH	Meta	F	30 Nov 1879	Ruda
EHRLICH	Minna	F	8 Apr 1882	Hindenburg O.S.
EHRLICH	Kurt	M	19 Nov 1881	Myslowice , Kattowitz
EHRLICH	Curt	M	4 Jun 1896	Hindenburg O. S.
EHRLICH	Rosa	F	6 Sep 1882	Hindenburg O.S.
EHRMANN	Rosalie	F	3 Jul 1874	Carls Colonie bei Ruda
EHRMANN	Elsa	F	5 Mar 1891	Stadtel, Namslau
EHRMANN	Gerda	F	28 Mar 1920	Stadtel, Namslau
EHRMANN	Hugo	M	7 Jun 1883	Oels
EHRMANN	Lotte	F	29 Mar 1911	Stadtel, Namslau
EICHEL	Marta	F	16 Aug 1882	Stadtel, Namslau
EIRLISCH	Alexander	M		Piotrkow Trybunalski,
EISENBERG	Lydia Elfrida	F	13 Dec 1904	Hindenburg, Germany
EISINGER–PHILIPP	Cela	F	15 May 1925	Kozienice, Poland
EISNER	Lotti	F	04 Feb 1921	Hindenburg
EISNER	Richard	M	1 Aug 1859	Zabrze, Hindenburg
EISNER	Hans	M	21 Jun 1921	
EISNER	Louis	M	30 Jul 1877	Hindenburg O.S.
EISNER	Martha	F	11 Jun 1878	Hindenburg
EISNER	Max	M	4 Oct 1867	Hindenburg O.S.
EISNER	Ruth	F	06 Dec 1908	Hindenburg O.S.
EISNER	Walter	M	21 Nov 1925	Hindenburg O.S.
EISNER	Wilhelm	M	12 Aug 1900	Hindenburg
EISNER	Alice	F	11 Jul 1903	Hindenburg
EISNER	Ernst	M	06 Nov 1906	Hindenburg O.S.
EISNER	Helene	F	06 Feb 1932	Hindenburg O.S.
EISNER	Hugo	M	7 Aug 1873	Hindenburg
EISNER	KSthe	U	08 Aug 1910	Zabrze, Schlesien
EISNER	Gertrud	F	22 Jul 1911	Hindenburg O.S.
EISNER	Gerda	F	12 Oct 1915	Kanigdhatte
EISNER	Hermann	M	7 May 1890	Antonienhatte
EISNER	Kate	F	1 Sep 1891	Cosel
EISNER	Max	M	28 Dec 1863	Hindenburg
EISNER	Walter	M	21 Mar 1924	Hindenburg
EISNER	Frieda	F	1 Feb 1896	Falkenberg O.S.
EISNER	Malvina	F		Svidnicka, Czechoslovakia

ELGER	Malvina	F	16 Aug 1924	Svidnicka, Czechoslovakia
ELGER	Johanna	F	24 Apr 1901	Marklowitz
ELIAS	Leopold	M	6 Jul 1898	Wittenberg
ELIAS	Maria	F	28 Jun 1872	Zabrze, Schlesien
ELIAS	Maria	F	28 Jun 1872	Hindenburg
ELIAS	Helene	F	21 Aug 1878	Rawicz Rawitsch
ELIAS	Victor	M	7 Nov 1879	Kobyla Gora
ELIAS	Gerda	F	03 Mar 1921	Lipine
ELSTER	Marie	F	28 Jun 1872	Hindenburg O.S.
ELTER	Rubin	M	01 Sep 1921	Szidliesz
ELTER	Herman	M	05 Apr 1905	Hindenburg
EMMERICH	Leon	M	09 Nov 1924	Hindenburg
ENGEL	Arthur	M	16 Oct 1903	Hindenburg
ENGEL	Rosa	F	6 May 1883	Zabrze, Schlesien
ENGEL	Alfred	M	17 Jan 1912	Hindenburg
ENGEL	Ernestine	F	24 Sep 1873	Biskupitz, Hindenburg
ENGEL	Rosa	F	6 May 1883	Hindenburg O. S.
ENGLER	Meta	F	15 May 1876	Hindenburg O. S.
EPSTEIN	Else	F	17 Sep 1900	Hindenburg O.S.
ERBRECHT	Louis	M	13 Feb 1866	Hindenburg O. S.
ERLAG	Theodor	M	25 Jan 1868	Zaborze, Hindenburg
ERLICH	Pepa	F	01 Oct 1946	
ERLICH	Kurt	M		
ERNST	Anton	M	06 May 1936	Hindenburg
ERNST	Bernhard	M	25 Jul 1921	Hindenburg
ERNST	Marie	F		Radom, Poland
FARSTER	Marie	F	01 Oct 1923	Radom, Poland
FARSTER	Martha	F	26 Apr 1897	Hindenburg O.S.
FARSTER	Georg	M	16 Dec 1903	Hindenburg O.S.
FARSTER	Margarete	F	23 Oct 1899	Hindenburg O. S.
FABER	Walter	M	3 Jul 1898	Hindenburg O.S.
FABISCH	Sarah	F		Kalisz, Poland
FABISCH	Friedericke	F	24 Aug 1893	Hindenburg O.S.
FACTOR	Ernestine	F	2 Sep 1868	Mochalla, Lublinitz
FAJT	Lena	F	20 Oct 1920	Zarki, Poland
FECHNER	Wladyslaw	M	03 Dec 1924	Zabrze
FECHNER	Heinrich	M	22 Jul 1882	Hindenburg O.S.
FECHNER	Seraphine	F	16 Oct 1872	Hindenburg O.S.
FELDBERG	Heinrich	M	22 Jul 1882	Hindenburg
FELDHEIN	Rosa	F	17 May 1906	Hindenburg
FELDHEIN	Marek	M	06 Oct 1946	
FELLMANN	Romana	F	06 Oct 1946	
FERENCI	Abraham	M	15 Jul 1925	Hindenburg
FERENCIK	Raza	F	06 1918	Nagykanizsa (Hungary)
FIEBIG	Irena	F	14 May 1914	Humenna (Czechoslovakia)
FIEDLER	Gunther	M	09 Dec 1909	Hindenburg O.S.
FINKELSTEIN	Charlotte	F	11 Jul 1915	Hindenburg O. S.

FINKELSTEIN	Ernst	M	16 Apr 1921	Hindenburg
FINKELSTEIN	Gunther	M	14 Sep 1912	Hindenburg
FINKELSTEIN	Rosa	F	21 Oct 1913	Zabrze, Schlesien
FINKELSTEIN	Bernhard	M	16 Aug 1876	Zaborze, Hindenburg O.S.
FINKELSTEIN	Rosa	F	21 Oct 1913	Hindenburg
FINKELSTEIN	Flora	F	4 May 1884	Beuthen O.S.
FINKELSTEIN	Max	M	13 Mar 1874	Hindenburg O.S. (Zaborze)
FINKIELSTEIN	Sally	F		Tarnow, Poland
FINKIELSZTEJN	Rota	F	06 Apr 1905	
FIREMAN	Sura	F	09 Apr 1905	
FISCHER	Helen	F	01 Apr 1918	Pionki (Poland), Russia
FISCHER	Kurt	M	4 Sep 1895	Hindenburg
FISCHER	Fritz	M	16 Apr 1896	Hindenburg
FISCHER	Leopold	M		
FISCHER	Else	F	23 Feb 1875	Hindenburg
FISCHER	Charlotte	F	15 Jan 1887	Dziedzitz
FISCHER	Gustav	M	14 Aug 1862	Tarnowitz
FISCHER	Jacob	M	5 Feb 1874	Hindenburg O.S.
FISCHER	Kurt	M	4 Sep 1895	Hindenburg O.S.
FISCHER	Rosa	F	23 May 1873	Hindenburg O.S.
FISCHER	Ernst	M	22 Feb 1898	Hindenburg O.S.
FITZEK	Peretz	M		Hindenburg, Germany
FLAM	Marie	F	04 Jun 1904	Hindenburg
FLANCBAUM	Chana	F	10 Nov 1925	Pionki, Poland
FLANCBAUM	Paula Lerman	F		Bialobrzegi, Poland
FLEISHER	Paula	F	12 Mar 1920	Bialobrzegi , Poland
FLEISCHER	Herta	F		
FLEISCHER	Kurt Emil	M	19 Jan 1913	Hindenburg
FLEISCHER	Leopold	M	26 Sep 1897	Hindenburg
FLEISCHER	Leopold	M	21 Mar 1905	Hindenburg
FLEISCHER	Hans	M	16 Mar 1934	Hindenburg O.S.
FLEISCHER	Amalie	F	21 Oct 1861	Hindenburg O.S.
FLEISCHER	Dieter	M	12 Sep 1933	Hindenburg
FLEISCHER	Ella	F	24 Jun 1924	Hindenburg
FLEISCHER	Gunter	M	08 Oct 1925	Hindenburg
FLEISCHER	Heinz	M	30 Jan 1927	Hindenburg
FLEISCHER	Josef	M	12 Jun 1872	Hindenburg
FLEISCHER	Kate	F	22 Jan 1922	Hindenburg
FLEISCHER	Leopold	M	26 Sep 1897	Hindenburg
FLEISCHER	Rudolf	M	18 Jun 1904	Hindenburg
FLEISCHER	Eva	F	14 Apr 1883	Kieferstadtel, Gleiwitz
FLEISCHER	Herbert	M	24 Apr 1910	Charlottenburg,
FLEISCHER	Herta	F	02 Apr 1901	Ruda
FLEISCHER	Paula	F	8 May 1897	Alt Berun, Pleay
FLEISCHER	Rosa	F	18 Sep 1892	Kieferstadtel, Gleiwitz
FLEISCHER	Leopold	M	03 Dec 1910	Hindenburg
FLEISCHER	Johanna	F	5 Jun 1889	Jaratschewo, Jarotschin

FLORIAN	Elfriede	F	27 Oct 1919	Hindenburg O.S.
FNRST	Rosemarie	F	29 Mar 1933	Hindenburg
FOGELMAN	Georg	M	16 Dec 1903	Zabrze, Schlesien
FOIT	Chana	F	15 Apr 1926	Radom
FOLLAK	Georg	M	17 Oct 1908	Hindenburg
FOLLAK	Bruno	M	28 Aug 1882	Schurgersdorf, Ratibor
FOLLAK	Christiana	F	1921 beF 22	Kanigshatte
FOLLAK	Gerry	M	24 Apr 1884	Schurgersdorf, Ratibor
FOLLAK	Ottilie	F	28 Aug 1854	Kostenthal, Cosel
FORREITER	Walter	M	30 Oct 1913	Kanigshatte
FOX	Max	M	11 Apr 1906	Hindenburg O.S.
FOX	Nina	F		Kozienice, Poland
FRANKEL	Nina	F	02 Apr 1926	Kozienice, Poland
FRAHLICH	Gerda	F	12 Jun 1913	Hindenburg O.S.
FRAHLICH	Max	M	04 Jan 1920	Hindenburg
FRAHLICH	Berta	F	15 Oct 1900	Hindenburg
FRAHLICH	Gerda	F	14 Dec 1927	Hindenburg
FRAHLICH	Ingrid–Maria	F	15 Oct 1926	Zaborze, Hindenburg
FRAHLICH	Kurt	M	23 Mar 1933	Hindenburg
FRAHLICH	Toni	F	24 Mar 1891	Orzesche, Pleay
FRAHLICH	Bertha	F	5 Dec 1879	Ratibor
FRAHLICH	Georg	M	27 Nov 1884	Laband, Gleiwitz
FRAHLICH	Kurt	M	15 Nov 1879	Laband, Gleiwitz
FRAHLICH	Moritz	M	9 Jul 1887	Radzionkau, Tarnowitz
FRAHLICH	Natalie	F	26 Apr 1890	Imielin
FRAHLICH	Kathe	F	24 Feb 1907	Hindenburg O.S.
FRANCUS	Max	M	04 Jan 1920	Hindenburg, Schlesien
FRANCUS	Genia	F		Radom, Poland
FRANIK	Golde	F	22 Dec 1925	Radom, Poland
FRANKEL	Georg	M	11 Sep 1905	Hindenburg/OS.
FRANZ	Rachela	F		Tomaszow, Poland
FREEDMAN	Bernhardt	M	11 Mar 1901	Grunsken
FRENKIEL	Sara	F		Warka, Poland
FREUND	Nina	F	05 Apr 1927	Radom, Poland
FREUND	Ewald	M	4 Mar 1895	Zabrze, Schlesien
FREUND	Friedericke	F		
FREUND	Ewald	M	4 Mar 1895	Hindenburg
FREUND	Friedrich	M	23 Nov 1901	Hindenburg O.S.
FREUND	Alma	F	13 Aug 1898	Beuthen O.S.
FREUND	Friedericke	F	25 May 1868	Brenskowitz, Kattowitz
FREUND	Moritz	M	10 Mar 1872	Bilitz
FREUND	Benjamin	M	23 Apr 1871	Biskupitz Kreis Hindenburg
FREUND	Hertha	F	28 Apr 1896	Hindenburg O.S.
FREUND	Arthur	M	6 Jan 1872	Biskupitz, Hindenburg
FREUND	Benjamin	M	23 Apr 1871	Hindenburg (Biskupitz)
FREUND	Kathe	F	15 Apr 1900	Zaborze, Hindenburg
FREY	Max	M	23 Jun 1870	Bielschowitz, Hindenburg

FREY	Franz	M	08 Oct 1928	Biskupitz, Hindenburg O.S.
FREY	Rose–Marie	F	09 Jan 1925	Biskupitz, Hindenburg O.S.
FREY	Ursula	F	10 Mar 1925	Biskupitz, Hindenburg O.S.
FREY	Albert	M	14 Jan 1879	Scharley, Beuthen
FREY	Irma	F	16 May 1898	Falkenberg
FREY	Siegmund	M	20 Jul 1885	Schewley
FRIEDEANDER	Anastasia	F	15 Apr 1896	Hindenburg O.S.
FRIEDLANDER	Erwin	U	16 Aug 1900	Hindenburg
FRIEDLANDER	Dagobert	M	6 Nov 1898	Zabrze
FRIEDLANDER	Friedrich	M	18 Feb 1890	Zabrze (Hindenburg)
FRIEDLANDER	Johanna	F	17 Aug 1887	Hindenburg
FRIEDLANDER	Dagobert	M	6 Nov 1897	Hindenburg OS.
FRIEDLANDER	Alfred	M	29 Aug 1887	Hindenburg
FRIEDLANDER	Rosa	F	19 Mar 1853	Weschawa, Tarnowitz
FRIEDLANDER	Alma	F	29 Mar 1881	Tichau, Pleay
FRIEDLANDER	Josef	M	9 Apr 1887	Hindenburg O.S.
FRIEDLANDER	Johanna	F	17 Aug 1887	Hindenburg O.S.
FRIEDLANDER	Alfred	M	29 Aug 1887	Hindenburg O.S.
FRIEDLANDER	Erwin	M	16 Aug 1900	Hindenburg
FRIEDLANDER	Heinrich	M	9 Jul 1895	Hindenburg OS
FRIEDLANDER	Johanna	F	17 Aug 1887	Hindenburg
FRIEDLER	Josef	U	9 Apr 1887	Hindenburg
FRIEDLSNDER	Sara	F		Hindenburg, Germany
FROEHLICH	Josef	M	9 Apr 1887	Zabrze, Schlesien
FROMM	Kurt	M		
FUERST	Emilie	F	27 Feb 1905	Hindenburg
FURST	Georg	M	16 Dec 1903	Hindenburg
FUTERHENDLER	Walter	M	Jul 1898	Hindenburg
GATZ	Chaja	F	01 Sep 1925	Tomaszow–Mazowiecki
GARTLER	Helene	F	15 Jan 1912	Pawlow (Paulsdorf)
GADIEL	Pauline	F	25 Nov 1884	Breslau
GAIDA	Margar.	F	25 May 1886	Hindenburg O.S.
GAIDETZKA	Marta	F	28 Nov 1901	Biskupitz, Hindenburg
GARGOSZ	Elsa	F	01 Jan 1920	Hindenburg O.S.
GARGOSZ	Franz	M	25 Sep 1902	Hindenburg
GASSMANN	Johann	M	28 Sep 1899	Zaborze/Hindenburg
GAWLIK	Alfred	M	24 Apr 1877	Hindenburg O.S.
GEBAUER	Bernhardt	M	22 Jul 1906	Hindenburg
GEIER	Hans	M	11 May 1934	Hindenburg O.S.
GELDBERG	Maria	F	14 Jul 1923	Piestany, Czechoslovakia
GELDBERG	Nadia	F		
GELDNER	Nadia	F	29 May 1926	Radom , Poland
GELFAND	Sylvia	F	1 Feb 1893	Hindenburg O.S.
GENIDA	Edita	F	02 Jan 1923	Hindenburg
GERGMANN	Veronika	F	18 Oct 1879	Hindenburg O.S.
GERICHTER	Ursula	U	20 May 1927	Hindenburg
GERICHTER	Friedrike	U	23 Sep 1875	Zabrze, Schlesien

GERSTEL	Anna	F	09 Oct 1922	Hindenburg O.S.
GERSTEL	Margareth	F	16 Apr 1892	Zabrze
GERSTEL	Alexander	M	9 Jul 1890	Zabrze, Schlesien
GERSTEL	Alexander	M	7 Nov 1880	Hindenburg/OS
GERSTEL	Elisabeth	M	26 Feb 1905	Hindenburg
GERSTEL	Cacilie	F	2 Mar 1886	Hindenburg O.S.
GERSTEL	Clare	F	17 Oct 1891	Hindenburg
GERSTEL	Eva	F	26 Feb 1932	Hindenburg
GERSTEL	Rosalie	F	15 Jul 1887	Hindenburg O.S.
GERSTEL	Wilhelm	M	19 Oct 1884	Hindenburg O.S.
GERSTEL	Arnold	M	1 Oct 1897	Bublitz
GERSTEL	Eva	F	3 Apr 1863	Piaayetzne, Tarnowitz
GERSTEL	Laura	F	7 Feb 1887	Groay Wilkowitz
GERSTENFELD	Philipp	M	14 Jan 1856	Koschentin, Bublitz
GIEL	Gertrude	F		Garbatka, Poland
GILLNER	Alexander	M	19 Jun 1892	Hindenburg
GIPSMAN	Elisabeth	F	26 Jun 1893	Hindenburg
GIPSMANN	Natan	M	19 Jan 1925	Hindenburg
GLACKSMANN	Charlotte	F	22 May 1869	Hindenburg
GLAGLA	Selma	F	18 Feb 1878	Ruda, Hindenburg
GLACKSMANN	Else	F	19 Jan 1923	Hindenburg O.S.
GLASER	Charlotte	F	22 May 1869	Hindenburg
GLASER	Willy	M	02 Mar 1905	Zabrze
GLASER	Rosa	F	9 Jun 1896	Zabrze, Schlesien
GLASER	Gertrud	F	7 Feb 1884	Zabrze
GLASER	Friedrich	M	12 Aug 1888	Hindenburg
GLASER	Selma	F	15 Apr 1861	Halemba
GLASER	Elf.	F	29 Dec 1872	Trockenberg, Tarnowitz
GLASER	Friedrich	M	12 Aug 1888	Hindenburg O.S.
GLASER	Gertrud	F	7 Feb 1884	Hindenburg
GLASER	Rosa	F	9 Jun 1896	Hindenburg O.S.
GLASS	Berthold	M	4 Aug 1870	Hindenburg O.S.
GLAVOS	Klara	F		Hindenburg, Germany
GLIKSTEIN	Wilhelm	M	01 Aug 1913	Hindenburg
GNAT	Bluma	F	05 Feb 1923	Hindenburg
GOERLICH	Chana	F	17 Nov 1914	Hindenburg
GOINKA	Alfred	M	1 Oct 1897	Hindenburg
GOLASH	Else	F	9 Oct 1887	Schillersdorf, Ratibor
GOLDBERG	Adolf	M	28 Oct 1894	Hindenburg O.S.
GOLDBERG	Regina	F	05 Mar 1921	Hindenburg
GOLDFARB	Sara	F	08 Apr 1905	
GOLDMANN	Pola	F	20 May 1925	Radom, Poland
GOLDMANN	Hugo	M	13 Apr 1904	Hindenburg O.S.
GOLDMANN	Heinz	M	05 Apr 1921	Zalenjo
GOLDMANN	Eugenie	F	27 Oct 1894	Hindenburg
GOLDMANN	Hugo	M	29 Jan 1874	Hindenburg O.S.
GOLDMANN	Arthur	M	19 Aug 1885	Ruda, Hindenburg

GOLDMANN	Alma	F	2 Jun 1886	Tichau
GOLDMANN	Max	M	15 Aug 1872	Hindenburg, Hindenburg
GOLDMANN	Tinka	F	22 Dec 1880	Gostyn
GOLDMANN	Alfred	M	17 Nov 1877	Hindenburg
GOLDMANN	Herbert	M	13 Apr 1904	Hindenburg O.S.
GOLDMANN	Leo	M	5 Jul 1875	Hindenburg O.S.
GOLDSCHMID	Siegfried	M	30 Oct 1876	Hindenburg O.S.
GOLDSCHMID	Else	F		Hildesheim, D
GOLDSCHMIDT	Philipp	M	4 Jun 1889	Malhlbach, D
GOLDSCHMIDT	Rudolf	M	26 Sep 1905	Gleiwitz
GOLDSTEIN	Adelheid	F	05 Oct 1911	Zaborze
GOLDSTEIN	Erna	F	01 Jun 1913	Hindenburg O.S.
GOLDSTEIN	Alfred	M	29 May 1903	Hindenburg O.S.
GOLDSTEIN	Dorothea	F	21 Apr 1874	Zabrze, Schlesien
GOLDSTEIN	Wilhelm	M	12 Jan 1883	Zabrze, Schlesien
GOLDSTEIN	Erna	F	15 Jan 1900	Breslau
GOLDSTEIN	Paula	F	19 Apr 1885	Lissa
GOLDSTEIN	Samuel	M	7 Oct 1873	Urbanowitz, PleÃƒÅ
GOLDSTEIN	Dorothea	F	21 Apr 1874	Hindenburg O.S.
GOLDSZAJDER	Wilhelm	M	12 Jan 1883	Hindenburg O.S.
GOLINER	Henia	F	17 Nov 1923	Kielce, Poland
GOLLASCH	Else	F	27 Sep 1897	Hindenburg O.S.
GOLLASCH	Adolf	M	28 Oct 1894	Hindenburg O/S
GOLLY	Wilhelm	M	22 Jun 1898	Hindenburg O.S.
GORNY	Klara	F	16 Sep 1893	Boesigweck
GORYTZKA	Joseph	M	21 Feb 1909	Hindenburg O. S.–
GORYTZKA	Barbara	F	07 Jul 1932	Hindenburg
GORYTZKA	Lieselotte	F	21 Nov 1930	Hindenburg
GORYTZKA	Marianne	F	0 Sep 1935	Hindenburg
GORYTZKA	Marie	F	01 Jul 1904	Hindenburg
GORYTZKA	Paul	M	18 Aug 1904	Hindenburg O.S.
GORYTZKA	Viktor	M	04 Jan 1900	Hindenburg
GOTLIEB	Helene	F	21 Mar 1913	Beuthen O.S.
GOTLIEB	Sally	F		Radom, Poland
GOULD	Sally	F	18 Jun 1924	Radom, Poland
GRATZ	Paula	F	31 Jun 1926	Radom, Poland
GRANBERG	Margot	F	18 Feb 1901	Hindenburg O. S.
GRANBERG	Fanny	F	23 Mar 1879	Hindenburg O.S.
GRANBERG	Artur	M	11 May 1881	Zaborze O.S.
GRANBERG	Elise	F	18 Nov 1881	Rybnik, Rybnik
GRANBERG	Flora	F	11 Jul 1870	Zaborze
GRANBERG	Dagobert	M	3 Sep 1877	Hindenburg O.S.
GRANBERGER	Adolf	M	28 Jan 1883	Hindenburg O.S.
GRANBERGER	Ruth	F	04 Oct 1920	Zabrze Hindenburg
GRANBERGER	Horst	M	21 Dec 1928	Liegnitz, Liegnitz
GRABERGER	Kurt	M	29 Jan 1887	Koschmieder, Lublinitz
GRANBERGER	Paula	F	10 Dec 1896	Kaningshatte

GRANBERGER	Rosa	F	12 Jun 1897	Kaningshatte
GRANBERGER	Werner	M	04 Jan 1924	Sprottau
GRATTNER	Wilhelm	M	13 Nov 1895	Lublinitz
GRATTNER	Alexander	M	04 Feb 1915	Jekaterinoslaw
GRABER	Lubow	F	30 Oct 1887	Charkow
GRABOWSKI	Fritz	M	27 Sep 1891	Hindenburg O.S.
GRAETZ	Fanny	F	2 Oct 1875	Kaningshatte
GRASSEL	Margot	F	18 Feb 1901	Hindenburg
GRATZER	Alice	F		Hindenburg, Germany
GRAU	Simon	M	09 Feb 1901	Hindenburg
GREGOR	Rosalie	F	12 Nov 1876	Ruda , Hindenburg
GREIMANN	Alois	M	09 Apr 1925	Hindenburg
GREY	Walter	M	26 Jun 1907	Hindenburg O.S.
GRIESE	Doris	F	21 Jun 1912	Hindenburg
GRIESE	Joachim	M	05 Aug 1919	Hindenburg O.S.
GRIESE	Martha	F	30 Jan 1889	Sohrau
GRISCHMANN	Robert	M	4 Dec 1885	Berlin
GRISCHMANN	Hanne–Liese	F	07 Sep 1921	Hobg.Ost
GRISHMAN	Minna	F	18 Nov 1882	Hobg.Ost
GRNNBERGER	Margo	F		Beuthen, Germany
GROAY	Ernst	M	25 Feb 1899	Zabrze, Schlesien
GROBERG	Anna	F	20 Nov 1892	Hindenburg O.S.
GROFFIG	Hanka	F	03 Nov 1924	Glowaczow
GROSMAN	Wilhelm	M	30 Dec 1908	Hindenburg
GRUBERG	Helen	F	01 Sep 1925	Tomaszow, Poland
GRUENBERG	Kate	F		Hindenburg, Germany
GRUENBERGER	Dagobert	M	3 Sep 1877	Zabrze, Schlesien
GRUENWALD	Kurt	M		
GRUENWALD	Heinz	M	23 Dec 1909	Hindenburg
GRUENWALD	Max	M	10 Oct 1871	Hindenburg
GRUINBERGER	Lubow	M		
GRUNER	Ernst	M	25 Feb 1899	Hindenburg
GRUNER	Paul	M	29 Nov 1893	Hindenburg
GRUNER	Martha	F	01 Jul 1904	Hindenburg O.S.
GRUNWALD	Paul	M	29 Nov 1893	Hindenburg
GRUNWALD	Max	M	10 Oct 1871	Hindenburg
GRUNWALD	Alfons	M	19 Nov 1876	Zabrze, Schlesien
GRZESIK	Elaine Lenka	F		Hundsdorf, Czechoslovakia
GRZESIK	Elfriede	F	17 May 1912	Paulsdorf Ost
GUSDORF	Erich	M	24 Jun 1912	Paulsdorf Ost
GUTERMAN	Klara	F	25 Mar 1881	Hindenburg
GUTHAUER	Elfreda	F		Kattowitz, Germany
GUTTENTAG	Hans	M	28 May 1905	Hindenburg O.S.
GUTTMANN	Sophie	F	18 Nov 1865	Zabrze
GUTTMANN	Dagobert	M	31 Aug 1879	Zabrze, Schlesien
GUTTMANN	Heinz	M	22 May 1918	Bobrawnik
GUTTMANN	Julia	F	11 Apr 1889	Pilzendorf, Beuthen

GUTTMANN	Philipp	M	14 Sep 1883	Tarnowitz
GWOSILZ	Dagobert	M	31 Aug 1873	Hindenburg O.S.
HANDLER	Hedwig	F	08 Sep 1913	Hindenburg O.S.
HARTEL	Marie	F	4 Jan 1888	Hindenburg
HARTEL	Willy	M	07 Sep 1910	Hindenburg
HARTEL	Hedwig	F	21 Dec 1878	Waissak, Leobschatz
HABERMANN	Hermann	M	5 Nov 1879	Strayburg
HACHULA	Leiser	M	3 Jul 1879	Lecowka, Solina
HADASCHIK	Stanislaw	M	01 Jul 1920	Hindenburg O/S
HADROSSEK	Robert	M	03 Jun 1903	Hindenburg O.S.
HAENDLER	Heinrich	M	05 Jul 1903	Hindenburg O.S.
HAHLO	Eugen	M	1 Aug 1863	Hindenburg O. S.
HAHN	Anna	F	29 Jun 1863	Zabrze (Hindenburg O. S.)
HAHN	Jadwiga	F		
HAHN	Ilse	F	05 Nov 1925	Hindenburg
HAJOK	Olga	F	21 Sep 1895	Hindenburg
HAJOK	Johann	M	06 Mar 1907	Hindenburg
HALADYN	Franz	M	13 Sep 1894	Hindenburg
HALAMUDA	Georg	M	05 Apr 1900	Hindenburg O.S. (Biskupitz)
HALLE, VON	Magdalena	F	12 Jul 1914	Hindenburg O. S.
HALMAGYI	Meta	F	16 May 1892	Hindenburg O. S.
HAMBURGE	Veronica	F		
HAMBURGER	Hermann	M	6 Feb 1897	
HAMBURGER	Klaus	M	10 Feb 1920	Hindenburg
HAMBURGER	Jakob	M	12 Jan 1872	Cempen
HAMMER	Helene	F	26 Apr 1899	Katowice
HAMMER	Ferdinar	M	13 Oct 1879	Hindenburg O.S.
HAMMER	Else	F	26 Aug 1879	Knigshatte
HANKE	Heinrich	M	7 Jul 1867	Rogau, Ratibor
HANSLIK	Ruth	F	21 Sep 1921	Hindenburg O.S.
HARRIS	Martha	F	05 Mar 1905	Hindenburg
HARRIS	Binnie	F		Radom, Poland
HARTMANN	Binne	F	17 Dec 1929	Radom, Poland
HARTMANN	Kate	F	22 Nov 1896	Zabrze, Schlesien
HASELEY	Vera	F	22 Jan 1933	Hindenburg O. S.
HATESAUL	Hedwig	F	22 Feb 1899	Hindenburg O. S.
HAUSDORFF	Hedwig	F	13 Sep 1902	Hindenburg O.S.
HAUSDORFF	Henriette	F	17 Jul 1884	Kroschnitz, Groay Strehlitz
HAVBRO	Siegfried	M	14 Jan 1885	Zawodzin, Kattowitz
HAWERKAMP	Gerda	F	03 Mar 1921	Hindenburg
HAYMANN	Friedericke	F	21 Nov 1885	Lienen, Tschlenburg
HECHT	Emma	F	22 Nov 1858	Hindenburg O. S.–Biskupitz
HECHT	Georg	M	01 Mar 1904	Hindenburg
HECHT	Lina	F	27 Jan 1874	Hindenburg
HECHT	Paul	U	15 Dec 1870	Pless / O.S.
HECHT	Heinrich	M	01 Oct 1901	Kochlowitz, Kattowitz

HECHT	Ilse	F	02 May 1905	Kochlowitz, Kattowitz
HECHT	Josef	M	06 Jul 1928	Gleiwitz O.S.
HECHT	Kurt	M	8 May 1896	Gleiwitz O.S.
HECHT	Ludwig	M	11 Jan 1871	Kostow, Pleay
HECHT	Rosalie	F	16 Sep 1875	Kochlowitz, Kattowitz
HECHT	Alma	F	17 Dec 1889	
HECHT	Bianka	F	3 Jul 1898	Adelnau
HECHT	Else	F	09 Aug 1908	Gleiwitz
HECHT	Paul	M	15 Dec 1870	Pless /Polen
HECHT	Julie	F	27 Dec 1868	Hindenburg (Poremba)
HECKER	Selma	F	21 Apr 1886	Hindenburg O. S.
HECKER	Erna	F	25 Jul 1897	Wruschen
HECKER	Karl	M	16 Feb 1894	Orlau
HECKER	Erna	F	25 Jul 1897	Hruscha
HEIDUK	Karl	M	16 Feb 1894	Freystadt Belau
HEILBORN	Hildegard	F	13 May 1916	Hindenburg
HEILIG	Marie	F	19 Feb 1852	Groay Strehlitz
HEIMAN	Berta	F	18 Oct 1912	Hindenburg
HEIMANN	Arthur	M		
HEIMANN	Amalie	F	18 Dec 110	Hindenburg
HEIMANN	Elfriede	F	27 Feb 1922	Hindenburg
HEIMANN	Max	M	23 Jul 1890	Ostrow, Lublinitz
HEIMANN	Max	M	1 Feb 1880	Strzelbin, Lublinitz
HEIMANN	Paula	F	24 Jun 1894	Oppeln O.S.
HEIMANN	Paula	F	30 Jun 1885	Birkenau, Gleiwitz
HEIMANN	Charlotte	F	28 May 1863	Kalina
HEIMANN	Helene	F	20 Jul 1895	Laurahatte
HEIMANN	Jakob	M	20 Aug 1862	Beuthen O.S.
HEIMANN	Gitta	F	25 Dec 1933	Hindenburg
HEIMANN	Arthur	M	3 Sep 1887	Katowice
HEIMANN	Rosa	F	21 Oct 1913	Hindenburg O.S.
HEIMANN	Elfriede	F	27 Feb 1921	Hindenburg O.S.
HEIMANN	Ernst	M	26 Aug 1916	Hindenburg O.S.
HEINALT	Julius	M	26 Apr 1905	Hindenburg O.S.
HEINALT	Gerhard	M	11 Jan 1873	Hindenburg
HELIOS	Gehardt	M	11 Jan 1913	Hindenburg
HELIOS	Agnes	F	14 Jan 1897	Hindenburg
HELIOS	Aug	M	15 Aug 1894	Hindenburg
HELIOS	Christine	F	08 Feb 1922	Hindenburg
HELLMANN	Renate	F	26 Oct 1925	Hindenburg
HELLMANN	Marie	F	8 Nov 1888	Patichau, Gleiwitz
HELMRICH	Gustav	M	2 Dec 1881	Wansen, Ohlau
HENIKE	Josef	M	13 Nov 1893	Hindenburg
HERGESELL	Wilhelm	M	28 Jul 1904	Hindenburg
HERLITZ	Arthur	M	19 Sep 1880	Hindenburg
HERLITZ	Agnes	F	14 Apr 1877	Kochlowitz
HERMASCH	Oskar	M	24 Oct 1872	Glatz

HERMASCH	Johann	M	30 Jan 1920	Hindenburg
HERMASCH	Klara	F	06 Aug 1902	Hindenburg
HERRMANN	Anna	F	20 Aug 1881	Muldenau, Gleiwitz
HERRMANN	Amanda	F	12 Dec 1879	Zabrze
HERRMANN	Ernst	M	2 Feb 1895	Beuthen
HERRMANN	Hans–Ulrich	M	20 Jun 1931	Beuthen
HERRNSTADT	Ilse	F	14 Oct 1909	Witkowo, Gnesen
HERRNSTADT	Gregor	M	02 Oct 1928	Hindenburg
HERRNSTADT	Ingeborg	F	30 Mar 1932	Hindenburg
HERRNSTADT	Iolmar	M	13 Oct 1933	Hindenburg
HERRNSTADT	Karl	M	07 Feb 1930	Hindenburg
HERRNSTADT	Alice	F	20 Feb 1937	Hindenburg
HERRNSTADT	Brigitte	F	17 Dec 1931	Hindenburg
HERRNSTADT	Eberhard	M	24 Jan 1929	Hindenburg
HERRNSTADT	Elfriede	F	12 Jun 1910	Hindenburg
HERRNSTADT	Hans	M	08 Apr 1907	Breslau
HERRNSTADT	Margarete	F	13 Nov 1883	Zagorze, Bendzin
HERRNSTADT	Helene	F	09 May 1907	Katowice
HERRNSTADT	Ignacia	F	29 Jan 1929	Katowice
HERZBERG	Kurt	M	08 Feb 1906	Katowice
HERZBERG	Hanns	M	14 Apr 1919	Hindenburg
HERZBERG	Herman	M	07 Nov 1929	Hindenburg O.S.
HERZBERG	Josef	M	14 Jul 1879	Hindenburg
HERZBERG	Max	M	23 Mar 1875	Hindenburg O.S.
HERZBERG	Oskar	M	17 Mar 1879	Hindenburg
HERZBERG	Selma	F	20 May 1877	Hindenburg
HERZBERG	Salo	U	16 Feb 1864	Zabrze, Schlesien
HERZBERG	Paul	M	22 Mar 1874	Zabrze, Bielitz
HERZBERG	Salo	M	16 Feb 1864	Hindenburg
HERZBERG	Margar.	F	24 Nov 1886	Landsberg O.S.
HERZBERG	Marie	F	18 Nov 1895	Kunrow, Rybnik
HERZBERG	Werner	M	28 Oct 1921	Gleiwitz O.S.
HERZBERG	Bruno	M	4 Aug 1871	Hindenburg O.S.
HERZBERG	Leopold	M	19 Sep 1871	Hindenburg
HERZKA	Salo	M	16 Feb 1864	Hindenburg O.S.
HERZKA	Gertrud de	F		Czechoslovakia
HERZKA	Franz	M		Germany
HERZKO	Thea B.	F		Germany
HERZKO	Ismar	M	4 Nov 1893	Hindenburg O.S.
HERZKO	Rosa	F	26 Oct 1891	Hindenburg Ost O.S.
HERZKO	Rudi	M	27 Jun 1915	Hindenburg
HERZKO	Elfriede	F	5 Nov 1885	Kochlowitz, Kattowitz
HERZKO	Joseph	M	26 Dec 1881	Krassow, Pleay
HERZKO	Rosa	F	26 Nov 1877	Zirkwitz, Trebnitz
HERZKO	Salomon	M	9 Jan 1864	Birkenthal, Kattowitz
HEYMANN	Rudi	M	27 Jun 1915	Hindenburg O.S.
HEYMANN	Hildegard	F	16 Feb 1907	Hindenburg

HEYMANN	Cacilie	F	8 Aug 1878	Horneck, Gleiwitz
HEYMANN	Erwin	M	02 Jun 1912	Horneck, Gleiwitz
HEYMANN	Marie	F	6 Dec 1871	Kanigshatte
HEYMANN	Willi	M	10 Sep 1907	Horneck, Gleiwitz
HEYMANN	Bernd	M	25 Nov 1932	Hindenburg O.S.
HIMMELFARB	Hildegard	F	16 Feb 1907	Hindenburg O.S.
HIMMELFARB	Hannelore	F	03 Jan 1928	Hindenburg
HIMMELFARB	Kurt	M	17 Jul 1923	Hindenburg
HIMMELFARB	Margarete	F	14 Aug 1893	Beuthen O.S.
HIRCHKOWITZ	Max	M	24 Sep 1886	Katowice
HIRSCH	Helene	F	11 Jan 1876	Katowice
HIRSCHBERG	Elsa	F	18 Jun 1884	Woischnik, Lublinitz
HIRSCHBERG	Martha	F	19 May 1871	Hindenburg O.S.–
HIRSCHMANN	Martha	F	19 May 1877	Klein–Zabrze, Schlesien
HITELMAN–MERMELSTAJN	Ernestine	F	9 Feb 1867	Hindenburg O.S.
HOFFMANN	Sara Hadari	F	22 Mar 1924	Oboczno
HOFFMANN–BERGER	Emmy	F	3 Feb 1865	Hindenburg O.S.
HOFMAN	Emma	F	3 Feb 1865	Hindenburg
HOLCMAN	Helen	F		Radom, Poland
HOLECZEK	Edith	F	01 Dec 1918	Hindenburg
HOLLANDER	Stanislaus	M	02 Nov 1920	Hindenburg
HOLLON	Betty	F	2 Apr 1898	Ruda, Hindenburg
HOLZ	Pauline	F	7 Jul 1866	Solarnia, Ratibor
HONIGBAUM	Berta	F	28 Nov 1868	Zabrze
HONIGBAUM	Rosa	F	7 Oct 1874	Hindenburg
HONISCH	Rosa	F	7 Oct 1874	Hindenburg O.S.
HOPPE	Heinrich	M	02 Mar 1910	Hindenburg
HORN	Hildegard	F	17 Jul 1896	Hindenburg
HORN	Dinah	F		Radom, Poland
HORN	Maria	F	7 Oct 1893	Hindenburg O.S.
HORNIG	Dinah	F	06 Apr 1929	Radom (Kielce , Poland
IGNATZEK	Ida	F	02 May 1912	Troplowitz
IGNATZY	Maria	F	16 Dec 1919	Hindenburg O.S.
ISAAC	Paul	M	20 Mar 1899	Hindenburg
ISAAC	Lina	F	20 Jul 1868	Hindenburg
ISAAC	Marta	F	1 Jan 1875	Krotoschin
ISAAC	Sibilla	F	22 May 1910	Krotoschin
ISRAEL	Georg	M	21 Apr 1908	Krotoschin
ISRAEL	Dieter	M	18 Sep 1926	Hindenburg
ISRAEL	Edith	F	20 Feb 1893	Lipine
ITZKOWITZ	Hanns	M	24 Apr 1892	Ratibor
IVANKOWSKI	Lonia	F		Ciechanow, Poland
JACOBI	Rosa	F		Hindenburg, Germany
JACOBI	Heinz	M	08 Mar 1926	Hindenburg
JACOBI	Miryam	F	06 Jan 1929	Hindenburg
JACOBI	Ernst	M	10 Jan 1925	Oppeln

JACOBI	Gerhard	M	01 Oct 1922	Oppeln
JACOBI	Leo	M	21 Nov 1920	Beuthen
JACOBI	Rosa	F	3 Dec 1890	Nikolai, Pleay
JACOBI	Artur	M	19 Feb 1886	Krotoschin
JACOBOWITZ	Maria	F	15 Jul 1893	Hindenburg O.S.
JACOBOWITZ	Hildegard	F	4 Nov 1887	Klausdorf, Zabrze
JACOBOWITZ	Salo	M	17 Apr 1870	Hindenburg O.S. (Zabrze)
JACOBSOHN	Dorothea	F	28 Dec 1910	Hindenburg
JACOBSON	Margarethe	F	4 Jan 1877	Hindenburg O.S. (Zaborze)
JACOBY	Mania	F		Radom, Poland
JACOBY	Elfirede	F	14 Jul 1890	Hindenburg
JAKOB	Elfriede	F	14 Jul 1890	Hindenburg
JALOWIETZKI	Horst	M	27 Apr 1914	
JANETZKI	Paul	M	31 Dec 1913	Hindenburg O. S.
JANIK	Wilhelm	M	20 Mar 1909	Hindenburg
JANTA	Leopold	M	15 Nov 1900	Hindenburg O.S.
JANTA	Karl	M	28 May 1916	Hindenburg
JANTA	Emanuel	M	8 May 1886	Deutsch Krawarn, Ratibor
JANY	Maria	F	1 Mar 1884	Suaetz, Rybnik
JANY	Josef	M	13 Mar 1890	Hindenburg
JASCHEK	Wolfgang	M	28 Apr 1920	Landsberg, Rosenberg
JASCHIK	Siegesmund	M	06 Nov 1907	Hindenburg
JASCHIK	Edmund	M	11 Sep 1887	Blechowka, Tarnowitz
JASCHIK	Felizitas	F	24 Dec 1899	Wiesnitza, Schelletz
JASCHKOWITZ	Herbert	M	23 Feb 1920	Cosel
JASCHKOWITZ	Heinz	M	12 Aug 1913	Hindenburg O.S.
JASCHKOWITZ	Helene	F	15 May 1884	Bodland, Rosenberg
JASCHKOWITZ	Josef	M	28 Sep 1885	Brieg
JAUSLY	Ruth	F	22 Aug 1913	Beuthen O.S.
JAUSLY	Helene	F	21 Feb 1900	Glogau
JAWORSKI	Kurt	M	5 Dec 1890	Kanigshatte
JENSEN	Rafael	M	22 Mar 1902	Hindenburg
JENSEN	Albine	F	12 Dec 1876	Hindenburg O. S.
JOLLES	Hans	M	20 Sep 1870	Hindenburg O. S.
JOLLES	Fritz	M	4 Mar 1881	Breslau
JONIK	Gertrud	F	2 Mar 1899	Namslau
JOREK	Erwin	M	04 Feb 1908	Hindenburg OS.
JOSEPH	Max	M	02 Oct 1910	
JUCZIK	Diter	M	09 Jun 1931	Hindenburg
JULIUSBURGER	Heinrich	M	09 Feb 1909	Hindenburg
JULIUSBURGER	Else	F	31 Jan 1895	Pilzendorf, Tarnowitz
JULIUSBURGER	Ernst	M	29 Jan 193	Klausberg, Beuthen
JULIUSBURGER	Josef	M	25 Apr 1893	Geschowitz, Rybnik
JULIUSBURGER	Peter	M	24 Dec 1934	Klausberg, Beuthen
JULIUSBURGER	Rudi	M	16 Dec 1920	Klausberg, Beuthen
JULIUSBURGER	Siegfried	M	22 Nov 1929	Klausberg, Beuthen
JURETZKO	Johanna	F	22 Feb 1854	Hindenburg

JUROK	Hedwig	F	05 Mar 1910	Hindenburg O.S.
JUSCZIK	Georg	M	12 Jan 1898	Hindenburg O. S.
KAUFMAN	Heinrich	M	09 Feb 1919	Hindenburg
KANIGSFELD	Margalit	F	15 Dec 1927	Hindenburg
KANIGSFELD	Heinz	M	18 Apr 1938	Hindenburg
KANIGSFELD	Erwin	M	23 Nov 1902	Radzionkau, Tarnowitz
KARNER	Selma	F	26 Jul 1898	Schoppinitz, Kattowitz
KARNER	Alma	F	02 Oct 1922	Hindenburg O.S.
KARNER	Ernst	M	11 Jun 1914	Hindenburg O.S.
KARNER	Ilse	F	19 Mar 1924	Hindenburg O.S.
KARNER	Margarete	F	21 Jan 1916	Hindenburg O.S.
KARNER	Arthur	M	16 Mar 1881	Bisenz
KARNER	Olga	F	23 Jun 1885	Gading
KARNER	Franz–Josef	M	31 Oct 191 2	Hindenburg O.S.
KAATZ	Margarete	F	21 Jan 1916	Hindenburg O.S.
KAATZ	Alex	M	10 Sep 1898	Hindenburg
KAC	Paul	M	5 Jan 1870	Schwersenz
KACZMARCZYK	Rysia	F	04 Feb 1946	
KAHN	Marie	F	20 Jun 1894	Hindenburg O. S.
KAINTOCH	Elfriede	F	12 Mar 1889	Ruda, Zabrze
KAINTOCH	Johann	M	26 Jun 1891	Hindenburg
KAISER	Johann	M	26 Jun 1891	Hindenburg
KAISER	Walter	M	21 Jun 1900	Hindenburg
KAISER	Natalie	F	9 May 1893	Tarnowitz
KAISER	Wilhelm	M	30 Mar 1885	Woisepnik, Lublinitz
KAISER	Henriette	F	16 Jul 1847	Woisepnik, Lublinitz
KAISER	Ernst	M	11 Nov 1919	Hindenburg O. S.
KAISIG	Ernst	M	4 Jan 1896	Hindenburg
KALLMANN	Eduard	M	27 Mar 1902	Hindenburg
KALLMANN	Johanna Sara	F	27 Feb 1905	Hindenburg
KALLMANN	Erna	F	27 May 1908	
KALLMANN	Arnold	M	09 Jul 1904	Zawodzie
KALLMANN	Arthur	M	13 Apr 1912	Hindenburg O.S.
KALLMANN	Hana	F		Hindenburg, Poland
KALLMANN	Arnold	M	09 Jun 1904	Zawodzie, Kattowitz
KALMUS	Edita	F	07 Feb 1908	Rybnik, Rybnik
KALOK	Paula	F	29 Dec 1876	Hindenburg O.S.
KALOK	Alfred	M	20 Oct 1908	Kreuzburg O.S.
KALUS	Elisabeth	F	12 Nov 1914	Oppeln O.S.
KALUS	Bruno	M	25 Aug 1904	Hindenburg
KAMBACH	Regina	F	6 Jun 1876	Hindenburg–Ost
KAMM	Otto	M	22 Jul 1906	Hindenburg O.S.
KAMM	Dorothea	F	28 Nov 1906	Hindenburg
KAMM	Werner	M	10 Jan 1938	Hindenburg O.S.
KAMM	Hermann	M	26 May 1912	Beuthen O.S.
KAMM	Susanne	F	19 Nov 1936	Beuthen O.S.
KAMMLER	Ruth	F	15 Nov 1908	Katowice

KAMMLER	Erich	M	16 Jun 1898	Hindenburg
KAMMLER	Ernst	M	20 May 1906	Hindenburg
KAMMLER	Heinrich	M	12 May 1908	Hindenburg
KAMMLER	Max	M	26 Jul 1900	Hindenburg
KAMMLER	Otto	M	25 Jun 1904	Hindenburg
KANDZIOR	Agnes	F	17 Oct 1868	Ottmachau
KANDZIOR	Florian	M	4 May 1894	Hindenburg
KANDZIOR	Florian		4 May 1894	Hindenburg
KANDZIOR	Georg	M	11 Feb 1890	Hindenburg
KANERT	Georg	M	11 Feb 1890	Hindenburg
KANERT	Alois	M	7 Oct 1891	
KANERT	Alois	M	7 Oct 1891	Reinschdorf, Cosel
KANERT	Anna	F	20 Sep 1899	
KANERT	Irene	F	01 Apr 1923	Langlieben, Cosel
KANERT	Josef	M	07 Oct 1924	Langlieben, Cosel
KANERT	Ruth	F	24 Nov 1928	Frabeln, Neustadt
KARDISH	Anna	F	20 Sep 1899	Klein Nimsdorf, Cosel
KARDISH	Ewa	F		Radom, Poland
KARLINER	Eva	F	11 Apr 1905	Radom, Poland
KARLINER	Hildegardt	F	04 Nov 1901	Lonkau, Pleay
KARLINER	Max	M	8 Feb 1874	Tworog, Gleiwitz
KARLINER	Paula	F	31 Jan 1880	Tichau, Pleay
KARLINER	Margarete	F	17 Apr 1894	Paulsdorf, Hindenburg
KARUPKE	Margot	F	1 Aug 1897	Hindenburg O.S.
KARWOTH	Irma	F	28 Sep 1917	Ruda, Hindenburg
KARWOTH	Franz	M	26 Sep 1885	Hindenburg
KARY	Franz	M	26 Sep 1885	Hindenburg (Zaborze)
KARY	Otto	M	06 Jan 1921	Hindenburg O.S.
KARY	Kathe	F	02 Apr 1917	Hindenburg
KASCHEK	Marta	F	28 Mar 1884	Myslowice
KASSEL	Fridrich	M	03 Dec 1904	Hindenburg
KATZ	Fritz	M	16 May 1873	Katowice
KATZ	Hermann	M	13 Mar 1886	Hindenburg
KATZ	Ernst	M	6 Apr 1890	Hindenburg OS
KATZ	Erwin	M	10 Mar 1888	Hindenburg, Hindenburg
KATZ	Selma	F	22 Jul 1870	Hindenburg–Ost
KAUDERS	Leo	M	26 Nov 1870	Hindenburg O.S.
KAUDERS	Kathe	F	5 Oct 1898	Hindenburg
KAWELL	Kate	F	5 Oct 1898	Hindenburg O.S.
KAWOREK	Rosalie	F	13 Jul 1866	Alt Tarnowitz
KAYSER	Vinzent	M	01 Feb 1911	Hindenburg
KEINS	Ilse	F	9 Jul 1899	Hindenburg O.S.
KELLER	Rosalie	F	10 Oct 1874	Hindenburg O.S.
KELLER	Eberhard	M	01 Oct 1925	Hindenburg O.S.
KERMEL	–Joachim	M	25 Dec 1923	Hindenburg O.S.
KIEF	Emma	F	2 May 1888	Hindenburg O.S.
KIKSMANN	Maryla	F	07 Apr 1905	

KIKSMANN	Marie	F	4 Aug 1890	Kanigshatte
KILSTEIN	Max	M	15 Dec 1895	Schoppinitz
KIMMELMAN	Efraim	M	08 Apr 1905	Hindenburg
KIMMELMAN	Mira Mary	F		Zoppot, Poland
KINDEL	Mira	F	17 Sep 1923	Zoppot (Danz)
KINDEL	Alfred	M	13 Apr 1938	Hindenburg
KINDEL	Annemarie	F	02 Feb 1937 7	Hindenburg
KINDEL	Marie	F	01 May 1915	Pilchowitz, Gleiwitz
KIPKA	Viktor	M	02 Jul 1911	Dombrowka, Tost
KIRSCHNER	Karlheinz	M	09 Jan 1930	Granberg
KITTLER	Helene	F	18 Nov 1872	Hindenburg O.S.
KITZLER	Marta	F	21 Nov 1900	Oppeln
KITZLER	Emmi	F	18 Sep 1893	Hindenburg
KIWI	Bernhard	M	16 Aug 1929	Hindenburg
KLABISCH	Erna	F	27 May 1908	
KLAFLER	Albert	M	01 Sep 1908	Hindenburg O. S.
KLAKA	Helena	F	08 Apr 1946	
KLAKA	Alfons	M	28 Dec 1896	Hindenburg
KLECZKA	Alfons	M	28 Dec 1896	Hindenburg O.S.
KLEEMANN	Margaretha	U	21 Mar 1905	Hindenburg
KLEIN	Franz	M	7 Aug 1887	Hindenburg O. S.
KLEMANN	Doris	F	20 Mar 1915	Hindenburg
KLEMANN	Emil	U	6 Jan 1881	Zabrze
KLEMANN	Franz	M	16 Aug 1927	Hindenburg
KLENNER	Peter	M	03 Dec 1884	Hindenburg
KLENNER	Gertrud	F	19 Nov 1884	Hindenburg
KLENNER	Margarete	F	28 May 1908	Hindenburg
KLENNER	Theodor	M	8 Sep 1881	Hindenburg
KLOSKA	Ingeborg	F	07 Mar 1932	Oppeln
KLOSSEK	Julian	M	29 Dec 1905	Hindenburg
KLUGER	Emil	M	17 Jun 1911	Hindenburg
KLUGER	Hans	M	0 Jun 1923	Hindenburg
KLUGER	Fanny	F	23 Jan 1884	Deutsch Weichsel, Pleay
KNAPFLER	Samuel	M	14 Jul 1880	Myslowice
KNOBEL	Margarete	F	1 Jul 1871	Hindenburg O. S.
KNOCHE	Szoszana	F	12 Apr 1926	Krasnobrud
KNOCHE	Heinrich	M	16 Jun 1887	Hindenburg, Germany
KNOCHE	Minna	F	24 Jan 1861	Laziewik, Beuthen
KNOCZALLA	Heinrich	M	16 Jun 1887	Hindenburg
KNOSSALLA	Joseph	M	19 Mar 1908	Hindenburg O. S.
KOCH	Arnold	M	05 Aug 1902	Ruda Slaska (Ruda)
KOCH	Aug	M	12 May 1900	Hindenburg
KOCHMANN	Mathilde	F	17 Aug 1889	Hindenburg O. S.
KOCHMANN	Erich	M	7 Nov 1886	Hindenburg
KOCHMANN	Kate	F	16 Sep 1899	Hindenburg
KOCHMANN	Erich	M	7 Nov 1886	Hindenburg O.S.
KOCHMANN	Kaete	F	16 Sep 1899	Hindenburg O.S.

KOCHMANN	Gerda	F	17 Apr 1926	Berlin
KOCHMANN	Ida	F	3 Feb 1864	Katscher, Leobschatz
KOCHMANN	Jacob	M	28 Mar 1873	Karlsegengrube, Kattowitz
KOCZY	Julius	M	21 Jun 1854	Neudorf, Gleiwitz
KOCZY	Hulda	F		
KOCZY	Florian	M	5 May 1892	Zaborze O.S.
KOCZY	Hulda	F	3 May 1888	Zaborze O.S.
KOFLOWSKI	Johanna	F	16 Mar 1862	Wyrau, Pleay
KOHN	Alfred	M	08 Mar 1905	Hindenburg
KOHN	Leopold	M	7 May 1874	Hindenburg
KOLOCZEK	Ilse	F		Beuthen, Germany
KOLODZIEJ	Georg	M	13 Mar 1915	Hindenburg
KOLOTZEK	Herbert	M	04 Apr 1021	Borsigwerk, Hindenburg
KOLOTZEK	Johann	M	03 May 1900	Hindenburg
KOLTON	Elisabeth	F	06 May 1920	Hindenburg
KOMAREK	Max	M	3 Oct 1892	Hindenburg
KONIETZNY	Erich	M	26 Sep 1911	Hindenburg
KONIETZNY	Adelheid	F	25 May 1899	Hindenburg
KONIETZNY	Alfons	M	23 Oct 1895	Hindenburg
KONIK	Werner	M	13 May 1922	Hindenburg
KONSKY	Marie	F	21 May 1897	Neu Ruda
KOPIETZ	Alfred	M	26 Aug 1899	
KOPLOWITZ	Bernhard	M	05 Feb 1905	Hindenburg
KOPLOWITZ	Mina	F	15 Jul 1861	Potempa, Gleiwitz
KOPPER	Ruth	F	21 Apr 1907	Ratibor
KORN	Walter	M	28 Mar 1905	Bielitz, Poland
KORN	Bruno	M	02 Oct 1911	Hindenburg
KOSIOLLEK	Georg	M	02 Mar 1906	Hindenburg OS
KOSLOWSKY	Maria	F	1 Jul 1863	Ruda, Hindenburg
KOSLOWSKY	Hedwig	F	12 Mar 1885	Hindenburg
KOSTERLITZ	Adolf	M	15 Nov 1883	Altendorf, Friedek
KOSTERLITZ	Ida	F	24 Oct 1890	Krotoschin
KOSTERLITZ	Jakob	M	15 Dec 1891	Staude, Pleay
KOSTERLITZ	Walter	M	4 May 1896	Hindenburg
KOSTERLITZ	Olga	F	8 Nov 1865	Hindenburg
KOSTKA	Ernst	M	27 Jun 1894	Hindenburg O.S.
KOTALA	Marie	F	3 Oct 1878	Jaratschewo, Jarotschin
KOTT	Eduard	M	5 Sep 1893	Hindenburg
KOTZOT	Barbara	F	3 Dec 1896	Hindenburg
KOTZOT	Richard	M	15 Sep 1902	Hindenburg
KOTZUR	Alois	F	01 Apr 1904	Hindenburg
KOWALIK	Walpurgis	F	07 Oct 1901	Hindenburg
KOZIAL	Anton	M	31 Mar 1891	Hindenburg
KOZIAL	Franziska	F	09 Feb 1902	Hindenburg
KOZIAL	Jochanna	F	29 Sep 1936	Hindenburg
KOZUBIK	Josef	M	28 Feb 1909	Hindenburg
KRAKAUER	Adelheid	F	28 Dec 1917	Hindenburg Nord Ost

KRAKAUER	Erich	M	19 Dec 1887	Zabrze, Schlesien
KRAKAUER	Emma	F	29 Oct 1878	Pleay
KRAKAUER	Erich	M	19 Dec 1887	Hindenburg O.S.
KRAKOWIAK	Herbert	M	3 Dec 1894	Hindenburg O.S.
KRAMARCZYK	Erna	F	13 Feb 1883	Wangerin
KRAMARCZYK	Hubert	M	8 Dec 1899	Hindenburg O.S.
KRAMARCZYK	Lothar	M	18 Sep 1929	Hindenburg O.S.
KRASNOBORSKA	Anna	F	23 Feb 1901	Soanitza, Gleiwitz
KRAUS	Dina	F	20 Dec 1924	Wysokie Mazowiezki
KRAUS	Mirjam	F	10 Oct 1913	Hindenburg, Germany
KRAUSE	Else	F		Hindenburg O.S.
KRAUSE	Rochus	M	05 Sep 1927	Hindenburg O.S.
KRAUSE	Eva	F		Radom, Poland
KRAWIETZ	Eva	F	20 Aug 1925	Radom, Poland
KRAWIETZ	Aug	M	23 Aug 1886	Hindenburg
KREBS	Wilhelm	M	14 Mar 1905	Hindenburg
KREBS	Rudolf	M	08 Nov 1907	Hindenburg
KREBS	Heinz	M	16 Apr 1922	Hindenburg
KREBS	Max	M	8 Jan 1898	Hindenburg
KREBS	Harry	M	17 Jul 1895	Hindenburg O.S.
KREBS	Ruth	F	19 Jun 1920	Hindenburg O.S.
KREBS	Ludwig	M	18 Jan 1888	Zabrze, Schlesien
KREBS	Harry	M	17 Jul 1895	Hindenburg
KREBS	Ludwig	U	18 Jan 1888	Hindenburg
KREBS	Harry	U	17 Jul 1895	Hindenburg
KREBS	Alice	F	31 Oct 1922	Hindenburg Ost
KREBS	Georg	M	17 Dec 1877	Hindenburg Ost
KREBS	Ludwig	M	18 Jan 1888	Hindenburg O.S.
KREBS	Selma	F	6 Oct 1888	Orzech, Tarnowitz
KREBS	Heinz	M	01 Apr 1922	Hindenburg
KREBS	Leopold	M	6 Dec 1858	Hindenburg O.S.
KREIAYIG	Paul	M	22 Dec 1879	Hindenburg O.S.
KRETSCHMANN	Elisabet	F	13 Sep 1879	Hindenburg O.S.
KROLL	Johanna	F	6 Jul 1870	Kaningshatte
KROMM	Josef	M	04 Aug 1912	Hindenburg
KROMM	Emma	F	3 Oct 1879	Eintrachthatte
KROMPET	Johanna	M	09 Nov 1905	Hindenburg O.S.
KRUMSCHMIDT	Erich	M	25 Jul 1913	Hindenburg
KRUPPA	Elisabeth	F	10 Feb 1906	Kanigshatte
KSIENZIK	Richard	M	22 Feb 1933	Hindenburg
KUBANEK	Heinrich	M	01 Jun 1913	Hindenburg O.S.
KUBANEK	Theophil	M	22 Feb 1904	Hindenburg
KUCHTA	Edmund	M	14 Oct 1900	Hindenburg
KUETTNER	Maria	F	15 Apr 1892	Hindenburg
KUHN	Walter	M	27 Oct 1901	Hindenburg
KUHN	Victor	M	11 Aug 1859	Zabrze
KUPFERBERG	Magdalene	F	09 Feb 1905	Hindenburg

KUPIETZ	Georg	M	11 Sep 1903	Hindenburg
KUPITZ	Heinrich	M	18 Jul 1897	Hindenburg
KURKA	Franz	M	29 Dec 1890	Hindenburg
KURKA	Theodor	M	31 Oct 1883	Hindenburg/Zaborze
KUTTERER	Theodor	M	31 Oct 1883	Hindenburg OS
KUTTNER	Rosa	F	29 Dec 1873	Konstadt, Kreuzburg
KWASCHNIK	Alfred	M	26 Aug 1899	
KWOCZALLA	Alois	F	16 May 1908	Hindenburg O.S.
KWORZALLA	Klara	F	05 Jun 1905	Hindenburg O. S.
KWOZALLA	Helene	F	14 Jul 1906	Hindenburg O. S.
KYTZLER	Erich	M	16 Apr 1902	Hindenburg O. S.
KYTZLER	Bernhard	M	16 Aug 1929	Hindenburg O.S.
KYTZLER	Emmi	F	18 Sep 1893	Hindenburg O.S.
KYTZLER	Josef	M	12 Apr 1894	Lonschnik, Neustadt
LARMER	Emma	F	18 Sep 1893	Hindenburg o/s
LARMER	Schapsa	F	3 Nov 1895	Hindenburg
LARMER	Anna	F	11 Apr 1900	Hindenburg
LAWENSTAMM	Rosa	F	10 Oct 1926	Hindenburg
LAWENSTAMM	Lotte	F	31 Aug 1918	Hindenburg
LAWENSTAMM	Hedwig	F	30 Sep 1893	Ruda
LABAND	Hermann	M	22 Apr 1891	Friedrichswille, Tarnowitz
LACH	Hedwig	F	31 Dec 1876	Zabrze
LACHMANN	Georg	M	23 Apr 1913	Hindenburg O.S.
LACHMANN	Ilse	F	02 Oct 1931	Hindenburg O.S
LACHMANN	Ayga	F	05 Jul 1901	Zarki
LAIBMAN	Wilhelm	M	02 Feb 1900	Radzionkau
LANDAU	Broniah	F	03 Apr 1905	Warsaw, Poland
LANDAU	Nat	M		Hindenburg, Germany
LANDNER	Kaete	F	12 Apr 1896	Hindenburg
LANDSBERG	Paula	F		Siemianowice , Kattowitz
LANDSBERGER	Ludwig	M	14 Nov 1893	Hindenburg
LANGE	Alfred	M	01 May 1914	Hindenburg
LANGE	Max	M	20 Oct 1885	Hindenburg
LANGE	Martin	M	1 Jun 1873	Ruda, Zabrze
LANGE	Max	M	20 Oct 1885	Hindenburg
LANGE	Ingeborg	F	20 Dec 1934	Hindenburg O.S.
LANGER	Ursula	F	15 May 1932	Hindenburg O.S.
LANTZEK	Adolf	M	18 Mar 1858	Brannitz, Tarnowitz
LARISCH	Anna	F	28 Nov 1895	Konradan, Groay Wartenb
LARISCH	Magda	F	8 Aug 1899	Hindenburg
LARISCH	Ursula	F	17 May 1929	Hindenburg
LARISCH	Johanna	F	24 Sep 1904	Hindenburg O.S.
LARISCH	Magda	F	8 Aug 1899	Hindenburg O.S.
LARISCH	Elisabeth	F	26 Sep 1896	Frauendorf, Oppeln
LARMER	Max	M	18 Aug 1892	Warschowitz, Pleay
LARMER	Anna	F	11 Apr 1900	
LARMER	Rosa	F	10 Oct 1926	

LASSONCZYK	Schapsn	F	11 Mar 1895	
LATOCHA	Franz	M	31 Mar 1905	Hindenburg
LAUDON	Alois	M	07 May 1902	Hindenburg
LAUE	Johanan	M	30 Jun 1915	Hindenburg Near Berlin
LAUER	Kurt	M	19 Feb 1883	Hindenburg O.S.
LAUTERBACH	Betty	F	01 Mar 1925	Hindenburg
LEDERER	Alma	F	24 Feb 1895	Hindenburg
LEFKOWITZ	Berta	F	30 Apr 1880	Hindenburg O.S.
LEIFER	Hannah	F		Jedlnia, Poland
LEIPZIGER	Ernestine	F	21 Jun 1893	
LEIPZIGER	Margarete	F	9 Jun 1875	Zaborze, Zabrze
LENTSCHATZ	Alfred	M	21 Feb 1903	Hindenburg O.S.
LENZA	Martin	M	23 Feb 1877	Kanigshatte
LERCH	Alois	F	09 Jun 1910	Hindenburg
LERMAN	Erich	M	9 Oct 1898	Hindenburg
LESCHCZINER	Paula	F	07 Mar 1920	Bialobrzegi
LESCHCZINER	Ernst	M	06 Mar 1905	Hindenburg
LESCHIK	Ernst	M	30 Sep 1892	Hindenburg
LESCHNITZER	Georg	M	15 Aug 1901	Hindenburg
LESCHNITZER	Herman	M	6 Oct 1875	Hindenburg
LESCHNITZER	Hugo	M	12 Jul 1879	Hindenburg
LESCHNITZER	Dagobert	M	12 Jul 1879	Hindenburg O.S.
LESCHZINER	Richard	M	4 Jul 1877	Hindenburg O.S.
LESCHZINER	Hedwig	F	22 May 1874	Kosten
LESCHZINER	Max	M	10 May 1875	Kanigshatte
LESZCZYNSKA	Artur	M	3 Jun 1881	Hindenburg
LESZCZINSKI	Hinda	F	15 Jun 1918	Lodz
LEVIN	Josef	M	17 Nov 1896	Hindenburg
LEVY	Ernestine	F	08 May 1901	
LEVY	Johanna	F	26 Aug 1856	Zabrze
LEWIN	Handel	F	26 Aug 1856	Hindenburg O.S.
LEWIN	Gerhard	M	31 Oct 1907	Hindenburg
LEWIN	Elfriede	F	28 Jan 1909	Hindenburg
LEWIN	Vally	F	10 Sep 1885	Hindenburg
LEWIN	Fritz	M	29 Nov 1911	Hindenburg
LEWIN	Fritz	M	29 Sep 1911 1	Hindenburg
LEWIN	Else	F	17 Jan 1884	Zabrze
LIAY	Ruth	F	21 Mar 1905	Ruda near Hindenb
LICHTENSTEIN	Magdalene	F	23 May 1920	Hindenburg O. S.
LIEBERMANN	Rita	F	01 Oct 1918	Tomaszow
LIEBERMANN	Ernestine	F	21 Jun 1893	
LIEBICH	Ernestine	F	21 Jun 1893	Kanigshatte
LIGENDZA	Helene	F	29 Sep 1864	Ruda, Hindenburg
LIHS	Roman	M	4 Aug 1891	Hindenburg
LINDSTEDT	Paul	M	12 Oct 1909	Hindenburg OS
LINZER	Gerhard	M	10 Sep 1921	Hindenburg
LISUK	Angela	F	16 Jan 1911	Hindenburg O.S.

LIUBCHENKO	Iwan	M	24 Mar 1905	
LIWO	Mikhail	M	01 Jan 1904	Snezhkovk
LOEBEL	Paul	M	25 Jun 1896	Ruda /Hindenburg
LOEBL	Elly	M	17–× ×¤×¨–15	Hindenburg
LOEBMANN	Hermine	F	10 Jan 1888	Mostras
LOEBMANN	Rudolfine	F	8 Sep 1881	Hindenburg
LOEWENSTEIN	Elisabeth	F	06 Jan 1911	Ruda Slas Hindenburg
LOEWY	Kate	F	16 Mar 1907	Hindenburg O. S.
LOEWY	Louise	F	22 Apr 1882	Hindenburg
LOMNITZER	Martha	F	13 Sep 1886	Hindenburg
LOMNITZER	Gertrud	F	12 Jun 1872	Hindenburg (Alt–Zabrze)
LOMNITZER	Margarete	F	17 Dec 1882	Hindenburg O. S.
LONDNER	Gertrud	F	12 Jun 1872	Hindenburg
LOOCK	Waldemar	M	15 Sep 1914	Hindenburg O. S.
LOOCK	Elfriede	F	30 May 1914	Hindenburg O.S.
LOOCK	Horst	M	08 Jan 1939	Hindenburg O.S.
LOOCK	Ingeborg	F	05 May 1933	Hindenburg O.S.
LORENTZ	Erwin	M	28 Feb 1905	Lichterfelde, Teltow
LORENTZ	Friedrich	M	12 Mar 1889	Gummersberg
LOTH	Gertrud	F	6 Feb 1887	Berlin
LUDWIG	Franz	M	3 Sep 1890	Hindenburg
LUDWIG	Georg	M	09 Apr 1914	Kanigshatte
LUNDNER	Barbara	F		Ujpest, Hungary
LUSTIG	Marie	F		Germany, Hindenburg
LUSTIG	Max	M	22 Oct 1882	Kanigshatte
LUSTIG	Manfred	M	05 Aug 1910	Pleay
LYNN	Max	M	22 Oct 1882	Kanigshatte
MABUS	Marsha	F		Bialystok, Poland
MACKE	Hedwig	F	15 Oct 1906	Hindenburg O. S.
MACKE	Elisabeth	F	26 Apr 1894	Zaborze
MANZER	Wilhelm	M	27 Jan 1889	Zaborze
MANZER	Benno	M	18 Sep 1866	Hindenburg O. S. (Zabrze)
MANZER	Kurt	M	27 Jul 1887	Hindenburg O.S.,
MACZIEJCZYK	Max	M	9 Dec 1859	Peiskretschau, Gleiwitz
MADETZKI	Anton	M	10 Dec 1903	Sosnitza, Hindenburg
MAGARAM	Franz	M	5 Apr 1865	Ruda Slaska, Zabrze
MAGEN	Frances	F		Suchedniow, Poland
MAGIERA	Gideon	M	16 Nov 1890	Hindenburg
MAINKA	Gabriele	F	31 Jan 1901	Hindenburg O. S.
MAINKA	Alfred	M	12 Aug 1914	Hindenburg
MAINKA	Silvester	M	29 Dec 1885	Hindenburg O.S.
MAINNSCH	Viktor	M	17 Oct 1893	Hindenburg
MAINNSCH	Viktor	M	27 Jul 1882	Hindenburg O.S.
MAIZNER	Ida	F	29 Aug 1889	Jargerndorf
MAJOWSKI	Lili	F	30 Oct 1921	Lodz, Poland
MALACHOWSKI	Roman	M	02 Aug 1908	Hindenburg
MALACHOWSKI	Erich	M	18 Dec 1899	Hindenburg

MALCHAREK	Erich	M	18 Dec 1899	Hindenburg
MALCHEREK	Edmund	M	27 Oct 1884	Hindenburg
MAMLOK	Edmund	M	27 Oct 1884	Hindenburg
MAMLOK	Meta	F	11 Jun 1875	Kanigshatte
MANASSE	Erwin	M	09 Feb 1903	Kanigsberg
MANDOWSKI	Arthur	M	20 Mar 1880	Breslau
MANDOWSKI	Paul	M	12 May 1886	Hindenburg
MANDOWSKI	Helene	F	4 Jun 1878	Hindenburg
MANDOWSKY	Kurt	M	14 Nov 1877	Hindenburg
MANDOWSKY	Kathe	F	31 Dec 1884	Hindenburg
MANTEL	Marta	F	25 Nov 1883	Hindenburg
MAREK	Vincenz	M	19 Jan 1878	Santwiesen
MARGULIS	Wilhelm	M	14 May 1920	Hindenburg
MARGULIS	Jozef	M	24 Apr 1946	
MARKUS	Roza	F	07 Sep 1924	Katowice, Poland
MASUREK	Walter	M	16 Nov 1911	Hindenburg/s
MATHEJA	Johanna	F	18 Aug 1893	Hindenburg
MATHEJA	Paul	M	13 Jun 1896	Hindenburg
MATHEJA	Erich	M	15 Nov 1933	Hindenburg O.S.
MATHEJA	Gunter	M	22 Dec 1935	Hindenburg O.S.
MATHEJA	Mathilde	F	07 Aug 1911	Hindenburg O.S.
MATYSEK	Georg	M	02 Nov 1911	Schlesiengrube Ost
MATYSEK	Franz	M	3 May 1896	Hindenburg
MAUS	Franz	M	3 May 1896	Hindenburg
MAUS	Gertrud	F	31 Dec 1882	Glogau
MAY	Karl	M	26 Jun 1893	Katowice
MAY	Alfred	M	7 Aug 1899	Zabrze–Hindenburg
MAY	Alfred	M	7 Aug 1899	Hindenburg Schlesien
MAY	Edith	F	28 Sep 1900	Hindenburg
MEDNER	Jeanette	F	11 Feb 1886	Petersdorf, Gleiwitz
MEIDNER	Wilhelm	M	20 Jan 1892	Zabrze–Hindenburg
MEIDNER	Rosa	F	12 Jan 1886	Zabrze, Schlesien
MEISE	Rosa	F	12 Jan 1886	Hindenburg
MEISNER	Meta	F	12 Mar 1908	Hindenburg O.S.
MEKLER	Harriet	F		Hindenburg, Germany
MELLER	Paula Ester	F		Radom, Poland
MELSON	Editha	F	22 Nov 1887	Hindenburg O.S.
MENDE	Gertrud	M	30 Jul 1920	Hindenburg
MENDEL	Heinz	M	24 Sep 1926	Hindenburg
MENDELSOHN	Frieda	F	8 Jul 1868	Hindenburg O.S.
MENKES	Dorothea	F	5 Mar 1860	Hindenburg
MERMERSZTAJN	Bertha	F	15 Jun 1917	Hindenburg
MESSOW	Natka	F	22 Mar 1923	Radom
MESSOW	Elfriede	F	12 Dec 1872	Zabrze
MESSOW	Elfriede	F	12 Dec 1872	Zabrze, Schlesien
METTBACH–STEINBACH	Elfriede	F	12 Dec 1872	Hindenburg O.S.
MEYER	Anne	F	17 Oct 1904	Hindenburg

MEYER	Charlotte	F	06 Mar 1905	Hindenburg
MEYER	Valli	F	7 Jan 1869	Hindenburg
MEYER	Walli	F	7 Jan 1869	Hindenburg O.S.
MEYER	Paula	F		Radom, Poland
MICHAELIS	Rose	F		Kielce, Poland
MICHAELIS	Fritz	M	11 Oct 1899	Hindenburg
MICHAELIS	Margarete	F	13 Oct 1871	Hindenburg
MICHALSKI	Julius	M	26 Jul 1866	Koschmin
MICHALSKI	Franz	M	31 Dec 1877	Ratiborhammer, Ratibor
MICHALSKI	Hedwig	F	23 Sep 1882	Kanigshatte
MICHALSKI	Paul	M	13 Sep 1894	Bolko, Oppeln
MICHALSKI	Emilie	F	26 Aug 1889	Hindenburg
MICHALSKI	Dagmar	F	18 May 1925	Katowice
MICHEL	Herta	F	29 Dec 1895	Katowice
MICHELSOHN	Lucia	F	24 Jun 1914	Hindenburg
MICHELSOHN	Marie	F	14 Dec 1881	
MILGROM	Charl.	F	22 May 1869	Hindenburg O.S.
MING	Esther	F	16 Dec 194	Radom (Kielce) Poland
MISCHOK	Helene	F	3 Aug 1890	Hindenburg O. S.
MBICH	Max	M	23 Oct 1912	Hindenburg O.S.
MNICH	Robert	M	6 Jun 1888	Hindenburg
MOELLER	Robert	M	6 Jun 1888	Hindenburg
MOHNKE	Gary	M		Hindenburg, Germany
MOHRHARDT	Gertrud	F	17 Mar 1905	Hindenburg
MOHRHARDT	Leo	M	8 Apr 1883	Hindenburg
MONDSCHEIN	Leo	M	8 Apr 1893	Hindenburg
MORGALLA	Renia	F		Kelce, Poland
MORGENSTERN	Karl	M	28 Sep 1903	Hindenburg O.S.
MORGENSTERN	Lothar Martin	M	25 Mar 1914	Hindenburg
MORGENSTERN	Samuel	M	7 Aug 1884	Hindenburg
MORGENSTERN	Nathan	M	4 May 1886	Hindenburg O.S.
MORGENSTERN	Eduard	M	17 Apr 1880	Hindenburg
MORGENSTERN	Hulda	F	19 Feb 1882	Nikolai
MORGENSTERN	Bronislawa	F		Aurelow, Poland
MORGENSZTERN	Branca	F	11 Mar 1918	Aurelow, Poland
MORON	Lajzer	M	25 Oct 190 8	Plock
MORZISCHEK	Paul	M	1 Jun 1884	Bielschowitz
MOSES	Stanislaus	M	24 Sep 1895	Hindenburg
MOTTEK	Herta	F	04 Mar 1901	Zabrze
MROSEK	Luise	F	10 Sep 1876	Hindenburg O.S.
MROSS	Friedrich	M	1907peS 82	Hindenburg O.S.
MROZEK	Gertrud	F	07 Mar 1905	Hindenburg
MROZEK	Ingeburg	F	15 Apr 1935	Hindenburg
MUENSTER	Oskar	M	01 Jun 1935	Hindenburg
MUENSTER	Max	M	28 Nov 1888	Zabrze
MUENZER	Max Mendel	M	28 Nov 1888	Zabrze
MUNZER	Kurt	M	27 Jul 1887	Hindenburg

MUSCHALSKI	Werner	M		Berlin, Germany
MUSCHIALIK	Ernst	M	31 Oct 1897	Hindenburg
MYSLOWITZER	Hilde	F	05 Aug 1923	Hindenburg O.S.
NADZIK	Berta	F	25 Dec 1877	Hindenburg O.S.
NAJDEN	Kajeta	F		
NANADZIK	Bejla Rachel	F	22 Oct 1921	Hindenburg (Germany)
NANZIG	Kajeta	F		
NAPHTALI	KÃƒÂ¤the	F	08 Nov 1906	Hindenburg O.S.
NATHANSOHN	Jettel	F	25 Mar 1863	Hindenburg O. S.
NEBEL	Paula Sarah	F	8 Feb 1894	Hindenburg
NEBEL	Rosa	F	24 Sep 1885	Zabrze
NEBEL	Else	F	08 Nov 1906	Zabrze
NEBEL	Rudolf	M	06 Jan 1923	Hindenburg
NEBEL	Erwin	M	19 Nov 1912	Hindenburg
NEBEL	Herbert	M	19 Mar 1908	Hindenburg
NEBEL	Hans	M	02 Sep 1915	Hindenburg
NEBEL	Marie	F	14 Dec 1881	
NEBEL	Salo	M	28 Mar 1876	Hindenburg Ost
NEBEL	Kurt	M	25 Sep 1906	Zabrze, Schlesien
NEBEL	Rudolf	M	06 Jan 1923	Biskupitz, Hindenburg O.S.
NEBEL	Luise	F	26 Mar 1888	Groay Strehlitz
NEBEL	Nathan	M	27 Jan 1869	Waldhof, Tarnowitz
NEBEL	Rosa	F	13 Sep 1871	Fannygrube, Kattowitz
NEBEL	Eva	F	18 May 1878	Golassowitz, Pleay
NEBEL	Fritz	M	13 May 1883	Brzezinka
NEBEL	Heinrich	M	10 Oct 1878	Dombrowa, Beuthen
NEBEL	Hans	M	25 Sep 1915	Hindenburg O. S.
NEBEL	Alexander	M	23 Feb 1941	Beuthe, Germany
NEBEL	Kurt	M	25 Sep 1907	Hindenburg O.S.
NEBENZAHL	Heinrich	M	15 Nov 1905	
	Helene	F	24 Feb 1896	Hindenburg
NEHAB	Helene	F	24 Feb 1896	Hindenburg O.S.
NEHAB	Frieda	F	15 Mar 1891	Zabrze, Schlesien
NEHAB	Frieda	F	15 Mar 1881	Hindenburg
NEIGEBAUER	Frieda	F	15 Mar 1891	Hindenburg O.S.
NEISSER	Josef	M	19 Mar 1874	Josefsdorf, Kattowitz
NEUGEBAUER	Karl	M	24 Feb 1903	Hindenburg
NEUGEBAUER	Franziska	F	19 Apr 1873	Hindenburg
NEUMANN	Irmgard	F	26 Feb 1920	Katowic
NEUMANN	Hedwig	F	13 Nov 1872	Hindenburg
NEUMANN	Laura	F	22 Dec 1886	Sossnitza, Hindenburg
NEUMANN	Ruth	F	28 Aug 1937	Hindenburg O.S.
NEUMANN	Gunther	M	12 Jun 1929	Hindenburg O.S.
NEUMANN	Theophil	M	27 Dec 1883	Podgradowitz
NEUMANN	Else	F	10 Jul 1922	Kanigshatte
NEUMANN	Johanna	F	02 Aug 1911	Glogau
NEUMANN	Julius	M	14 Mar 1889	M. Gestrau

NEUMANN	Margarete	F	27 Jul 1924	Kanigshatte
NEUMANN	Olga	F	1 Apr 1898	Schoppinitz
NEUMANN	Gerda	F		Kanigshatte
NEUMANN	Klara	F	01 Aug 1903	Hindenburg O.S.
NEUMARK	Margot	F	28 Sep 1890	Hindenburg O.S.
NEWRZELLA	Ida	F	7 Jul 1872	Hindenburg O.S.
NEWRZELLA	Hans	M	05 Feb 1923	Hindenburg
NICOLAITZIK	Hedwig	F	9 Feb 1897	Hindenburg
NIEDZIELLA	Eduard	M	03 Jan 1905	Hindenburg
NIERLICH	Johann	M	20 Nov 1918	Hindenburg Ost.
NIEROBA	Max	M	10 Jun 1909	Hindenburg O.S.
NIEROBISCH	Heinrich	M	06 Jun 1913	Hindenburg
NIEROBISZ	Paul	M	26 May 1867	Hindenburg
NIERYCHLO	Paul	M	26 May 1867	Hindenburg O.S.
NIESTROJ	Rudolf	M	23 Jun 1930	Hindenburg
NIESTROJ	Flora	F	5 Jun 1880	Tarnowitz
NIKLAS	Constantin	M	3 May 1876	S.A.Annaberg, Groay
NISSENBAUM	Kurt	M	27 Oct 1905	Schwieben O.S., Gleiwitz
NISSENHOLZ	Lucy	F		Sandomierz, Poland
NISSENHOLZ	Bernhard	M	8 Jul 1881	Oppeln O.S.
NOACK	Sali	F	4 Feb 1885	Osviecian
NOLEPPA	Ruth	F	26 Dec 1891	Hindenburg O.S.
NORD	Heinrich	M	18 Jan 1893	Hindenburg O. S.
NORMAN	Dorothea	F		Warsaw, Poland
NOTHMANN	Yokheved	F	06 May 1926	Radom , Poland
NOTHMANN	Kurt	M	09 Jun 1918	Hindenburg
NOTHMANN	Jeny	F	17 Mar 1870	Dembowa Gora, Lublinitz
NOTHMANN	Ella	F	25 Oct 1876	Hindenburg O.S.
NOTHMANN	Kurt	M	23 Jan 1918	Hindenburg O.S.
NOWAK	Salomon	M	29 Nov 1876	Hindenburg O.S.
NOWARKA	Georg	M	13 Feb 1913	Hindenburg
NOWARKA	Paul	M	6 Jan 1884	Hindenburg
NOWARRA	Longiuus	M	15 Mar 1888	Hindenburg
OBERLANDER	Blima	F		Hindenburg, Germany
OCHMANN	Cacilie	F	12 Jul 1863	Bujakow, Zabrze
OCHMANN	Elisabeth	F	15 Jan 1919	Hindenburg O.S.
OFFOZARCZYK	Alfred	M	28 Feb 1885	Hindenburg O.S.
OFFOZARCZYK	Erwin	M	13 Jan 1897	Hindenburg O.S.
OFFOZARCZYK	Gerta	F	31 May 1928	Hindenburg O.S.
OFFOZARCZYK	Rosa	F	15 Feb 1902	Hindenburg O.S.
OLESCH	Werner	M	08 Sep 1905	Hindenburg O.S.
OPIELA	Wilhelm	M	23 Mar 1905	Hindenburg
OPIELKA	Franz	M	22 Oct 1900	Hindenburg
ORDON	Alfred	M	01 Apr 1904	Hindenburg
ORDON	Theodor	M	6 Nov 1886	Hindenburg
ORLIK	Theodor	M	6 Nov 1886	Hindenburg
ORYMEK	Helene	F	27 Aug 1895	Warschau

ORZECHOWSKI	Dorothea	F	13 Mar 1922	Hindenburg
ORZECHOWSKI	Herbert	M	03 Feb 1936	Hindenburg
ORZECHOWSKI	Albert	M	13 Aug 1906	Roayberg, Beuthen
OTTE	Helene	F	0 Aug 1908	Blumenthal, Hannover
PACH	Johann	M	12 Sep 1885	Pilsendorf
PAKULSKA	Viktor	M	12 Feb 1899	Hindenburg
PAPRZYSKI	Bronislawa	F	01 Jan 1946	
PAUTSCH	Hedwig	F	25 Sep 1895	Vilkowo
PAWELLEK	Jutta	F	20 Jun 1932	Hindenburg
PAWLENKA	Annemarie	F	14 May 1917	Hindenburg
PAWLENKA	Hedwig	F	22 Sep 1889	Tarnowitz
PAWLENKA	Johann	M	7 Feb 1888	Schillersdorf, Ratibor
PAWLINKA	Johanna	F	29 Feb 1920	Schoppinitz
PAWLITZEK	Bernhard	M	20 May 1907	Hindenburg
PEGA	Wilhelm	M	20 Jun 1906	Hindenburg O.S.
PEGA	Dietrich	M	19 Aug 1926	Hindenburg
PEGA	Erika	F	22 Oct 1924	Hindenburg
PEGA	Ingeborg	F	28 Jul 1928	Hindenburg
PEGA	Else	F	10 Nov 1902	Rathenow
PEREPELITSA	Fritz	M	29 Jun 1890	Peterschatz, Groay
PERES	Dmitrii	M		Mikhailovka
PERES	Armin	M	09 Jul 1926	Hindenburg
PERL	Ursula	F	13 Sep 1927	Hindenburg
PERL	Steffi	F	21 Dec 1931	Hindenburg
PESE	Rosalie	F	18 Oct 1864	Hindenburg O.S.
PESE	Natalie	F	10 Apr 1865	Zabrze, Schlesien
PETERMANN	Natalie	F	10 Apr 1865	Hindenburg
PETZAL	Robert	M	05 May 1909	Hindenburg
PFIFFERLING	Kurt	M	11 Jun 1888	Hindenburg O.S
PFIFFERLING	Else	F	30 Mar 1900	Hindenburg O.S.
PFINGST	Anna	F	4 Jun 1884	Hindenburg O.S.
PHILIPP	Else	F	15 Nov 1905	Hindenburg O.S.
PHILIPPSON	Wally	F	20 Feb 1889	Hindenburg O.S.
PICK	Ruth	F	16 Jun 1906	Hindenburg
PICK	Paul	M	20 Jun 1902	Zabrze, Schlesien
PICK	Walter	M	29 Sep 1903	Zabrze, Schlesien
PICK	Edith	F	08 Sep 1918	Alt Repten, Tarnowitz
PICK	Irmgard	F	16 May 1921	Alt Repten, Tarnowitz
PICK	Paula	F	15 Sep 1887	Pniowitz, Tarnowitz
PICK	Walter	M	29 Sep 1923	Hindenburg O.S.
PICK	Ernestine	F	23 Dec 1922	Pilzendorf, Beuthen O.S.
PICK	Salo	M	31 Aug 1888	Stollarzowitz, Beuthen O.S.
PICTRUS	Paul	M	20 Jan 1902	Hindenburg
PIECHOTTA	Rudolf	M	10 Jun 1905	Hindenburg O.S.
PIECZKA	Josef	M	11 Sep 1915	Hindenburg O.S.
PIELKA	Josef	M	24 Apr 1872	Hindenburg–Saborce
PIERUSCHEK	Rudolf	M	09 Jan 1905	Hindenburg

PIERUSCHEK	Georg	M	01 Jan 1909	Hindenburg
PIETRKOWSKI	Anna	F	4 Feb 1892	Hindenburg O.S.
PIETRKOWSKI	Hariet	F	8 Jul 1897	Hindenburg
PIETRYGA	Harriet	F	8 Jul 1897	Hindenburg
PIETRZIK	Stefan	M	22 Dec 1892	Hindenburg
PIETRZIK	Waldemar	F	09 Jun 1909	Hindenburg
PIETRZIK	Barbel	F	25 May 1925	Hindenburg
PIETRZIK	Erich	M	26 Aug 1927	Hindenburg
PIETRZIK	Gisela	F	26 Oct 1905	Hindenburg
PIETRZIK	Hedwig	F	08 Oct 1908	Hindenburg
PIETRZIK	Horst	M	13 Feb 1938	Hindenburg
PIETRZIK	Marie	F	22 Nov 1884	Hindenburg
PIETRZIK	Franz	M	16 Feb 1878	Petersdorf, Gleiwitz
PIETZKA	Luise	F	27 Jan 1927	
PINKUS	Paul	M	05 Jan 1904	Hindenburg
PINKUS	Heinrich	M	31 Jan 1893	Hindenburg
PINKUS	Elli Margot	F	15 Nov 1922	Hindenburg
PINKUS	Alfred	M	24 Mar 1882	Hindenburg
PINKUS	Miriam	F		Hindenburg, Silesia
PINKUS	Selma	F	21 Jan 1883	Kleinitz, Granberg
PINKUS	Kurt	M	15 May 1886	Hindenburg
PINKUS	Hermann	M	14 May 1883	Hindenburg O.S.,
PINKUS	Heinrich	M	31 Jan 1893	Hindenburg O.S.
PINKUS	Max	M	14 Jun 1888	Hindenburg O.S.
PISE	Rosa	F	28 Aug 1874	Hindenburg O.S.
PITZKO	Natalie	F	10 Apr 1865	Hindenburg O. S.
PLITZKO	Ernst	M	09 Dec 1917	Hindenburg
PLOCH	Alois	M	06 Jul 1920	Hindenburg O.S.
PLONSKI	Paul	M	15 Jan 1894	Hindenburg
PLONSKI	Bessi	F	19 Jun 1895	Hindenburg
PLOTKE	Betty	F	19 Jun 1895	Hindenburg O.S.
PLUSCHKA	Siegfried	M	24 Jun 1873	Koschmin
PNIOWER	Berta	F	04 Jul 1913	Hindenburg
PNIOWER	Alma	F	3 Apr 1875	Lublinitz
POAY	Max	M	1 May 1872	Loslau
PODBIELSKI	Suse	F	29 May 1913	Hindenburg O.S.
PODBIELSKI	Julius	M	7 Aug 1877	Johannisburg
PODBIELSKI	Sella	F	7 Apr 1888	Gostyn, Posen
POHORILLE	Hans	M	25 Oct 1911	Koscierzyna (Berent)
POLAP	Chaim	M	7 Jul 1882	Buczacz
POLLACK	Hildegard	F	24 Aug 1915	Groay Paniow, Pleay
POLLACK	Ferdinand	M	21 Apr 1862	Zabrze O.S.
POLLACK	Else	F	2 Apr 1885	Hindenburg
POLLACK	Eugen	M	25 Oct 1882	Hindenburg O.S.
POLLACK	Leo	M	9 Aug 1895	Hindenburg Ost
POLLACK	Marianne	F	15 Nov 1923	Hindenburg
POLLACK	Max	M	17 Dec 1872	Hindenburg O.S.

POLLACK	Hulda	F	19 Sep 1863	Zabrze, Schlesien
POLLACK	Adolf	M	4 Feb 1868	Hindenburg
POLLACK	Lisa	F	15 Dec 1868	Hindenburg
POLLACK	Else	F	2 Apr 1885	Hindenburg
POLLACK	Hulda	F	19 Sep 1863	Hindenburg
POLLACK	Clara	F	2 Feb 1867	London
POLLACK	Erna	F	17 Dec 1894	Hallen, Gelsenkirchen
POLLACK	Martin	M	28 Aug 1921	Oppeln O.S.
POLLACK	Polly	F	10 Dec 1879	Antonienhatte
POLLACK	Ernst	M	24 Jan 1894	Hindenburg
POLLACK	Hulda	F	19 Sep 1863	Hindenburg O. S.
POLLACK	Ralph	M		Beuthen, Germany
POLLACK	Eva	F	08 Apr 1926	Klausberg, Beuthen O.S.
POLLACK	Hanna	F	23 Mar 1898	Katowice
POLLACK	Adolf	M	4 Feb 1868	Hindenburg O.S.
POLLACK	Alfred	M	1 Sep 1888	Hindenburg O.S.
POLLACK	Elsa	F	2 Apr 1885	Hindenburg O.S.
POLLACK	Georg	M	11 Nov 1889	Hindenburg O.S.
POLLACK	Lina	F	15 Dec 1868	Hindenburg O.S.
POLLAK	Martin	M	9 Nov 1891	Hindenburg O.S.
POLLOCK	Hugo	M	20 May 1868	Hindenburg O.S. (Zabrze)
POLOCZEK	Cacilie	F	22 Nov 1878	Hindenburg O.S.
POLOCZEK	Franz	M	16 Jan 1911	Hindenburg
POLOMSKI	Vincenz	M	16 Jan 1884	Hindenburg O.S.
POMERANC	Elisabeth	F	07 Mar 1905	Hindenburg
POMERANC	Frania	F		
POMERANC	Hela	F	06 Apr 1922	Radom
PORADA	Rita	F		Radom, Poland
PORMEBKA	Elfriede	F	10 Sep 1909	Hindenburg O.S.
POSPIECH	Fried.	M	26 Jan 1908	Hindenburg O.S.
POTSTADA	Paul Mathias	M	02 May 1902	Hindenburg
POTSTADA	Erich	M	11 Apr 1914	Hindenburg
POTSTADA	Ernst	M	01 Jun 1922	Hindenburg
POTSTADA	Franz	M	3 Oct 1887	Hindenburg
PRACHER	Selma	F	1 Oct 1886	Birkenau, Gleiwitz
PRAGER	Leo	M	23 Jul 1872	Gleiwitz
PRAGER	Doris	F	21 Jun 1900	Hindenburg
PRAGER	Helga	F	01 Jul 1925	Hindenburg
PRAGER	Wilhelm	M	25 Jun 1899	Hindenburg O.S.
PRAGER	Bruno	M	19 Jul 1891	Hindenburg
PRAGER	Ernst	M	18 Dec 1887	Hindenburg
PRAGER	Julie	F	8 Jul 1858	Hindenburg
PRAGER	Rudi	M	13Aep 1932	Hindenburg
PRAGER	Ruth	F	18 Apr 1938	Hindenburg
PRAGER	Alice	F	19 Nov 1899	Lundenburg
PRAGER	Else	F	14 Sep 1897	
PRAGER	Johanna	F	24 Jul 1903	Leipzig

PRAGER	Lili	F	14 May 1925	Hindenburg
PRAGER	Gunther	M	01 Oct 1904	Hindenburg
PRAGER	Lili	F	14 May 1925	Hindenburg
PRESTON	Margot	F	01 Jun 1930	Hindenburg
PREUAY	Anna	F		Hindenburg, Germany
PREUAY	Elfriede	F		Hindenburg O.S.
PREUSS	Oskar	M	17 Jun 1878	Bialla, Johannisburg
PREUSS	Hugo	U	15 Apr 1886	Zabrze, Schlesien
PRUSKO	Helen	F	01 May 1923	Staszow, Poland
PUDLO	Pauline	F	16 May 1902	Hindenburg O.S.
PULVERMACHER	Bruno	M	27 Jul 1899	Hindenburg
PULVERMACHER	Helene	F	15 Jul 1876	Hindenburg
PUSKAUER	Margarete	F	8 Aug 1883	Hindenburg O.S.
PUSKAUER	Daniel	M	11 Jun 1873	Kreuzburg O.S.
PYKA	Johanna	F	20 Feb 1877	Potempa, Gleiwitz
PYRSKALLA	Richard	F	03 Apr 1912	Hindenburg
PYSIK	Bernhard	M	08 May 1912	Hindenburg O. S.
RASCHER	Karl	M	12 Jul 1912	Hindenburg O.S.
RAHMER	Rudolf	M	16 Feb 1924	Hindenburg O.S.
RECHNITZ	Margarethe	F	24 Feb 1870	Hindenburg O.S.
RECHNITZ	Martha	F	17 Aug 1877	Zabrze, Schlesien
REICHENBAUM	Martha	F	17 Aug 1877	Hindenburg O.S.
REICHENBAUM	Erna	F	06 Oct 1926	Milowka
REIF	Heinrich	M	18 Nov 1885	Hindenburg
REINHOLD	Heinrich	M	18 Nov 1885	Zaborze,
REMBAUM	Veronika	F	3 Feb 1895	Biskupitz, Hindenburg
RESNICK	Danka	F	02 Mar 1929	Ciechanow
RESNIK	Anne	F	01 Nov 1939	Hindenbury
RESNIKOW	Anne Herzog	F		Hindenburg, Germany
RESPONDEK	Frieda	F	2 Jan 1893	Hindenburg O.S.
REST	Theodor	M	16 Apr 1884	Hindenburg O.S.
RETZLICK	Wilhelm	M	08 Mar 1909	Hindenburg–Zaborze
REZNIK	Adelheid	F	07 Sep 1912	Hindenburg
RICE	Helen	F	01 Mar 1922	Grajec, Poland
RICHTER	Barbara	F		Lublin, Poland
RICHTER	Betty	F	17 May 1876	Hindenburg
RIESENFELD	Herta	F	10 May 1896	Hindenburg O.S.
RIESENFELD	Grethel	F	15 Apr 1876	Gleiwitz, Tost–Gleiwitz
RIESENFELD	Olga	F	8 Jun 1871	Gleiwitz, Tost–Gleiwitz
RIGOLL	Bertha	F	7 Feb 1866	Rosenberg O.S.
RIGOLL	Olga	F	23 May 1902	Hindenburg
RIGOLL	Rita	F	31 Oct 1929	Hindenburg
RINN	Viktor	M	30 Sep 1903	Heydebreck, Cosel
ROBERT	Erna	F	07 Jan 1901	Hindenburg O.S.
ROBERT	Egon	M	25 Oct 1921	Hindenburg O.S.
ROBERT	Margarete	F	10 Jan 1891	Breslau
ROGON	Horst	M	01 May 1920	Hindenburg O.S.

ROGON	Franz	M	20 Nov 1920	Hindenburg
ROLLNIK	Ernst	M	13 Dec 1895	Hindenburg/OS
RONES	Gertrud	F	8 Mar 1892	Kunzendorf b. Hindenburg
ROSENBAUM	Pauline	F	14 Dec 1882	Hindenburg O.S.
ROSENBAUM	Iser	M		
ROSENBAUM	Eleonora	F	04 Sep 1905	Hindenburg O.S.
ROSENBERG	Louis	M	2 Jul 1884	Bielszowice, Hindenburg
ROSENBERG	Fritz	M	3 Sep 1898	Hindenburg
ROSENBERG	Fritz	M	3 Sep 1898	Hindenburg
ROSENBLUM	Yetta	F	28 Mar 1923	Radom, Poland
ROSENBUND	Liba Malka	F	05 Oct 1920	Tomaszow
ROSENBUND	Simon	M	9 Dec 1872	Zabrze
ROSENKRANZ	Simon	M	9 Dec 1872	Hindenburg O. S.
ROSENKRANZ–KATZENELENBOGEN	Sally	F		Zaklikow, Poland
ROSENMEYER	Aliza Franka	F	23 Sep 1924	Oboczno
ROSENTHAL	Amalie	F	17 Jul 1876	Hindenburg O.S.
ROSENTHAL	Else	F	2 Feb 1886	Zabrze, Schlesien
ROSENTHAL	Elfriede	F	25 May 1894	Zabrze, Schlesien
ROSENTHAL	Else	F	2 Feb 1886	Hindenburg
ROSENZWEIG	Elfriede	F	25 May 1894	Hindenburg O. S.
ROSINSKI	Regina	F	02 Jan 1924	Radom
ROSSA	Boleslaw	M	24 Mar 1919	Hindenburg
ROSSAU	Franz	M	3 Dec 1894	Dammfelderhammer
ROTH	Lucie	F	10 Nov 1910	Hindenburg–Ost (Zaborze)
ROTH	Werner	M	12 Aug 1920	
ROTH	Gunter	M	13 May 1923	Hindenburg
ROTH	Herbert	M	22 May 1922	Hindenburg O.S.
ROTH	Rudolf	M	24 Feb 1891	Hindenburg O.S.
ROTH	Egon	M	04 Apr 1929	Hindenburg O.S.
ROTH	Jenni	F	5 Sep 1870	Pappelau, Oppeln
ROTH	KÃƒÂ¤the	F	19 Jun 1898	Einbeck, Hannover
ROTH	Margarete	F	22 Oct 1896	Kanigshatte
ROWEK	Heinrich	M	6 Aug 1894	Hindenburg
ROYAL	Erna	F	26 Feb 1907	Hindenburg O.S.
ROZOK	Hanka	F	23 Jan 1923	Radom, Poland
RUMMLER	Heinrich	M	21 Mar 1905	Hindenburg
RUSSEK	Erich	M	27 Nov 1903	Hindenburg O.S.
RUSSEK	Jgnatz	M	05 Aug 1910	Hindenburg
RUSSEK	Johanna	F	27 Feb 1929	Hindenburg
RUSSEK	Waltraud	F	11 Apr 1936	Hindenburg
RUSSEK	Werner	M	31 Jul 1923	Hindenburg
RUSSEK	Stefan	M	2 Sep 1889	Hindenburg
RUSSEK	Lucie	F	6 May 1897	Ornontowitz, Pleay
RUSSEK	Otto	M	10 Nov 1897	Kanigshatte
RUSSEK	Ignatz	U	05 Aug 1910	Hindenburg
RUSZCZYNSKI	Rudolph	M		Javornik, Czechoslovakia

RUTMAN	Helene	F	13 Oct 1899	Hindenburg O.S.
RUTTNER	Eugenia	F	28 Mar 1926	Lwow, Poland
RYCZKE	Serena	F		Senta, Yugoslavia
SAYMANN	Mira	F	17 Sep 1923	Zoppot
SAYMANN	Emmy	F	17 Sep 1887	Hindenburg O.S.
SASSER	Helene	F	23 Mar 1884	Hindenburg O.S.
SACHS	Robert	M	25 Aug 1917	Zabrze
SACHS	Dorothea	F	3 Dec 1873	Hindenburg
SACHS	Hermann	M	12 Oct 1877	Hindenburg
SALINGER	Dorothea	F	3 Dec 1873	Hindenburg O.S.
SALOMON	Mania	F	23 Feb 1924	Radom, Poland
SALOMON	Paula	F	12 Oct 1872	Kangingshatte
SALOMON	Sally	M	5 Sep 1872	Dyck, Deutsch Krone
SALSITZ	Ilona	F		Kralovo, Czechoslovakia
SALWICZEK	Norman	M		Hindenburg, Germany
SALWICZEK	Edyta	F		
SALWICZEK	Max	M	18 Feb 1909	Hindenburg O.S.
SALWICZEK	Willibald	M	27 Jul 1935	Hindenburg O.S.
SALWICZEK	Wolfgang	M	10 Aug 1936	Hindenburg O.S.
SALWIG	Edith	F	05 May 1910	Tworog
SALZMANN	Chanka	F	08 Dec 1927	Garbadka
SAMET	Bella	F	01 Mar 1925	Garbadka
SAMET	Elfriede	F	16 Dec 1916	Hindenburg
SAMET	Siegfried	M	27 Jul 1928	Hindenburg
SAMOL	Hella	F	17 Sep 1900	Kalbuszara
SAMOL	Maks	M	12 Oct 1898	Hindenburg
SANDBERG	Maks	M	12 Oct 1898	Hindenburg
SANDBERG	Ismar	M	19 Dec 1909	Hindenburg
SANDBERG	Josef	M	27 Oct 1884	Beuthen O.S.
SANDBERG	Lina	F	13 Mar 1897	Brinnitz
SARNA	Ismar	M	19 Dec 1909	Hindenburg O.S.
SARNETZKY	Dina	F	20 Dec 1924	Wysokie, Poland
SCHACHER	Magdalene	F	1 Sep 1896	Hindenburg O.S.
SCHANFELD	Erna	F	31 Oct 1901	Zaborze, Hindenburg
SCHANFELD	Ernestine	F	29 Dec 1868	Lublinitz
SCHANFELD	Lieselotte	F	23 Jan 1921	Hindenburg O.S.
SCHANFELD	Heinrich	M	05 Feb 1904	Hindenburg O.S.
SCHANFELD	Louis	M	24 Nov 1877	Neuberun, Pleay
SCHANFELD	Gerhard	M	05 Sep 1924	Hindenburg, Schlesien
SCHATTAN	Lieselotte	F	23 Jan 1921	Hindenburg, Schlesien
SCHATTAN	Friedrich	M	1 Aug 1897	Proskau, Oppeln
SCHATTAN	Rosa	F	15 Sep 1902	Stadtel, Namslau
SCHALLER	Margarete	F	19 Jun 1896	Hindenburg Nord Ost
SCHALLER	Guido	M	12 Jul 1870	Hindenburg O.S.
SCHAEFER	Jacques	U	15 Feb 1874	Zaborze Kreis Hindenburg
SCHAEFER	Alice	F	7 Aug 1893	Eisleben
SCHAEFER	Ernst	M	13 Jul 1021	Breslau

SCHAFFNER	Josef	M	3 Apr 1881	Nikolai, Pleay
SCHAJOR	Valeska	F	6 Feb 1891	Hindenburg O.S.
SCHALL	Josef	M	10 Nov 1880	Hindenburg O.S.
SCHALL	Elisabeth	F	30 Dec 1933	Hindenburg Ost
SCHALL	Heinrich	M	05 Jun 1927	Hindenburg Ost
SCHALL	Irmgard	F	06 May 1926	Hindenburg Ost
SCHALL	Wilhelm	M	07 Mar 1932	Hindenburg Ost
SCHALL	Minna	F	29 Dec 1861	Zabrze, Schlesien
SCHALL	Bronislawa	F	20 Oct 1901	Bielschowitz
SCHALL	Georg	M	14 Sep 1919	Paulsdorf
SCHALL	Hildegard	F	24 Aug 1921	Paulsdorf
SCHALL	Theodor	M	2 Sep 1894	Ruda
SCHALL	Alfred	M	14 Jul 1865	Hindenburg O.S.
SCHALLAMACH	Minna	F	29 Dec 1861	Hindenburg O.S.
SCHALLAMACH	Arno	M	29 Apr 1932	Hindenburg
SCHALLAMACH	Hilde	F	04 Dec 1905	Hindenburg
SCHALLAMACH	Ruth	F	02 Oct 1929	Hindenburg
SCHALLAMACH	Arno	M	29 Apr 1932	Hindenburg
SCHALLAMACH	Hilde	F	04 Dec 1905	Hindenburg
SCHANFELD	Ruth	F	02 Oct 1929	Hindenburg
SCHATTAN	Elizabeth	F		
SCHEEMANN	Alfred	M	31 Jul 1911	Hindenburg
SCHEEMANN	Hulda	F	28 May 1892	Tichau
SCHEEMANN	Margot	F	06 Apr 1924	Schkeuditz, Merseburg
SCHEINWECHSLER	Friedrich	M	12 Jan 1889	Katowice
SCHENDZIELORZ	Sara	F	13 Nov 1882	Klein–Zabrze, Schlesien
SCHENK	Gertrud	F	16 Sep 1918	Hindenburg O. S.
SCHENK	Doris	F	14 Sep 1883	Labau, Rosenberg
SCHEWIOLA	Max	M	6 Apr 1885	Breslau
SCHEYER	Paul	M	12 Jan 1901	Hindenburg
SCHEYER	Ludwig	M	12 Nov 1884	Hindenburg
SCHIFFER	Sigmar	M	17 May 1889	Hindenburg O.S.
SCHIFTAN	Marie	F	2 Jun 1891	Hindenburg O.S.
SCHIFTAN	Nathan	M	23 Jun 1895	Proskau/Oppeln
SCHIFTAN	Hanne	F	23 Sep 1933	Hindenburg
SCHIFTAN	Berta	F	6 May 1899	Bierdzan, Oppeln
SCHIFTAN	Nathan	M	23 Jun 1895	Proskau, Oppeln
SCHIFTAN	Ruth	F	14 May 1925	Illnau, Oppeln
SCHILLER	Friedrich	M	11 Mar 1905	Proskau, Germany
SCHILLER	Armin	M	16 Aug 1891	Hindenburg
SCHILLER	Adolf	M	7 Jul 1861	Zabrze, Schlesien
SCHILLER	Lina	F	28 Nov 1866	Kosten
SCHILZER	Ludwig	M	19 Feb 1889	Hindenburg O.S.
SCHINDLER	Cacilie	F	4 May 1897	Hindenburg O.S.
SCHINDLER	Else	F	28 Apr 1887	Hindenburg
SCHINDLER	Hans	M	27 Jul 1916	Hindenburg
SCHINDLER	Ernst	M	30 Oct 1911	Hindenburg

SCHINDLER	Bianka	F	8 Jun 1870	Tost, Gleiwitz
SCHINDLER	Kurt	M	01 Apr 1905	Hindenburg
SCHIPP	Sara	F	2 Jul 1858	Hindenburg O.S.
SCHIROKAUER	Ewald	M	2 Oct 1899	Hindenburg O.S.
SCHIROKAUER	Nathan	M	3 Nov 1886	Schlesiengrube, Beuthen
SCHIROKAUER	Rosa	F	9 Dec 1897	Gleiwitz
SCHLEIN	Siegfried	M	30 Nov 1922	Klaisberg, Beuthen
SCHLEIN	Doris	F	20 Mar 1915	Hindenburg
SCHLESINGER	Elisabeth	F	14 Sep 2909	Hindenburg
SCHLESINGER	Fritz	M	19 Apr 1915	Hindenburg
SCHLESINGER	Heinrich	M	12 Oct 1892	Hindenburg
SCHLESINGER	Kurt	M	02 Aug 1907	Zabrze
SCHLESINGER	Dagobert	M	14 Aug 1910	Kanigshatte
SCHLESINGER	Rosa	F	25 Apr 1895	Hindenburg O.S
SCHLESINGER	Curt	M	12 Nov 1893	Hindenburg O.S.,
SCHLESINGER	Edith	F	11 Jul 1898	Zabrze, Schlesien
SCHLESINGER	Gertrud	F	29 Jan 1881	Zabrze, Schlesien
SCHLESINGER	Max	M	01 Aug 1906	Tarnowitz
SCHLESINGER	Dagobert	M	14 Aug 1910	Kanigshatte
SCHLESINGER	Elisabeth	F	18 Nov 1898	Hindenburg O.S.
SCHLESINGER	Edith	F	11 Jul 1898	Hindenburg O. S.
SCHLESINGER	Gerda	F	16 Nov 1922	Hindenburg
SCHLESINGER	Herbert	M	22 Jan 1902	Hindenburg O. S.
SCHLESINGER	Julie	F	5 Aug 1897	Hindenburg O.S.
SCHLESINGER	Kurt	M	02 Apr 1907	Hindenburg O. S.
SCHLESINGER	Edgar	M	15 Feb 1901	Hindenburg O.S.
SCHLESINGER	Erika	F	03 Dec 1922	Hindenburg O.S.
SCHLESINGER	Gertrud	F	29 Jan 1881	Hindenburg O. S.
SCHLESINGER	Heinrich	M	12 Oct 1892	Hindenburg O.S.
SCHLOKOPF	Ilse	F	02 Feb 1924	Hindenburg O.S.
SCHLOKOPF	Stefanie	F	01 May 1928	Hindenburg
SCHMIDT	Katharina	F	13 Jan 1887	Kobier, Pleay
SCHMIDT	Brigitte	F	24 Jan 1929	Hindenburg O.S.
SCHMIDT	Renate	F	21 Apr 1935	Hindenburg O.S.
SCHMIDT	Gertrud	F	24 Aug 1899	Breslau
SCHMIDT	Paul	M	20 Apr 1897	Gleiwitz
SCHMIDT	Wolfgang	M	05 Jul 1924	Breslau
SCHMILGEIT	Margarete	F	24 Jun 1917	Oppeln
SCHMITZ	Elfriede	F	12 Jan 1914	Hindenburg, Labiau
SCHMITZ	Selma	F	26 Feb 1896	Hindenburg
SCHMUL	Selma	F	26 Feb 1896	Hindenburg
SCHMULOWITZ	Helene	F	8 Nov 1873	Hindenburg O.S.
SCHMULOWITZ	Alfred	M	1 Feb.1885	Zabrze
SCHMULOWITZ	Berthold	M	26 Jul 1881	Hindenburg
SCHMULOWITZ	Fedor	M		Hindenburg
SCHNEIDER	Dorothea	F	23 Oct 1879	Hindenburg O.S.
SCHNEIDER	Roman	M	13 Jul 1897	Hindenburg

SCHNURAWA	Erna	F	17 Mar 1918	Paulsdorf/Hindenburg
SCHOENFELD	Julie	F	15 Feb 1854	Klein Kotulin, Gleiwitz
SCHOENFELD	Lotte	F	13 Nov 1906	Klein Zabrze
SCHOENFELD	Gerhard	M	05 Sep 1924	Hindenburg O.S.
SCHOENFELD	Henriette	F	26 Aug 1894	Hindenburg O.S.
SCHOLTIS	Alfred	M	29 May 1894	Kanigshatte
SCHOLZ	Elisabeth	F	11 Mar 1903	Hindenburg
SCHOLZ	Richard	M	08 Mar 1912	Hindenburg O.S.
SCHOLZ	Wanda	F	20 May 1897	Hindenburg
SCHREIBER	Elfriede	F	06 Aug 1913	Hindenburg O. S.
SCHREIBER	Gertrud	F	28 Feb 1893	Hindenburg O.S.
SCHUBAK	Margaret	F	24 May 1897	Hindenburg O.S.
SCHUBAK	Barbara	F		Bialystok, Poland
SCHUBERT	Barbara	F	27 Dec 1924	Bialystok, Poland
SCHUBERT	Hedwig	F	17 Nov 1932	Hindenburg
SCHULA	Johannes	F	26 Jul 1936	Hindenburg
SCHULENBURG	Georg	M	28 Apr 1904	Hindenburg
SCHULTHEIAY	Marie	F	09 Mar 1909	Hindenburg
SCHULZ	Liselotte	F	08 Nov 1906	Hindenburg O.S.
SCHULZE	Rosa	F	5 Oct 1887	Hindenburg O.S.
SCHULZE	Ida	F	27 Aug 1864	Hindenburg, Osterburg
SCHUMNIK	Charlotte	F	29 Apr 1910	Hindenburg O.S.
SCHUPACK	Klara	F	25 Aug 1893	Ruda, Hindenburg
SCHUSTER	Balla	F		Zawiercie, Poland
SCHUSTER	Norbert	M	6 Dec 1898	Hindenburg O.S.
SCHUSTER	Herbert	M	18 Jul 1900	Hindenburg O.S.
SCHUSTER	Rosalie	F	1 Nov 1865	Orzech, Tarnowitz
SCHUTZ	Walter	M	30 Jun 1902	Hindenburg O.S.
SCHUTZ	Arthur	M	05 Jan 1904	Zabrze
SCHUTZ	Georg	M	15 Apr 1929	Hindenburg
SCHWARTZ	Hanelore	F	9 Sep 1888	Knischwitz, Strelno
SCHWARTZ	Jean	F		Radom, Poland
SCHWARZ	Eva	F		Zwolen, Poland
SCHWARZ	Elfriede Irma	F	21 Aug 1895	Hindenburg
SCHWARZ	Elfriede	F	21 Aug 1895	Hindenburg
SCHWARZ	Zilla	F	28 Oct 1938	Hindenburg
SCHWARZ	Betty	F	12 Jul 1891	Zaborze, Hindenburg
SCHWARZ	Hedwig	F	12 Oct 1931	Hindenburg
SCHWARZ	Minna	F	12 Nov 1900	Ckrunow
SCHWARZ	Sigmund	M	08 Jul 1927	Ckrunow
SCHWARZ	Jakob	M	15 Jul 1894	Zawiercia
SCHWARZ	James	M	30 May 1884	Breslau
SCHWARZ	Berta	F	14 Feb 1924	Ckrunow
SCHWEITZER	Gunter	M		Hindenburg, Germany
SCHWEITZER	Emma	F	18 Mar 1905	Hindenburg
SCHWERIN	Emma	F	08 Mar 1904	Hindenburg O.S.
SCHWERIN	Hedwig	F	19 Oct 1884	Antonienhatte, Kattowitz

SCHWIERCYNA	Jenny	F	3 Jul 1872	Bielschowitz, Hindenburg
SCHYMA	Paul	M	15 Jan 1880	Hindenburg
SCHYMATZEK	Kate	F	26 Apr 1904	Hindenburg
SCHYMETZKA	Franz	M	01 Jun 1902	Hindenburg
SEDLACZEK	Max	M	06 Oct 1901	Hindenburg
SEDLACZEK	Alfred	M	20 Nov 1912	Hindenburg
SEDLACZEK	Anna	F	18 Swp 1922	Hindenburg O.S.
SEDLACZEK	Helene	F	11 Dec 1915	Hindenburg
SEDLACZEK	Kurt	M	17 Oct 1913	Hindenburg O.S.
SEDLACZEK	Sophie	F	9 May 1886	Hindenburg O.S.
SEIDEL	Rudolf	M	19 Aug 1889	Dobrkow, Pilsen
SEIDEL	Wilhelm	M	31 Jul 1902	Hindenburg
SEIDEL	Edeltraud	F	0 Jul 1927	Hindenburg
SEIDEL	Helene	F	4 Apr 1894	Hindenburg
SEIDEL	Paul	M	7 Jan 1891	Hindenburg
SEIDEL	Rudi	M	11 Dec 1920	Hindenburg
SEIDEL	Wilhelm	M	31 Jul 1902	Hindenburg
SEIDEMANN	Erwin	M	05 Jun 1918	Hindenburg O.S.
SEIDEMANN	Charlotte	F	15 Jun 1917	Hindenburg
SEIDEMANN	Selma	F	17 Jul 1883	Hindenburg
SEIDEMANN	Hertha	F	16 Jun 1914	Woitnik, Lublinitz
SEIDEMANN	Max	M	24 Jul 1883	Czuchow, Rybnik
SEIDLER	Helene	F	13 Sep 1891	Hindenburg O.S.
SEIWKA	Gertrud	F	5 Apr 1888	Poremba / Kr.Hindenburg
SELIGER	Erich	M	15 Apr 1892	Hindenburg O.S.
SEMMLER	Magda	F	30 Apr 1890	Hindenburg O.S.
SEMMLER	Karl	M	17 May 1904	Hindenburg
SEMMLER	Anna	F	15 May 1870	Lindau, Leobschatz
SERYNEK	Max	M	29 Sep 1869	Petersdorf, Gleiwitz
SEZESS	Hilda	F	03 Jan 193	Hindenburg
SHEVCHUK	Emil	M	13 Jun 1906	Hindenburg O.S.
SHIBE	Ivan	U	01 Oct 1917	Kamenets–Podolskaia
SHNEYDER	Anna	F	06 Jun 1922	Sandomierz , Poland
SHOEN	Aron	M		
SHYLIT	Manya	F		Radom, Poland
SIEDNER	Henia	F		Kozienice, Poland
SIEDNER	Kurt	M	26 May 1894	Hindenburg O. S.
SIEGEL	Alfred	M	7 Jun 1893	Zaborze, Hindenburg O.S.
SIEGMUND	Marta	F	15 Jul 1880	Hindenburg O.S.
SILBERMANN	Ernestine	F	18 Nov 1855	Hindenburg
SILBERSTEIN	Max	M	20 Mar 1870	Hindenburg O.S.
SILBERSTEIN	Alfred	M	21 May 1895	Zabrze
SILBERSTEIN	Siegfried	M	30 Jul 1883	Hindenburg
SIMENAUER	Ruth	F		Hindenburg, Germany
SIMENAUER	Wilhelm	M		Germany
SIMONI	Laura	F	10 Jul 1866	Biskupitz, Hindenburg
SINGER	Hanna	F	9 Dec 1894	Hindenburg O.S.

SIROTA	Josefine	F	20 Mar 1905	
SIROTA	Fay	F		Radom, Poland
SKIBA	Fay	F	15 May 1926	Radom , Poland
SKOLUDEK	Konrad	M	30 Nov 1911	Hindenburg
SKROBANEK	Fritz	M	27 Nov 1894	Hindenburg O.S.
SKROBEK	Lydia	F	24 Jun 1910	Hindenburg O.S.
SKUPNY	Viktor	M	4 Oct 1892	Zaborze, Hindenburg
SLAMOVICH	Karl	M	15 Sep 1909	Hindenburg
SLICOKA	Bella	F		
SLICOKA	Arnold	M	26 Jan 1896	Hindenburg O.S.
SLIWKA	Elli	F	15 May 1900	Beuthen O.S.
SLIWKA	Wilhelm	M	04 Jan 1903	Hindenburg
SLIWKA	Helmut	M	31 Dec 1933	Hindenburg O.S.
SLIWKA	Herbert	M	09 Oct 1923	Hindenburg O.S.
SLIWKA	Ingeborg	F	28 Jun 1934	Hindenburg O.S.
SLIWKA	Leo	M	10 Jun 1927	Hindenburg O.S.
SLIWKA	Marie	F	02 Aug 1900	Hindenburg O.S.
SLIWKA	Rosa	F	25 Feb 1925	Hindenburg O.S.
SLIWKA	Rudolf	M	01 Mar 1900	Hindenburg O.S.
SLIWKA	Werner	M	17 Aug 1936	Hindenburg O.S.
SLOMKA	Irmgard	F	15 Jun 1922	Hindenburg O.S.
SLOWIG	Alois	F	2 Nov 1894	Hindenburg
SLOWIG	Ernst	M	15 Apr 1899	Hindenburg
SMARSLIK	Ernest	M	15 Apr 1899	Hindenburg
SMUDA	Paul	M	22 Jul 1903	Hindenburg
SMUDA	Cazilie	F	14 Jul 1923	Hindenburg
SMUDEL	Valeska	F	9 Feb 1894	Hindenburg
SMYRZEK	Josef	M	06 Jan 1903	Hindenburg
SNSSMANN	Luise	F	25 Mar 1905	Hindenburg
SOER	Helene	F	23 Mar 1884	Zabrze, Schlesien
SONNENFELD	Mira	F	02 Sep 1923	Bialystok, Poland
SONSKY	Martha	F	11 Jan 1900	Hindenburg O.S.
SORSKY	Eduard	M	4 Oct 1869	Hindenburg
SORSKY	Erich	M	16 Jul 1898	Hindenburg
SORSKY	Eva	F	15 Nov 1873	Hindenburg
SOWA	Eduard	M	9 Mar 1867	Hindenburg O.S.
SOWA	Albert	M	25 Mar 1905	Hindenburg
SOWA	Ilse	F	25 Sep 1911	Hindenburg O.S.
SPERLICH	Klara	F	16 Mar 1900	Hindenburg O. S.
SPERLICH	Jadwiga	F		
SPERLICH	Lieselotte	F	15 Dec 1930	Hindenburg
SPERLICH	Hedwig	F	18 Sep 1899	Hindenburg
SPERLICH	Heinz	M	03 Oct 1928	Hindenburg
SPERLICH	Lieselotte	F	15 Dec 1930	Hindenburg
SPITZ	Paul	M	07 Mar 1901	Kreuzendorf, Leobschatz
SPITZ	Ernst	M	16 Jul 1916	Hindenburg
SPITZ	Arthur	M	22 May 1878	Cosel O.S.

SPRAI	Rose	F	21 Oct 1886	Oberglogau, Neustadt O.S.
SPRENTZ	Salo	M	10 Sep 1884	Zabrze, Schlesien
SPRINGER	Vinzent	M	21 Jan 1895	Hindenburg O.S.
SPRINGER	Dora	F	24 Jul 1926	Hindenburg
SPRINGER	Moses	M	14 Jan 1918	Hindenburg
SROKA	Eugen	M	04 Jul 1918	Hindenburg O.S.
STALLMACH	Tauba	F		Radom, Poland
STALLMACH	Hedwig	F	12 Apr 1893	Orzesche, Pleay
STALLMACH	Kurt	M	01 Jun 1912	Kanigshatte Ost
STANGASSINGER	Maria	F	27 Nov 1928	Kanigshatte Ost
STANIEK	Hans	M	15 Jan 1894	Hindenburg
STANIEK	Gerhard	M	26 Aug 1901	Hindenburg O.S.
STANIEK	Annemarie	F	02 Feb 1929	Tost, Gleiwitz
STANIEK	Otto	M	05 Jan 1925 5	Hundsdorf, Wiesbaden
STANIK	Annemarie	F	02 Feb 1929	Hindenburg
STANIK	Walter	M	25 Jan 1916	Hindenburg
STANITZEK	Gertrud	F	10 Feb 1894	
STANLEY	Georg	M	04 Jul 1914	Hindenburg
STAPLER	Susy	F	3 Sep 1897	Hindenburg O. S.
STARK	Kurt	M	04 Jun 1909	Hindenburg
STARK	Hugo	M	24 May 1902	Hindenburg
STARKULLA	Heinz	M	04 Oct 1922	Borsigwerk, Hindenburg
STAVSKI	Ingeborg	F	10 Dec 1923	Borsigwerk, Hindenburg
STAWSKI	Yacob	M		Hindenburg, Germany
STEBEL	Adolf	M	26 Dec 1875	Hindenburg O. S.
STEIN	Sophie	F	16 May 1899	Hindenburg O.S.
STEINBERG	Hedwig	F	20 Jun 1872	Pleay
STEINITZ	Lillian	F	18 Feb 1924	Vienna, Austria
STEINITZ	Alma	F	14 Nov 1877	Ruda, Zabrze
STEINITZ	Walter Israel	M	05 Oct 1910	Hindenburg O S
STEINITZ	Kurt	M	14 Jan 1907	Hindenburg
STEINITZ	Walter	M	05 Oct 1910	Hindenburg
STEINITZ	Bertha	F	26 Oct 1869	Kunzendorf
STEINITZ	Kurt	M	14 Jan 1907	Hindenburg/OS
STEINITZ	Josef	M	07 Aug 1901	Hindenburg O.S.
STEOCZOWSKI	Kurt	M	14 Aug 1907	Hindenbur, Germany
STERN	Clara	F	19 Aug 1913	Hindenburg O. S.
STERN	Ilse	F		Hindenburg, Germany
STEUER	Curt	M	21 Jan 1887	Hindenburg O. S.
STEUER	Albert	M	20 Feb 1868	Hindenburg
STIASTNY	Hugo	M	4 Apr 1870	Hindenburg
STIASTNY	Walter	M	07 Mar 1925	Hindenburg O.S.
STIEBEL	Jeny	F	12 May 1890	Gleiwitz O.S.
STOEGER	Anna	F	24 Nov 1869	Hindenburg
STRAUCH	Janet	F		Sadowa, Poland
STRAUSS	Margot	F	11 Jan 1907	Hindenburg
STRAUSS	Tommy	M		Beuthen, Germany

STRAUSS	Gunter	M	15 Jul 1925	Beuthen
STRAUSS	Meier	M	28 Jan 1890	Sterbfritz, Schlachtern
SUCHOWSKI	Marie	F	30 Jan 1889	Katowice
SUCHOWSK	Theodor	M	9 Nov 1896	Hindenburg
SUISKY	Theodor	M	9 Nov 1896	Hindenburg
SUSSMANN	Wilhelm	M	26 Mar 1905	Hindenburg
SVET	Rose	F	27 Jan 1874	Hindenburg
SWIATOWICZ	Regina	F		Radom, Poland
SWIERCZ	Fela Zipora	F		Warsaw, Poland
SYRZISKO	Josef	M	07 Aug 1919	Hindenburg
SZEPSEL	Izydor	M	7 Sep 1899	Hindenburg
SZYMA	Eva	F	20 Aug 1925	Radom
SZYMA	Richard	M	24 Mar 1901	Hindenburg
TATERKA	Magdalene	F	15 Apr 1916	Hindenburg O. S.
TATERKA	Frank	M		Katowice, Poland
TATERKA	Alice	F	11 Jun 1896	Gilgenberg, Osterode
TATERKA	Jaques	M	23 Feb 1893	Krojanke, Flatow
TEICHNER	Franz	M	24 Jun 1922	Katowice
TERALLA	Leopold	M	18 Jan 1871	Hindenburg O.S.
TERNER	Rudolf	M	17 Apr 1896	
THALER	Ruth	F		Hindenburg, Germany
THAU	Anna	F	17 Oct 1858	Nikolai Pleay
THAU	Alfred	M	19J an 1917	Hindenburg
THAU	Marga	F	27 Feb 1909	Zabrze, Schlesien
THAU	Ernst	M	22 Dec 1920	Hindenburg
THAU	Heinz	M	08 Oct 1913	Hindenburg O.S.
THIELE	Marga	F	02 Feb 1907	Hindenburg O.S.
THIELEN	Rosa	F	19 Sep 1906	Hindenburg O. S.
TICHAUER	Wilhelm	M	28 Feb 1914	Bielschowitz, Hindenburg
TICHAUER	Anna	F	28 Mar 1876	Kanigshatte
TICHAUER	David	M	24 Oct 1926	Klausberg, Beuthen
TICHAUER	Eugen	M	11 Jul 1878	Birkental, Kattowitz
TICHAUER	Florentini	F	5 Aug 1898	Pilzendorf, Beuthen
TICHAUER	Hans–Lutz	M	07 Feb 1920	Birkental
TICHAUER	Heimann	M	3 Mar 1880	Beuthen O.S.
TICHAUER	Liesbeth	F	17 Jan 1891	Beuthen O.S.
TICHAUER	Lutz	M	10 Apr 1930	Klausberg, Beuthen
TICHAUER	Margarete	F	18 Mar 1880	Tarnowitz
TICHAUER	Moritz	M	8 Aug 1898	Beuthen O.S.
TICHAUER	Moritz	M	11 Aug 1860	Gillowitz, Pleay
TICHAUER	Regina	F	28 Jan 1881	Birkental
TICHAUER	Rudolf	M	24 Jul 1905	Gleiwitz
TILS	Max	M	6 May 1891	Hindenburg O.S.
TILS	Elisabeth	F	12 Oct 1893	Frankfurt
TILS	Hans	M	18 Jul 1930	Manheim Ruhr
TIRALLA	Johann	M	12 Jan 1893	Schleiden
TIRALLA	Eva	F	25 Sep 1935	Hindenburg O.S.

TIRALLA	Rudolf	M	17 Apr 1896	Zaborze, Hindenburg
TIRALLA	Therese	F	24 Aug 1931	Hindenburg
TIRALLA	Gertrud	F	21 Nov 1905	Kaminitz, Beuthen
TIRALLA	Luzie	F	06 Jan 1901	Lipine
TISCHLER	Paula	F	19 Nov 1867	Orzech, Tarnowitz
TKOCZ	Johanna	F	12 Sep 1905	Hindenburg
TOCZEK	Stefan	M	22 Dec 1892	Hindenburg
TOKARSKI	Arthur	M	22 Nov 1908	Hindenburg O. S.
TOKARSKI	Josef	M	24 Mar 1908	Hindenburg
TONDERA	Edmund	M	11 Nov 1911	Hindenburg
TORKA	Heinrich	M	11 Jul 1903	Hindenburg
TOTSCHEK	Martha	F	26 Jul 1883	Hindenburg, Naugard
TOTSCHEK	Heinz	M	08 May 1925	Hindenburg O.S.
TOTSCHEK	Marianne	F	22 Dec 1930	Hindenburg O.S.
TOTSCHEK	Else	F	25 Jan 1900	Hindenburg Ost
TOTSCHEK	Rose–Marie	F	22 Feb 1928	Hindenburg
TOTSCHEK	Heinz	M	08 May 1925	Hindenburg
TOTSCHEK	Arthur	M	23 Nov 1886	Kornowatz, Ratibor
TOTSCHEK	Elisabeth	F	9 May 1899	Freystadt
TOTSCHEK	Erich	M	30 Jan 1890	Rosenberg
TOTSCHEK	Kurt	M	26 Jul 1893	Kanigshatte
TOTSCHEK	Paul	M	1 May 1895	Kanigshatte
TOTSCHEK	Rosa	F	15 Dec 1897	Kocon
TOTSCHEK	Toni	F	18 Jun 1873	Rudahammer
TOTSCHEK	Heinz	M	08 May 1925	Hindenburg, Schlesien
TOTSCHEK	Marie	F	14 Jul 1884	Katowice
TRACHT	Herbert	M	27 Nov 1904	Hindenburg O.S.
TRACINSKI	Leon	M		Kiev, Soviet Union
TRACINSKI	Eva	F	18 Jun 1896	Longeville, Metz
TRACINSKI	Walther	M	14 Mar 1884	Birkental, Kattowitz
TRAUBE	Katharina	F	26 Jun 1896	Hindenburg O.S.
TRAUBE	Kunegunda	M	10 1910	
TRAUGOTT	Friedericke	F	5 Apr 1877	Kanigshatte
TRAUGOTT	Elfriede	F	23 Jul 1904	Hindenburg
TRAUGOTT	Rosa	F	18 Sep 1882	Labau, Rosenberg
TREUMANN	Margarete	F	17 Mar 1879	Hindenburg
TRIBISCH	Margarete	F	17 Mar 1879	Hindenburg O.S.
TUCHS	Emil	M	17 Jun 1903	Hindenburg
TUNTKE	Gerhard	M	06 May 1919	Hindenburg
TYCKA	Gertrud	F	24 Oct 1894	Hindenburg O.S.
UCKO	Georg		05 Dec 1909	Hindenburg
UCKO	Martin	M	9 Jun 1884	Zabrze, Schlesien
UCKO	Sally	M	9 Feb 1893	Hindenburg O.S.
UCKO	Lotte	F	12 Jan 1931	Hindenburg O.S.
UCKO	Bernd	M	15 Jun 1926	Gleiwitz O.S.
UCKO	Gertrud	F	05 Mar 1900	Pleay
UCKO	Martin	M	9 Jun 1884	Hindenburg O.S.

UHEREK	Ernst	M	13 Jun 1929	Hindenburg O.S.
ULFIG	Klaus	M	21 Oct 1923	Hindenburg O.S.
ULFIG	Paul	M	30 Apr 1891	Hindenburg
UNGER	Paul	M	30 Apr 1891	Hindenburg
UNGER	Curt	M	15 Nov 1900	Hindenburg
URBAINCZYK	Erwin	M	26 May 1903	Hindenburg
URBANCZYK	Werner	M	02 Dec 1909	Hindenburg
USEREK	Alois	M	26 May 1886	Hindenburg O.S.
VAYNSHTAYN	Hermann	M	1 Jun 1896	Hindenburg O.S.
VAYS	Maashah	F	28 Jun 1913	Bialystok (Poland), Russia
VEYS	Drazel	F	19 Aug 1925	Radom , Poland
VAN DICKEN	MatÃŒyah	F	09 Sep 1927	Przytyk , Poland
VASERMAN	Maria	F	12 Mar 1905	Hindenburg
VERMEL	Cesia	F	04 Apr 1924	Garbatka , Poland
VETH	Margot	F	02 Oct 1923	Hindenburg
VICTOR	Elly	F	13 Nov 1911	Hindenburg O. S.
VICTOR	Mirjam	F	31 Jan 1928	Hindenburg
VICTOR	Eva	F	29 Oct 1930	Hindenburg
VOGEL	Hanne	F	03 Nov 1932	Hindenburg
VOGEL	Elisabeth	F	16 Dec 1906	Hindenburg O.S.
VOGELHUT	Siegmund	M	30 Mar 1900	Hamburg
VOGELHUT	Runia	F		Krakow, Poland
VOGT	Runia	F	22 Sep 1928	Cracow, Poland
VOGT	Walter	M	16 Jul 1910	Zabrze
VOGT	Grete Katz	F	13 Mar 1886	Hindenburg
VUPEL	Grete	F	13 Mar 1886	Hindenburg O.S.
WACHSMANN	Walter	M	23 Mar 1905	Hindenburg
WACHSMANN	Marga	F	06 Apr 1908	
WACHSMANN	Suse	F	24 Feb 1916	Hindenburg
WACHSMANN	Betty	F	12 Apr 1887	Breslawitz, Militsch
WACHSMANN	Bruno	M	3 Nov 1883	Zalas
WACHSMANN	Edgar	M	12 Apr 1883	Laurahatte
WACHSMANN	Ernst	M	14 Oct 1876	Laurahatte, Kattowitz
WACHSMANN	Walter	M	23 Feb 1910	Beuthen O.S.
WACHSNER	Ella	F	13 Nov 1891	Katowice
WACLAVCZYK	Fanny	F	6 Aug 1861	Hindenburg O.S.
WACLAVCZYK	Josef	M	17 Feb 1921	Hindenburg O.S.,
WACLAVCZYK	Ruth	F	07 Feb 1915	Hindenburg O.S.
WACZLAWSKI	Pauline	F	25 Dec 1885	Stubendorf, Groay Strehlitz
WADULLA	Johann	M	3 Mar 1880	Hindenburg
WAGNER	Heinrich	M	15 Jul 1903	Hindenburg
WAHLER	Elisabeth	F	26 Feb 1886	Hindenburg O. S.
WAHLER	David	M	12 Jul 1938	Hindenburg
WAHLER	Karl	M	11 Nov 1936	Hindenburg
WAHLER	Rachel	F	18 Aug 1934	Hindenburg
WAHLER	Arthur	M	13 Dec 1901	Schalkrippen, Alzen
WAIGLAWSKE	Luise	F	04 Apr 1908	Siemianowice, Kattowitz

WAJSKOPF	Johann	M	3 Mar 1880	Hindenburg O.S.
WAJSKOPF	Sala	F		
WALENZYK	Zofia	F	01 Apr 1905	Tomaszow
WALENZYK	Paul	M	22 Jan 1897	Hindenburg
WALLACH	Paul	M	22 Jan 1897	Hindenburg
WALLACH	Luise	F	17 Apr 1916	Hindenburg
WALTER	Genovefa	F	03 Jan 1915	Hindenburg O.S.
WARTENBERGER	Handel	F	6 Nov 1874	Hindenburg O.S.
WARTSKI	Sara	F	24 Oct 1870	Zaborze, Hindenburg
WARZECHA	Max	M	19 Oct 1899	Hindenburg
WARZECHA	Erich	M	28 Nov 191	Hindenburg
WARZECHA	Herbert	M	31 Jul 1913	Hindenburg
WARZECHA	Erich	M	28 Nov 1910	Hindenburg
WARZECHA	Herbert	M	31 Jul 1913	Hindenburg
WARZECHA	Erich	M	28 Nov 1910	Hindenburg
WASSERTEIL	Cesia	F		Garbatka, Poland
WASSERTHEIL	Abraham	M	25 Mar 1928	Hindenburg, Germany
WAWRZINEK	Nathan	M	04 Apr 1926	Hindenburg
WEBER	Franziska	F	30 Sep 1897	Hindenburg O.S.
WEBER	Emanuel	M	07 Feb 1900	Hindenburg
WEGEMUND	Charlotte	F	09 Jan 1906	Hindenburg O.S.
WEGEMUND	Berta	F	21 Jun 1911	Hindenburg O.S.
WEGEMUND	Dorothea	F	08 Aug 1938	Hindenburg O.S.
WEGEMUND	Peter	M	28 Jan 1934	Hindenburg O.S.
WEGEMUND	Wilhelm	M	21 Jan 1931	Hindenburg O.S.
WEIAY	Wilhelm	M	29 Oct 1906	Katowice
WEIAY	Martha	F	29 Jul 1876	Meaugschatz, Brieg
WEIAY	Gerhard	M	08 Aug 1903	Hindenburg
WEIABLUM	Johanna	F	30 May 1871	Hindenburg O.S.
WEIABLUM	Gertrud	F	04 Mar 1930	Hindenburg O.S.
WEILER	Max	M	15 May 1931	Hindenburg O.S.
WEILER	Kurt	M	03 Dec 1900	Nikolai, Pleay
WEICH	Meta	F	14 May 1905	Kanigsbach
WEINER	Fritz	M	08 Jul 1902	Hindenburg
WEINSTEIN	Sylvia	F	15 Jan 1931	Parczew, Poland
WEINSTEIN	Alexander	U	18 Mar 1914	Hindenburg
WEINSTEIN	Friedrich	U	06 Nov 1915	Hindenburg
WEINSTEIN	Alexander	U	18 Mar 1914	Hindenburg
WEINSTEIN	Friedrich	U	06 Nov 1915	Hindenburg
WEINSTEIN	Alexander	U	18 Mar 1914	Hindenburg
WEINSTEIN	Friedrich	U	06 Nov 1915	Hindenburg
WEINSTEIN	Else	F	6 Aug 1883	Hindenburg
WEINSTEIN	Alexander	M	18 Mar 1914	Hindenburg
WEINSTEIN	Friedrich	M	06 Nov 1915	Hindenburg
WEINSTEIN	Ella	F	6 Aug 1883	Hindenburg O.S.,
WEINSTOCK	Arthur	M	22 Sep 1878	Beuthen
WEIS	David	M	15 Dec 1912	Hindenburg

WEISER	Gustav	M	30 Oct 1897	Hindenburg
WEISS	Bruno	M	23 Oct 1900	Hindenburg O.S.
WEISS	Gerhard	M	03 Aug 1912	Hindenburg
WEISS	Ruth	F	19 Jul 1908	Hindenburg O.S.
WEISS	Johanna	F	2 Oct 1888	Tichau
WEISS	Ludwig	M	16 Apr 1899	Ackerfelde, Gleiwitz
WEISS	Benno	M	12 Dec 1886	Schildberg
WEISS	Daniel	M	11 Aug 1874	Gostyn
WEISS	Elsa	F	15 Aug 1880	Oppeln
WEISS	Gizella	F		Czechoslovakia
WEISS	Rosa	F	18 May 1929	Klausberg, Beuthen O.S.
WEISSBERGER	Alma	F	24 Sep 1894	Groay Chelm, Pleay
WEISSBERGER	Oskar	M		
WEISSENBERG	Ilona	F		Budapest, Hungary
WEISSENBERG	Helene	F	1 Dec 1880	Zaborze
WELKE	Arthur	M	14 Mar 1879	Katowice
WENDRINER	Regina	F	13 Dec 1887	Laurahatte
WENDRINER	Wally	F	01 Jan 1906	Hindenburg
WENGRZIK	Dorothea	F	15 May 1874	Hindenburg
WERNER	Wilhelm	M	10 Jan 1879	Hindenburg O.S.
WERNER	Alice	F	17 Sep 1905	Hindenburg
WETMORE	Ruth	F	12 Jun 1930	Hindenburg
WIDERA	Irma	F	26 Apr 1909	Hindenburg
WIELAND	Ernst	M	30 Dce 1919	Hindenburg
WIENER	Mathilde	F	1 Oct 1876	Hindenburg O.S.
WIENER	Artur	M	12 Oct 1883	Hindenburg
WIENSKOWITZ	Ellen	F	28 Dec 1926	
WIENSKOWITZ	Paul	M	17 May 1890	Hindenburg O.S.
WIENSKOWITZ	Berndt	M	19 Jun 1922	Beuthen O.S.
WIENSKOWITZ	Lilli	F	29 Jun 1924	Beuthen O.S.
WIERCIMOK	Hans	M	23 Jul 1894	Hindenburg O.S.
WIERCIMOK	Recha	F	13 Jan 1864	Gleiwitz
WIERCIMOK	Annemarie	F	10–×¡×¤×˜–20	Katowice
WIEREZINEK	Gertrude	F	27 Oct 1891	Roayberg, Beuthen O.S.
WIERNY	Recha	F		
WIERUSZOWSKI	Herbert	M	01 Oct 1921	Gleiwitz
WIESCHALKA	Rosa	F	02 Feb 1903	Hindenburg O.S.
WIESCHOK	Marie	F	16 Nov 1898	Zabrze Hindenburg
WILCZEK	Paul	M	16 Mar 1911	Hindenburg O.S.
WILETZY	Reinhold	M	21 Jul 1905	Hindenburg
WILK	Klara	F	16 Apr 1902	Hindenburg O.S.
WILK	Anna	F	23 Jan 1898	Hindenburg O.S.
WILK	Josef	M	25 Nov 1889	Hindenburg O.S.
WILLIAMS	Josef	M	27 Nov 1918	Hindenburg
WILMAN	Rose	F	10 Jun 1927	Radom, Poland
WINTER	Sara	F		Hindenburg
WINTER	Helmut	M		Hindenburg, Germany

WIRSZTEL	Helen	F		Hindenburg, Germany
WISCHNITZER	Marie	F	05 May 1923	Bialystok, Poland
WISCHNITZER	Helmut	M		
WISCHNITZER	Alfred	M	28 Jan 1910	Hindenburg Nord Ost
WISCHNITZER	Erwin	M	06 Apr 1911	Hindenburg Nord Ost
WISCHNITZER	Hellmut	M	09 Nov 1917	Hindenburg Nord Ost
WISCHNITZER	Josef	M	7 Jan 1880	Slemien
WISNIA	Sophie	F	3 Apr 1887	Lachowitz
WISNIA	Fela	F	02 Sep 1929	Radom
WISNIA	Esther–Masza	F	22 Sep 1927	Radom, Poland
WITOSZA	Fela	F	02 Sep 1925	Radom, Poland
WITOSZA	Marta	F	23 May 1893	Hindenburg
WITT	Anton	M	17 Jan 1892	Sassetz, Pleay Ost
WIZENBERG	Johann	M	07 Feb 1901	Hindenburg O.S.
WOHL	Hinda	F	30 Jul 1913	Radom (Kielce) Poland
WOHLGEMUTH	Ruth	F	5 Nov 1898	Alt Zabrze
WOITZIBE	Gerhard	M	30 Jun 1927	Hindenburg O.S.
WOITZIK	Ruth–Christa	F	01 Oct 1912	Hohenlinde
WOITZIK	Georg	M	14 Dec 1911	Hindenburg
WOJNAR	Georg	M	14 Dec 1911	Hindenburg
WOLF	Emil	M	01 May 1908	Hindenburg
WOLF	Herbert	M		
WOLF	Gusta	F	27 Mar 1915	Hindenburg
WOLFF	Walter	M		Breslau, Germany
WOLFF	Margot	F	17 Feb 1927	Hindenburg O.S.
WOLFF	Dieter	M	10 Aug 1935	Hindenburg O.S.
WOLFF	Erich	M	23 Jul 1930	Hindenburg O.S.
WOLFF	Gerh.	M	14 May 1917	Hindenburg
WOLFF	Herbert	M	13 Jun 1900	Hindenburg O.S.
WOLFF	Adelheid	F	09 Jun 1904	Hindenburg O.S.
WOLFF	Alfred	M	17 Oct 1937	Hindenburg O.S.
WOLFF	Kurt	M	9 Feb 1899	Hindenburg
WOLFF	Felicia	F	6 May 1889	Zabrze, Schlesien
WOLFF	Felicia	F	6 May 1889	Hindenburg
WOLFF	Lucie	F	24 Sep 1889	Peiskretschau, Gleiwitz
WOLFF	Karoline	F	15 Jul 1866	Stanonitz, Rybnik
WOLFF	Karl	M	30 Sep 1866	Kaniglich, Rybnik
WOLFF	Berta	F	02 Feb 1900	Hindenburg O.S.
WOLKOWICZ	Adolf	M	2 Feb 1862	Ruda Slaska, Hindenburg
WORZMAN	Eda	F	01 Mar 1922	Tomaszaw, Poland
WOSNITZKA	Sari	F	28 Aug 1926	Sighe , Romania
WOWRO	Dorothea	F	14 Sep 1910	Hindenburg
WOWRO	Anton	M	31 Aug 1898	Hindenburg
WROBEL	Anton	M	31 Aug 1898	Hindenburg
WROBEL	Hildegard	F	06 Dec 1914	Biskupitz
WROBEL	Johanna	F	12 Jul 1869	Woiska, Gleiwitz
WRONKER	Eva	F		Radom, Poland

WYCISLO	Johanna	F	3 Jun 1879	Beuthen O.S.
WYCISLO	Wilhelm	M	25 Jun 1904	Hindenburg OS
WYGAS	Wilhelm	M	25 Apr 1904	Hindenburg
WYGAS	Edyta	F		
WYGAS	Egon	M	27 Dec 1942	Hindenburg
WYGAS	Edith	F	26 May 1909	Brynek, Gleiwitz
YACOBOVITCH	Karl	M	14 Apr 2903	Kanigshatte
YAKSCHIK	Moshe	M	27 Mar 1920	Hamburg, Germany,
YUDELEVICZ	Klara	F	25 Jun 1905	Hindenburg O.S.
ZACHARIAS	Zelda	F		Janowiec, Poland
ZACHARIASZ	Werner	M		Hindenburg, Germany
ZACHARIASZ	Herschel	M		Bedzin, Poland
ZACZEK	Erna	F		Gleiwitz, Germany
ZAHNERT	Richard	M	24 Aug 1909	Hindenburg
ZAHNERT	Hans	M	01 Oct 1939	Gleiwitz
ZAHNERT	Magda	F	22 Jul 1899	Scharley
ZAIFMAN	Walter	M	30 Sep 1899	Deschowitz, Groay
ZAMORY	Zenia	F	05 Oct 1935	Radom , Poland
ZEBROWSKI	Leo	M	03 Apr 1905	Hindenburg, Dorotheastr 41
ZEGMAN	Rosa	F	31 Oct 1867	Hindenburg O.S.
ZEPLER	Anna	F		Radom, Poland
ZERNIK	Amalie	F	12 Apr 1866	Hindenburg O.S.
ZIGMUNDZYK	Bernhard	M	21 Aug 1871	Zabrze
ZIMMELS	Thomas	M	28 Dec 1907	Hindenburg
ZIMMER	Irma	F	04 Aug 1908	Hindenburg O.S.
ZIMMERMANN	Helene	F	16 Dec 1908	Hindenburg O.S.
ZIMMERMANN	Emma	F	27 Nov 1873	Hindenburg O.S.
ZIMMERMANN	Heinz	M	14 Nov 1936	Hindenburg O.S.
ZIMMERMANN	Edith	F	27 Mar 1937	Lonkau, Pleay
ZLOTLOW	Else	F	1 Jun 1875	Kanigshatte
ZMUDA	Guta	M		Radomsko, Poland
ZOLTY	Friedrich	M	26 Dec 1911	Hindenburg in n
ZOLTY	Doris	F		Garbatka, Poland
ZORAWIK	Doris	F	15/??/1920	Garbatka (Kielce), Poland
ZORICHTA	Richard	M	6 Apr 1896	Hindenburg
ZYLBERMAN	Wilhelm	M	31 May 1920	Hindenburg
ZYLBERSZTAJN	Froim	M	03 May 1918	Jadow
ZYLBERSZTAJN	Sara Ruchla	F	17 Oct 1925	Hindenburg

Please note: The index below does not include the names in the alphabetized
tables on pages 178 – 185, 186 – 195 and 196 – 248.

Index